$2130

# COMPUTER ARCHITECTURE

COMPUTER SCIENCE SERIES

COMPUTER SCIENCE SERIES

# COMPUTER ARCHITECTURE
## Second Edition

Caxton C. Foster

*Professor of Computer Science*
*University of Massachusetts*
*Amherst, Massachusetts*

**VNR** VAN NOSTRAND REINHOLD COMPANY
NEW YORK   CINCINNATI   ATLANTA   DALLAS   SAN FRANCISCO
LONDON   TORONTO   MELBOURNE

Van Nostrand Reinhold Company Regional Offices:
New York   Cincinnati   Atlanta   Dallas   San Francisco

Van Nostrand Reinhold Company Foreign Offices:
London   Toronto   Melbourne

Manufactured in the United States of America

Published by Van Nostrand Reinhold Company
135 West 50th Street, New York, N.Y. 10020

Published simultaneously in Canada by
Van Nostrand Reinhold Ltd.

15  14  13  12  11  10 9 8 7 6 5 4

**Library of Congress Cataloging in Publication Data**

Foster, Caxton C   1929–
  Computer architecture.

  (Computer science series)
  Includes bibliographical references and index.
  1. Computer architecture.   I. Title.
QA76.9.A73F67   1976        621.3819′52        76-25245
ISBN 0-442-22434-6

*For Mary Lou*

*"When we mean to build,*
*We first survey the plot, then draw the model;*
*And when we see the figure of the house,*
*Then must we rate the cost of the erection . . ."*

William Shakespeare

# PREFACE TO THE SECOND EDITION

It is now nine years since I started writing the first edition of this book and six years since it was published. When the publishers kindly suggested a second edition was due, I expected that I would have to scrap most of the original and start from scratch. Perhaps there are some who believe this would have been a good idea. Nonetheless, when I approached the task seriously, I discovered that it was more a case of adding than subtracting.

The field of computer architecture has not so much changed as expanded. New machines, new organizations, and new technologies have eclipsed the old in some instances, but the same old methods of indexing, to take an obvious example, still persist. So this new edition is fatter than the old and, I suppose, the price will be higher, as well.

To be more specific, I have added sections on tri-state output circuits, more detail on flip-flops and integrated circuitry, magnetic bubble storage, charge coupled devices, semi-conductor memories, and read only memories. The elementary machine, BLUE, has been redesigned with current circuit elements, and a micro-programmed version of BLUE has been added to illustrate this important design tool. There is an expanded discussion of interrupt and hand shaking techniques, a new chapter on microprocessors, and the chapter on giant machines has been completely rewritten, using up to date examples. Finally, I have included a brief discussion of STARAN, ILLIAC IV, and the Hypercube machines as examples of array processors.

Questions remain scattered throughout the text, but they have been numbered for ease of reference, and several have been added. Last, but not least, all the logic diagrams have been redrawn using contemporary symbols for AND's and OR's.

I would especially like to thank those students who have suffered through COINS 335/635 for their patience over the years and their many helpful suggestions.

Caxton C. Foster
*Amherst, Massachusetts*

# PREFACE TO THE FIRST EDITION

The field of computer architecture, or "the art of designing a machine that will be a pleasure to work with" is only gradually receiving the recognition it deserves.

This art, one cannot call it a science, is one step more abstract than that of a logical designer, which in turn is abstracted from the study of electronic circuits. The logical designer is unconcerned with whether his gates are made from NPN or PNP transistors, or indeed whether they use transistors at all. He deals with gates as black boxes and his forte is the arrangement and organization of these black boxes to provide, with minimum cost and maximum speed and reliability, a unit, which, when presented with appropriate inputs, generates appropriate outputs.

The computer architect in turn is unconcerned with the insides of an adder or a shift register. His job is to assemble the units turned out by the logical designer into a useful, flexible tool that is called a computer.

There are three areas a computer architect should be familiar with in order to do his job well. First, he should be a competent machine-language programmer, preferably with experience in software systems. This is not a prerequisite for reading this book, nor is the subject covered herein. But if a man doesn't know what a device is used for, he sometimes has trouble doing a good job of designing it.

Second, a computer architect must know the nature of the building blocks he is going to be working with. He must know about number systems, about storage mechanisms, and something about logical circuitry. These topics are covered in the first four chapters of this book.

Finally, and perhaps most central, he should be exposed to the problems that must be solved and how others have sought to solve them.

This book is organized as follows. Chapters 1–4 provide a background to the field. Chapter 1 discusses some of the many methods of representing information inside a computer. Chapter 2 is a brief review of elementary switching circuits. Chapter 3 covers the more common physical devices that have been used for storing information. Chapter 4 considers how these devices can be put together to provide storage for computers.

Chapter 5 presents a case study in depth of the design of a general-purpose computer called BLUE.

Beginning with Chapter 6 we start to present the reader with some of the choice points he will meet in designing a computer, in this case, various addressing structures. From here on we discuss the problems, indicate generally how they might be solved and ask the reader to provide a detailed solution. Chapter 7 discusses problems that arise in input and output control; Chapter 8 treats some of the instructions that are found in other computers. Chapter 9 looks at a few of the larger machines available today and concludes with a detailed study of a hypothetical machine designed to work in a time-sharing environment. This time the study is not at the logical gate level, as it was in Chapter 5, but at the functional level: What capabilities should the machine have?

Chapters 10 and 11 are concerned with some of the nonstandard approaches to computer architecture. The former discusses multi-processors and distributed logic computers, while the latter deals with Holland-type machines—what they can do and how they are organized.

This book is an outgrowth of a course called Comparative Machine Design that has been taught several times at the University of Massachusetts to Computer Science graduate students and upper level engineering undergraduates. We have called for a prerequisite of one course in machine language programming, but this is more to establish interest and maturity than because of content. Depending on how many of the questions posed are explored in class and how many are left to the students, the course may extend for one or two semesters.

Finally I would like to thank the many students who have helped to shape the content and the approach; Mrs. Noble for valiantly typing the several drafts; Professor John A. N. Lee of the University of Massachusetts and Professor Sidney Michaelson of the University of Edinburgh for their helpful suggestions while the manuscript was in preparation; and most of all my wife, Mary Lou, who has served as technical editor, urging me time and again to rewrite the obscurer sections until, as she put it, "a non-expert in the field will have a chance at understanding what you're trying to say."

CAXTON C. FOSTER

*Amherst, Mass.*
*July, 1970*

# CONTENTS

# COMPUTER
# ARCHITECTURE

# 1 | THE REPRESENTATION OF INFORMATION

*"For deeds doe die however noblie donne*
*And thoughts of men do as themselves decay,*
*But wise words taught in numbers for to ronne*
*Recorded by the muses, live for ay."*
*Edmund Spenser*

Man's machines fall into two general categories: those that deal with energy and those that deal with information. An electric motor is an example of the first type of machine. It absorbs electrical energy and produces mechanical energy. A transistor radio is an example of the second type of machine. To be sure, it requires energy to operate, but the less the better. It is designed to absorb a signal in the RF band and produce one in the audio band. A computer is also an example of an information processing machine. It absorbs programs and data and produces "results." It is quite difficult to frame a definition of a computer that will exclude transistor radios, TV sets, and even automobile odometers (milagemeters). We are not going to try. We know, and if we don't now we will by the time we have finished this book, what a computer is. It's one of those "things" made by IBM, Control Data, Honeywell, etc., that are so maddeningly literal, difficult to get along with, and expensive to buy or rent.

Since these devices deal with information, we must spend time in finding out what forms information must assume to be intelligible to these machines. The sub-class of information processing machines we are concerned with deals with discrete, quantized signals. They are called digital computers.

In most cases, signals will be restricted to one of two states: off-on, zero-one, false-true. We will find that this simple vocabulary will be sufficient to express everything we wish to tell a computer.

This chapter will be concerned with some of the many different ways that have been invented for the representation of information. In particular, we will be concerned with ways of writing down numbers because many of the applications of computers have to do with numbers. We will see that the other symbols of interest, such as, letters, punctuation, etc., can be represented as numbers.

The Roman Numerals are a counting scheme based on 5's and 10's (V's and X's). The Romans had symbols for 1, 5, 10, 50, 100, 500, 1000 (CIƆ), 10,000 (CCIƆƆ) and 100,000 (CCCIƆƆƆ) but no larger units. To express a number like 1,000,000 they would write down the symbol for 100,000 ten times. The national budget of even a small country would require several lines just to indicate the total.

In our modern number system, we have what is called a "positional" number system. The meaning of a particular symbol is modified by the position in which it occurs. Thus, 1234 means $4 \times 10^0 + 3 \times 10^1 + 2 \times 10^2 + 1 \times 10^3$. We use ten different symbols 0 to 9, and by way of the positional value that can be assigned to them, we can represent any number whatsoever. Unlike the Romans, we do not need more than those ten symbols. The Babylonians used a similar method, but it was forgotten by Mediterranean civilization, and it was not until about the year 1200 that the concept was reintroduced into western thought from India, via the Arabs, hence to be called Arabic numbers.

We use a number system based on ten, called the decimal system. Other than the fact that we have ten fingers, there is no particular attraction to the decimal number system. Many people have urged the adoption of a duo decimal (base 12) system. Such a scheme has the advantage that the base can be divided evenly by many more numbers than can ten. The likelihood of this scheme being adopted is probably remote, however attractive it might be. Even the British gave up the 12 pence to the shilling in 1971 and converted to a decimal coinage.

The introduction of digital computers and the technology on which they are based has recently given rise to considerable interest in number systems in which the "weight" assigned to each succeeding leftward position in a number is *not* ten times as great as its right hand neighbor. The factor by which the weight increases as we move leftward in a number is called the "base" or "radix." In the decimal system, this factor is of course 10, and enumerating the weights from right to left we have

$$1 = 10^0$$
$$10 = 10^1$$
$$100 = 10^2$$
$$1000 = 10^3 \quad \text{etc.}$$

## BINARY NUMBERS

Other weighting schemes are possible; let us look at one. The ancients usually counted to five on one hand. Had they stumbled on the idea of positional notation, they could just as easily have counted up to 31. On the pad of your right thumb, draw the number 1; on your index finger, 2; on your middle finger, 4; ring finger, 8; and little finger, 16. Beginning with a closed fist for zero, we count as follows:

$$1 = \text{thumb}$$
$$2 = \text{index}$$
$$3 = \text{thumb and index}$$
$$4 = \text{middle}$$
$$5 = \text{middle and thumb}$$
$$15 = \text{ring and middle and index and thumb}$$
$$31 = \text{all five fingers extended}$$

To represent a particular configuration of fingers, let us write down a 1 if the finger is out straight and a 0 if it is bent down. There must be five digit positions, and we let the rightmost correspond to the thumb.

Then, the number 25 shown in Fig. 1.1 would be written as 11001. We translate to familiar decimal numbers by adding up the numbers exposed. Thus,

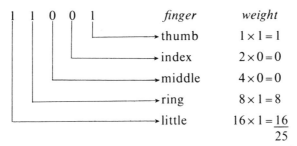

More formally, we multiply the weight of a position by the value of the digit shown in that position (0 or 1) and sum up the result. Thus,

$$25 = 1 \times 16 + 1 \times 8 + 0 \times 4 + 0 \times 2 + 1 \times 1$$

Notice that each succeeding finger (as we move to the left) has a weight of twice the preceding one.

---

*Question 1.1:* If we extend this scheme to include both hands, what will be the value of the left-most finger? What will be the largest number that can be expressed with all ten fingers?

---

Fig. 1.1 Configuration for the number $25_d$ in binary.

The radix of a positional number system is the weight of any position divided by the weight of the position immediately to its right.

The system we have just described has a radix (ratio of successive weights) of two and is called the "binary" number system. Each position is called a "bit" or binary digit. It is the system most often used in modern digital computers.

The word "digital" is actually derived from the word for "finger," so we should not be ashamed of doing what these paragons of modern technology do—counting on our fingers.

We will examine the binary system in more detail later. Meanwhile, let's look at some other schemes for counting.[1]

## TRINARY NUMBERS

We will leave out the thumb this time, because it is not flexible enough, and will still count up to 80 on the fingers of one hand.

On the *ends* of the four fingers of the right hand write the numbers:

27    9   3   1

and on the pads of the same fingers write

54   18   6   2

Now we have three possible positions for each finger: fully closed, exposing no number; partially extended, exposing the number on the end; and fully extended, exposing the number on the pad. Let us represent those positions respectively by: 0, 1, and 2.

Fig. 1.2 Configuration for the number 69$_d$ in trinary.

*The number 69 will be:* (See Fig. 1.2.)

| representation: | 2 | 1 | 2 | 0 |
|---|---|---|---|---|
| number exposed: | 54 | 9 | 6 | – |

The shorthand notation: 2222 will represent $54 + 18 + 6 + 2 = 80$. The nota-tation: 1111 will represent $27 + 9 + 3 + 1 = 40$.

Let us formalize this number system. The index finger can be said to represent either 0, 1, or 2 times three to the zero power. The middle finger 0, 1, or 2 times three to the first. The ring finger 0, 1, or 2 times three squared, and the little finger 0, 1, or 2 times three cubed. The ratio of successive weights is thus three, and the system is called "trinary."

## SOME OTHER METHODS

There are two things to be noted from the discussion so far. First, the larger the radix, the bigger the number that can be expressed with a given number of positions, or conversely, the smaller the radix, the more po-sitions are required to express a given number. Second, we need as many different symbols as the value of the radix. For radix ten, we need the ten digits 0 to 9.

Note that in no system is there a single symbol to represent the radix itself. It is always represented by the combination: 10.

Thus the figure pair we usually call "ten" can represent 2, 3, or "one more than nine." To eliminate confusion, we will subscript numbers with their radix (using a "$d$" for decimal numbers) whenever there might be ambiguity. We can then write that

$$5_d = 101_2 = 12_3$$

The subscripts will always be in decimal.

---

*Question 1.2:* Using the symbol "t" for "one more than nine" and "e" for "two more than nine," represent the numbers $143_d$ and $318_d$ in the duo decimal (radix = 12) system. What does 1 et 5 represent in decimal?

---

As we have noted, the small radixes require a large number of positions. This can become exceedingly cumbersome to write out if large numbers are involved. Because the binary system is widely used, two "shorthand" notations have evolved for handling this problem. They are called "octal" and "hexadecimal" (or "hex") notation. They are, of course, proper notations in their own right with radices of 8 and 16, respectively.

Table 1.1 shows various ways of representing the first few integers. Notice that in hex, symbols have had to be invented to represent the numbers from 10 to 15. The letters *a* through *f* are commonly used to make life easier for the typesetters.

Octal and binary are related one to the other. If we group the bits of the binary notation three at a time, we can predict the value of the octal digit. Thus,

$$000 \rightarrow 0$$
$$001 \rightarrow 1$$
$$010 \rightarrow 2$$
$$011 \rightarrow 3$$
$$100 \rightarrow 4$$
$$101 \rightarrow 5$$
$$110 \rightarrow 6$$
$$111 \rightarrow 7$$

For example, the bit pattern 101110 would imply an octal number of 56 or $5 \times 8 + 6 = 46$. Similarly, if we group bits four at a time, we obtain a predictor of the hex symbol.

Table 1.1 shows six different number systems. Many more exist. One might be tempted to ask if there is a "best" system. If by best one means "most familiar," then the decimal system wins hands down. If by best one means "least expensive," then the question has another answer. Let us suppose that we wish to represent the numbers from 0 to $N$, where $N$ is some large integer. We assume that the "cost" of a single digit is propor-

TABLE 1.1

| Decimal | Binary | Octal | Hex | Trinary | Noval |
|---|---|---|---|---|---|
| 0 | 0 | 0 | 0 | 0 | 0 |
| 1 | 1 | 1 | 1 | 1 | 1 |
| 2 | 10 | 2 | 2 | 2 | 2 |
| 3 | 11 | 3 | 3 | 10 | 3 |
| 4 | 100 | 4 | 4 | 11 | 4 |
| 5 | 101 | 5 | 5 | 12 | 5 |
| 6 | 110 | 6 | 6 | 20 | 6 |
| 7 | 111 | 7 | 7 | 21 | 7 |
| 8 | 1000 | 10 | 8 | 22 | 8 |
| 9 | 1001 | 11 | 9 | 100 | 10 |
| 10 | 1010 | 12 | a | 101 | 11 |
| 11 | 1011 | 13 | b | 102 | 12 |
| 12 | 1100 | 14 | c | 110 | 13 |
| 13 | 1101 | 15 | d | 111 | 14 |
| 14 | 1110 | 16 | e | 112 | 15 |
| 15 | 1111 | 17 | f | 120 | 16 |
| 16 | 10000 | 20 | 10 | 121 | 17 |
| 17 | 10001 | 21 | 11 | 122 | 18 |
| 18 | 10010 | 22 | 12 | 200 | 20 |
| 19 | 10011 | 23 | 13 | 201 | 21 |
| 20 | 10100 | 24 | 14 | 202 | 22 |
| Octal | Y Y Y Y | | | | |
| Binary | $\widetilde{XXX}$ $\widetilde{XXX}$ $\widetilde{XXX}$ $\widetilde{XXX}$ | | | | |
| Hex | Z Z Z | | | | |

tional to the number of values $v$ that the digit can take on, so that the cost of representing the number $N$ will be

$$C = v \cdot p \qquad (1)$$

where $p$ is the number of positions required to represent the number $N$ in radix $v$. The largest number that can be shown with $p$ positions is less than $v$ to the $p$ power, so that we have

$$N < v^p . \qquad (2)$$

Solving this for $p$ we get

$$p > \frac{\log_e N}{\log_e v} . \qquad (3)$$

Substituting in (1), $$C \geq \log_e N \frac{v}{\log_e v} . \qquad (4)$$

The cost of representing $N$ has a minimum when $v$ is equal to $e$, the base of the natural logarithms, but both $v=2$ and $v=3$ are quite close to this value, with $v=3$ having slightly lower cost.

These then are the "best" radices to use, with 3 being slightly better than 2. Yet we said above that the binary system is the most often used. The reason for this is that many physical devices naturally have two readily distinguishable states, and relatively few have three. Consider an ordinary mouse trap. It is easy to decide, perhaps by poking it, whether it is set or sprung. Just exactly *when* it is half set or sprung is hard to judge. Further, it is not a stable state that will persist and *be the same* half an hour from now.

---

*Question 1.3:* Name some common things that have two states. Name some that have three. Are these states "stable"? That is does it take some definite action or application of energy to change from one to the other?

---

Most computers built today use the binary system to represent numbers. Trinary computers have been proposed several times, but never built to my knowledge. Later we will see how even computers that operate in the decimal system are really disguised binary machines. Thus Aristotle, with his two-valued logic and the law of the excluded middle, would be quite at home in a computer factory.

## NEGATIVE NUMBERS

We have discussed above various methods of representing the positive integers. We must now broaden our sights a bit and look at ways of representing negative integers.[2]

In conventional arithmetic, we prefix a minus sign to negative numbers and occasionally put a plus sign in front of positive numbers when there might be ambiguity. This is called a "sign and magnitude" representation. First, one finds out whether a number is positive or negative and then how large it is. This method has been used in several computer designs, usually with one bit reserved for the sign position, zero meaning plus and one meaning minus. It has the tremendous advantage of familiarity and also of readability. A five is a five and has the same bit pattern regardless of whether it is plus five or minus five. Figure 1.3 shows an example of this.

*Number*     *Sign Bit*

+5      0  00.......................0101

−5      1  00.......................0101

Fig. 1.3  A sign and magnitude representation of plus and minus five.

## Modular Arithmetic

Before discussing the other two methods used to represent negative numbers, we must digress a bit and discuss modular arithmetic.  We define an
integer $M$, called the *modulus of our arithmetic*, and note that for any integer $X$, we can find an integer $k$ such that

$$X = k \cdot M + \rho \tag{5}$$

where $\rho$ is called the residue and is unique and is constrained by

$$0 \leq \rho < M$$

In modular arithmetic we consider two numbers to be identical if they
have the same residues.  Table 1.2 shows some examples.

TABLE 1.2   SOME INTEGERS MODULO 3

| | |
|---|---|
| 1. | 0*3+1 |
| 2. | 0*3+2 |
| 3. | 1*3+0 |
| 4. | 1*3+1 |
| 5. | 1*3+2 |
| 6. | 2*3+0 |
| 7. | 2*3+1 |

In modulo 3 then, we treat $0, 3, 6, \ldots$ as being identical, $1, 4, 7,$ as being
identical, and $2, 5, 8, \ldots$ as being identical.

In a digital computer, we often have fixed word lengths of, say $b$-bits.
If we take our modulus to be

$$M = 2^b$$

we can do modular arithmetic simply by ignoring any bits in the results to
the left of the $b$th position.

If we add two numbers together, the residue of their sum is equal to the
sum of their residues.  Thus, taken modulo 5:

$$17 + 21 = 3*5 + 2 + 4*5 + 1 = 38 = 7*5 + 3$$

As another example, consider the sum of 19 and 23:

$$19+23=(3*5+4)+(4*5+3)=7*5+7=8*5+2=42$$

*Radix Complement*

Now we are ready to examine the next way of representing negative numbers. From equation 5 we may write

$$X = X + M \qquad (6)$$

where the sum is taken modulo $M$. By extension, we may write

$$-X = M - X \qquad (7)$$

if once again the arithmetic is done modulo $M$. These equations hold because both sides have the same residue. Now let us consider a number system taken modulo 12 in which we wish to represent both positive and negative integers. Consider Table 1.3.

TABLE 1.3

| Number | | Representation |
|---|---|---|
| 0 | | 0 |
| 1 | | 1 |
| 2 | | 2 |
| 3 | | 3 |
| 4 | | 4 |
| 5 | | 5 |
| $-1 = 12 - 1$ | $=$ | 11 |
| $-2 = 12 - 2$ | $=$ | 10 |
| $-3 = 12 - 3$ | $=$ | 9 |
| $-4 = 12 - 4$ | $=$ | 8 |
| $-5 = 12 - 5$ | $=$ | 7 |
| $-6 = 12 - 6$ | $=$ | 6 |

Let us see what happens if we add the numbers 3 and $-1$. We expect a sum of 2. Three plus minus one is $3+11$ which equals 14 or 2 modulo 12.

Again, $-2$ plus $-2$ is 10 plus 10 which equals 20 or 8 modulo 12. 8 modulo 12 is the representation of minus 4.

The interested reader is urged to explore other combinations. For example, what is the product of 2 and $-3$?

Caution should be exercised however. With the assignment of Table 1.3, we cannot have positive numbers greater than 5 or negative numbers less than $-6$. Observe what happens if we try to add 4 and 4. The answer is 8, which *means* minus 4 and is obviously in error. Many computers store negative numbers in radix complement mode and they must be provided with special circuits to alert the programmer when he inadvertently makes a mistake of this kind.  These are called "overflow circuits" and will be discussed below.

---

*Question 1.4:* Can you guess what phenomenon these circuits are designed to detect?

---

Let us consider a TWO's (radix) complement binary computer with $b$-bits per word.  We take $2^b$ as our modulus and further we let the left-most bit of each word function as a sign bit, with a 0 there indicating positive numbers and a 1 indicating negative numbers.  This means that in a binary machine using radix complement (TWO's complement) arithmetic, the largest positive integer that can be stored in $b$-bits is

$$2^{b-1} - 1$$

and the most negative number that can be stored is

$$-2^{b-1}.$$

We do our arithmetic on positive numbers between 0 and $2^b - 1$.  In the ordinary course of events, the computer doesn't "know" that we are considering the left-most bit of every word to be a sign bit.  It gets added, subtracted, multiplied, and divided just like the rest of the bits.  There is, however, a monitor circuit installed which checks for "unwarranted changes of sign" and when these occur, the monitor generates what is called an "arithmetic overflow" signal.  An unwarranted change of sign would occur if we added two positive numbers and got a negative result.

---

*Question 1.5:* Under what other conditions could an arithmetic overflow signal be generated?  Can one arise from subtraction?

---

To find the radix complement representation of a negative number, we can use a trick to simplify our work.  From equation 7 we can write that

$$-X = M - X = (M - 1) - X + 1 \tag{8}$$

The reason this is convenient is because with $M$ being a power of the radix ($r$), the number $(M - 1)$ consists of a string of digits each being $(r - 1)$.  For example, if $r = 10$, $m = 1000$ and we have

$$M - 1 = 999$$

and our subtraction can never generate a "borrow" from the next higher place.

Table 1.4 shows the integers that can be represented in a four bit word if two's complement arithmetic is used.

If $r$ is the radix, we need have only $r$ entries in our subtraction table to determine the difference between any digit and $r-1$. We "complement" each digit by subtracting it from $r-1$ and then add one to the resulting number, in accordance with equation 8.

TABLE 1.4   FOUR BIT TWO's COMPLEMENT NUMBERS AND THEIR MEANINGS. THE LEFT-MOST BIT IS THE SIGN BIT

| Binary Numbers | Their Meaning |
|---|---|
| 1000 | −8 |
| 1001 | −7 |
| 1010 | −6 |
| 1011 | −5 |
| 1100 | −4 |
| 1101 | −3 |
| 1110 | −2 |
| 1111 | −1 |
| 0000 | 0 |
| 0001 | 1 |
| 0010 | 2 |
| 0011 | 3 |
| 0100 | 4 |
| 0101 | 5 |
| 0110 | 6 |
| 0111 | 7 |

As an example, modulo 10,000,

$$-123 = (9999 - 123) + 1 = (9876) + 1 = 9877 \qquad (12)$$

In the binary system, taking the "TWO's complement" can be expressed in a different way, but it is the same operation. We can say, "To get the TWO's complement of a binary number replace every zero by a one and every one by a zero. Then add one to the result."

---

*Question 1.6:* Another way to say this is "complement every bit to the left of, but not including, the right-most ONE." Give some examples. Why does this work out?

---

The major advantage of this scheme of representing negative numbers is the way in which it permits simplification of computer's hardware. One needs no "subtracter" circuits, only an "adder." When we wish to subtract $B$ from $A$, we take the complement of $B$ and add that to $A$.

*Diminished Radix Complement* (1's comp.)

As you will have noted above, any carry out of the sign position is just quietly forgotten in radix complement arithmetic. Such is not the case with the following scheme called "diminished radix complement."

In this scheme, we also do modular arithmetic and identify $X$ with $X + M$, where $M$ is the modulus. We also employ the trick of equation 8 and write that

$$X = X + M = (X + (M - 1)) + 1 \tag{15}$$

but we postpone adding in the final one until it is absolutely necessary. (See Table 1.5.) Therefore, in "NINE's complement," radix ten, modulus

TABLE 1.5    FOUR BIT ONE's COMPLEMENT
NUMBERS. THE LEFT-MOST BIT
IS AGAIN THE SIGN BIT

| Binary Number | Its Meaning |
|:---:|:---:|
| 1000 | −7 |
| 1001 | −6 |
| 1010 | −5 |
| 1011 | −4 |
| 1100 | −3 |
| 1101 | −2 |
| 1110 | −1 |
| 1111 | −0 |
| 0000 | 0 |
| 0001 | 1 |
| 0010 | 2 |
| 0011 | 3 |
| 0100 | 4 |
| 0101 | 5 |
| 0110 | 6 |
| 0111 | 7 |

10000 arithmetic we say that

$$-123 = 9999 - 123 = 9876 \tag{16}$$

Let us now add 456 to that and examine the result.

$$456 - 123 = 0456 + 9876 = 10332 \tag{17}$$

If we merely throw away the carry out of the sign digit (the left-most one) we get the wrong answer. It will be one too small. The clue then is to take the carry out of the sign position (if there is one) and add it into the low order (right-most) position of the result. Thus

$$10332 = 1 + 0332 = 333 \qquad (18)$$

as required. This is not difficult to do in practice.

Designers like to use the same circuits over and over again, since this reduces cost. In a radix complement adder, all the digit positions are the same except for the right-most one. They all must have inputs for the two digits and for the carry from the next less significant position to their right. But the least significant position has no right-hand neighbor and, consequently, either must have a special circuit or else must leave the carry input unused. Quite often the second solution is the one chosen. When this is the case, "adding in the carry out of the sign position" requires nothing more than connecting a single wire. Utilizing this otherwise idle portion of the circuit warms the cockles of a penny-pinching designer's heart.

The second and perhaps more understandable advantage of diminished radix complement notation (in binary it is called "ONE's complement") is the fact that it is easy to implement the complementation process. As we will see in the next chapter, when we look at flip-flops, the normal output and its one's complement are equally available. It is merely a matter of selecting which one you want when.

A third advantage to diminished radix complement notation is that with a little practice, it is almost as easy to read as sign and magnitude. (See Table 1.5.)

With all these advantages, the reader may well ask why it has not swept all before it and become *the* way of representing negative numbers. The answer is more emotional than technical. Programmers in general do not like one's complement arithmetic. The reason is that there are two ways of writing down "zero," namely "all zeros" and its one's complement, "all ones." This second representation called "minus zero" is always getting in the way, particularly when generating an address (see Chapter 4) and when one is testing the accumulator to see if it contains a positive number or not, one normally tends to think of zero as being positive.

Programmer preference for two's complement notation has lead to its adoption by most computer manufacturers.

## NON-INTEGERS

So far we have considered only the representation of integers. Unfortunately, not all the world is made up of followers of Diophantus, and there are those who insist on using non-integral numbers, like seven and one-half, for instance. Once one has opened the door to seemingly innocuous numbers like seven and one-half, one finds a whole troop of monsters like $e$ and $\pi$ and 7.4999 coming in at its heels. The obvious solution to this problem is to introduce a "decimal point" into our notation, or giving it its more general name, a "radix point." This permits a reasonable approximation to most of the numbers of interest, limited only by the number of digits that are employed.

The positional notation is extended to the right of the radix point in exact symmetry with its use for integers. The least significant position of an integer has a weight of $r^0$ or 1. The first position to the right of the radix point has a weight of $r^{-1}$, the next of $r^{-2}$, and so on. In decimal notation we write

$$1.234$$

and mean

$$1 \times 10^0 + 2 \times 10^{-1} + 3 \times 10^{-2} + 4 \times 10^{-3}.$$

If that number was considered to be in octal, we would mean

$$1 \times 8^0 + 2 \times 8^{-1} + 3 \times 8^{-2} + 4 \times 8^{-3}.$$

The only question that remains is where to put the radix point. Most large modern computers give the programmer three possible choices which he may employ at will, and even, if he dares, may use first one and then another.

*Fixed Point*

The first is simple. It is immediately to the right of the least significant digit. But this is just the integer notation we have discussed before. Consequently, the multiply and divide operations, which assume that "binal point" location, are called "integer multiply" and "integer divide." The next option is to place the binal point immediately to the right of the sign bit and before the first information bit. This convention implies that all numbers are less than one. Therefore, the two operations are called "fractional multiply" and "fractional divide." Integer multiply can cause an overflow to occur if the product is larger than the modulus. Integer divide causes trouble only if you attempt to divide by zero, since the next smallest integer is one and dividing by one serves only to waste machine time. Fractional multiply never causes trouble, because the product of two numbers less than one is itself less than one and hence can be represented. Fractional divide will cause a "divide check," which is a form of overflow if the divisor is less than the dividend in absolute magnitude, since this would generate a number larger than *one*, which cannot be represented with this convention.

### Floating Point

The third option is called "floating point" to distinguish it from the preceding two.[3,4] It is the one which is usually used to manipulate what the compiler writers like to call "real numbers," as distinct from integers. In scientific notation, it is usual to write down a number as a digit between one and nine, followed by a decimal point and some more digits. Then, multiply this by ten to an appropriate power. The first part is called the mantissa and the latter the exponent. The correct names for these parts of a number are the "signicand" and the "exrad," but they are hardly ever used. Thus,

$$123 = 1.23 \times 10^2$$
$$5482 = 5.482 \times 10^3$$
$$0.0187 = 1.87 \times 10^{-2} \tag{19}$$
$$-257.3 = -2.573 \times 10^2$$

where for example, 1.23 is the mantissa and 2 is the exponent.

In digital computers, the same scheme is used to store floating point numbers, but with certain modifications. First, we have one bit to represent the sign of number, then several bits to represent the exponent, and finally several more bits to represent the mantissa, so scaled that it lies between one-half and one.* Thus the number,

$$\pm m \cdot 2^x$$

is represented by

$$\pm, x, m$$

where $x$ is adjusted so that the first bit of $m$ is a one if the number is positive and zero if it is negative. Suppose, for example, we wish to represent the number eleven, which has an integer bit pattern of 1011. We must divide this by $2^4 = 16$ to get it to lie between one-half and one. It might be represented in floating point as—

| 0 | 100 | 1011 |
|---|-----|------|
| sign | exponent | mantissa |

Translating this back to decimal we would read

$$+2^4 \cdot (\tfrac{1}{2} + \tfrac{1}{8} + \tfrac{1}{16}) \text{ or} + 11$$

But how would we represent the number one-eighth? This clearly should be "plus, two to the minus two, times one-half." But we have not yet shown how to write down negative exponents. The way this is most often done in computers is by using what is called an "excess two to the $n$th" notation where $n$ varies considerably between various machines. Let us

---

*There are some machines that have the exponent represent powers of 16 rather than powers of 2. In these cases, the mantissa is adjusted until it lies between one-sixteenth and one.

*Handwritten top margin:* 5d = 101   normalized = .1010 and in so doing you moved binal pt. 3 places left

suppose that in a particular machine there are seven bit positions set aside
to hold the exponent. The scheme works like this. An exponent of zero is
represented by the bit pattern 1000000 or in decimal, 64. Plus one is represented by 1000001 or 65, and minus one by 0111111 or 63. The largest
number that can be represented with seven bits is 127, and this is taken
to mean an exponent of plus 63. The smallest is zero, which implies a
multiplication by two to the minus 64th power. If you prefer, you can
consider the left-most bit of the exponent to be a sign bit (where a one
means plus and a zero means minus) and the exponent expressed in two's
complement notation.

Thus, we would actually write $11_d$ as

|  0  | 1000100 | 1011 |
|-----|---------|------|
| sign | exponent | mantissa |

*Handwritten:* to convert to dec.# E = 68 − 64 = 4 or $2^4$ ① Can then move mantissa binal pt 4 places to right : .1011 ⟹ 1011. Then decode binary: $11_d$

and we would write one-eighth as

|  0  | 0111110 | 1000 |
|-----|---------|------|
| sign | exponent | mantissa |

*Handwritten:* or ② can figure $2^4 = 16$ times decimal rep of m = .1011 : $16 \times (1 \times 2^{-1} + 1 \times 2^{-3} + 1 \times 2^{-4})$ $= 16 \times (\frac{1}{2} + \frac{1}{8} + \frac{1}{16}) = 16 \times 11$

(plus, two to the minus two, times one-half). The number "zero" is usually represented in floating point notation as a string of all zeros.

The four arithmetic operations (add, subtract, multiply, and divide) in
floating point deserve special attention. Suppose we have two numbers

$$\pm M_1 \cdot 2^{X_1} \text{ and } \pm M_2 \cdot 2^{X_1}$$

They will be represented as

$$S_1 E_1 M_1 \text{ and } S_2 E_2 M_2$$

where $S$ represents the sign bit (1 for minus, 0 for plus). The product of
these two numbers should be found by multiplying the two mantissas and
adding the exponents,

$$M_1 \cdot M_2 \cdot 2^{X_1 + X_2}$$

but we note firstly that we cannot simply add the two exponent fields that
we have since

$$E_1 = X_1 + 64 \text{ and } E_2 = X_2 + 64$$

the sum would be too large by 64. Therefore, we let the exponent of the
product

*Handwritten:* in excess-64 (i.e., still 64 over real value)

$$E_p = E_1 + E_2 - 64 = X_1 + X_2 + 64$$

Secondly, we cannot just multiply the two mantissas together because
their product may be less than a half. The process of bringing the product
back to the range between one-half and one is called "normalization."

We find an integer $K$ such that,

$$\tfrac{1}{2} \leq M_1 \cdot M_2 \cdot 2^K < 1. \tag{20}$$

We must subtract this number $K$ from the final value of the exponent. The result of a floating multiply will therefore be given as

$$S_p E_p M_p \tag{21}$$

where

$$S_p = 0 \text{ if } S_1 = S_2$$
$$1 \text{ if } S_1 \neq S_2$$
$$E_p = E_1 + E_2 - 64 - K$$
$$M_p = M_1 \cdot M_2 \cdot 2^K$$

**($K$ being selected to satisfy equation 20)**

As an example, consider the multiplication of 11 by one-eighth. Adding exponents and subtracting off the excess "excess 64" we get

10000100 + 0111110 = 10000010 or 2 + 128
less 64 gives 1000010 or 2 + 64.

Multiplying mantissas we have

.1011 * .1000 = .01011.

But this must be normalized by shifting left one position (multiplying by 2) and then subtracting one from the exponent. The result is

$$\underbrace{0}_{sign} \quad \underbrace{1000001}_{exponent} \quad \underbrace{.1011}_{mantissa}$$

The reader should verify that this really does represent eleven-eights.

The process of floating division is analogous. The quotient $n_1$ divided by $n_2$ is

$$S_q E_q M_q$$

where

$$S_q = 0 \text{ if } S_1 = S_2$$
$$= 1 \text{ if } S_1 \neq S_2$$
$$E_q = E_1 - E_2 + 64 - k \tag{22}$$
$$M_q = (M_1/M_2) \cdot 2^k$$
$$\text{for } k \text{ selected such that}$$
$$\tfrac{1}{2} \leq (M_1/M_2) 2^k < 1$$

In order to add or subtract two floating point numbers, we must adjust them so that they both have the same value of exponent. Suppose that $n_1$

is larger than $n_2$. We find a number $j$ such that

$$j = X_1 - X_2 \tag{23}$$

We modify $n_2$ by adding $j$ to the exponent and dividing the mantissa by $2^j$,

$$n_2 = S_2(E_2 + j) M_2/2^j$$

and then add or subtract the mantissas of $n_1$ and $n_2$ as required. The result is then normalized à la equation 20.

As an example, let us add 11 and 3 to get, we hope, 14. Firstly, the number 3 will be stored as 2 plus 64 times (one-half plus one-fourth) or:

(11)  0  1000100  .1011

(3)     0    1000010    .1100

     sign     exponent     mantissa

and must be shifted right two places so that its exponent will be the same as that of the other number. Thus, we modify the representation of 3 to have:

     0     1000100     .0011

     sign     exponent     mantissa

Now that the exponents are the same, we can add the mantissas:

$$+\begin{array}{r} .0011 \\ .1011 \\ \hline .1110 \end{array}$$

and finding that we do not need any normalization in this case, we end up with

     0     1000100     .1110

     sign     exponent     mantissa

---

*Question 1.7:* Add 11 and 7. Subtract 7 from 11.

---

All these operations are carried out by hardware and are available on most computers of today. Their existence has relieved the programmer of the tedious task of keeping track of where the binal point is (or should be) to avoid overflow and/or loss of significance. The penalty that one must pay is twofold. One, floating point operations are generally much slower than fixed point, by factors of 2 or 5. Two, given a fixed word size in a computer, using up some of the bits to hold the exponent, leaves less to store the value of a number, and hence, a given number will be represented with fewer significant digits than is possible in fixed point. Nonetheless, the simplicity of using floating point is so great that these penalties are gladly accepted by most programmers for scientific computations where there is a large range of values that numbers may assume and where it is often difficult to predict in advance where within the range a particular set of data may fall.

## OTHER SCHEMES OF REPRESENTING NUMBERS

Although two is the most common radix in use in modern computers, there is a large class of machines, those designed primarily for business data processing, that use the normal decimal system internally. There are even some that permit the programmer to use both decimal and binary arithmetic.

Since devices with ten stable states, one for each digit from 0 to 9, are not too common,* these decimal machines fall back on using bistable (two state) devices and combining these in groups of four (or more) to represent each decimal digit.

Before discussing some of these schemes, we should point out two disadvantages and two advantages of a decimal computer.

Decimal arithmetic is more complicated than binary. Figure 1.4 shows the addition and multiplication tables for binary arithmetic.

The $10 \times 10$ tables for decimal addition and multiplication are well known.

Implementing tables with four entries is about 25 times simpler and cheaper than implementing tables with 100.

Using four bistable devices to represent 10 possible states is inefficient. Four bistable devices can store 16 distinct states. Using 32 bits in a "decimal" machine, one can store only 8 decimal digits (4 bits per digit) confining one's self therefore to numbers less than $10^8$. On the other hand, if the 32 bits are used to store a binary number, we may have $2^{32}$, which is somewhat larger than $4 \times 10^9$, a gain of one-and-a-half significant figures.

|     | Sum |     |     | Product |     |
| --- | --- | --- | --- | --- | --- |
|     | 0   | 1   |     | 0   | 1   |
| 0   | 0   | 1   | 0   | 0   | 0   |
| 1   | 1   | 10  | 1   | 0   | 1   |

Fig. 1.4 Addition and multiplication tables for binary arithmetic.

*Mechanical desk calculators use notched wheels with ten or more notches in them, but moving mechanical parts are too slow for use in high-speed computers.

Decimal computers have the great advantage of using a familiar number system that does not require training to learn.  Or rather, say, that most people are already trained in their use.  The second advantage is even more important.  A large proportion of business data processing involves reading in information prepared by people and putting out other information intended to be consumed by people.  This means that both input and output must be in decimal and, if the machine is binary, there must be a translation at each end.  If the amount of actual computing to be done is small, then this translation becomes an appreciable part of the work load of the machine.  Avoiding this translation by using a decimal machine then becomes worthwhile.

## Codes For Decimal Digits

Let us consider a way of mapping the 10 decimal digits onto the 16 possible states of four bistable devices.  There are 16 ways of choosing the state which will represent zero.  Once that choice has been made, there are still 15 states remaining unchosen, any of which may be used to represent the number 1.  Following this through, we will have 7 states unassigned, any one of which may be chosen to represent the number 9.  The total number of codes that exist for representing the decimal digits in 4 bits is the product of all these ways or

$$\frac{16!}{6!} = 29,059,430,400,$$

or about $3 \times 10^{10}$ possible codes.  We will not examine all of them here, but we will look at one or two of special interest.

The first and most obvious, and actually the most widely used code, is the "8, 4, 2, 1" code in which the 10 decimal digits are assigned to the patterns which correspond to the first 10 binary numbers.  The appropriate correspondences have already been shown in Table 1.  This is commonly called "Binary Coded Decimal," or BCD for short.  (To represent the decimal number 56 for example, we use four bits to store the 5 and another four bits to store the 6.  Thus, 56=0101 0110).  It is only one of several possible "weighted" codes where each of the four positions is given a weight and the digit being represented can be found by adding up the weights of those positions containing ones.

---

*Question 1.8:* Write down the 10 decimal digits and next to them the patterns that correspond to the following weighted codes:  8421, 7421, 4221, 4321.  Note that in some cases there is more than one way of representing a particular digit.

---

It is not even necessary for all the weights to be positive. 8, 4, −2, −1, and 6, 4, 3, −2, are perfectly good weighted codes for example.

An advantage of the 8421 system is that the sum of two digits is the sum of their representations. For example:

$$3 + 5 = 8 \text{ or } 0011 + 0101 = 1000$$

If the resulting sum is greater than nine, one must generate a "carry" signal and translate the resulting number.

The 8, 4, −2, −1 code has the interesting property that the nine's complement of the digit *decimal* may be found by taking the one's complement of the representation. Several other weighted codes share this property, as do some non-weighted codes. A code which has received some attention in the past is known as the "excess three" or XS3 code. We represent the digit zero by the binary pattern 0011, one by 0100, two by 0101, and so forth. The digit being represented can be discovered by subtracting three from the value that the representation would have in binary. The reason for interest in this code is that it combines the two features we have mentioned above. The NINE's complement *order digit XS3 code* is found by taking the ONE's complement of the *BCD* bits and the sum of two digits can be discovered by taking the sum of their representations and then subtracting three.

XS - 3 :  add as in binary except, if is a carry, add 3 to sum
_____
          no carry, subtract 3 (or add (0s comp of 3 = 1(0))

*Question 1.9:* Generate the assignment table for the XS 3 code. Show with some examples that the sum of the representations of pairs of digits produces a new representation that is too large by "three" to represent the sum of the digits. 9's comp. of all values ; 2 ex. showing why it works.

_____
'0s comp of the binary digit (bit) = 9s comp plus 1.

Scott contains an excellent discussion of these and other codes.[5]

## Non-Numeric Representations

Although numerical analysts would have you believe that computers are devices for performing arithmetic at great speed, a slightly more general viewpoint might suggest that computers are really devices for performing logical operations rapidly that have, by dint of a lot of hard work, been made capable of doing arithmetic as well. To lend credence to this point of view, it is necessary to be able to enter symbols other than numbers into the computer.

Now there are 10 digits, 26 letters, and a dozen or so punctuation marks in common usage—roughly 50 to 60 symbols not counting upper and lower case letters. To represent this many symbols, we will need at least six bits per symbol. Six bits limits us to 64 distinct bit patterns, and they may be assigned in any desired fashion, one to each of the characters. There are two cautions to be observed in selecting a particular set of assignments. First, it will be convenient for the translation of decimal numbers into internal binary if the digits are represented by the bit patterns whose binary value corresponds to the value of the digit. Second, it will be convenient for sorting names and other symbolic information if we maintain a relationship between the binary value of the bit pattern and the normal lexicographic ordering of the letters:    namely $A, B, C, \ldots$, with perhaps the "space" preceding $A$. One can then say that $A$ precedes $B$ both in alphabetic sequence and in the value of the representation.

Many machines have been built which utilized a 6 bit code for representing the characters. More recently, there has been a movement toward 8 bit codes. There are several reasons behind this change.

To begin with, 6 bits are not enough to include lower case letters as well as upper case. As computers move into more general use, there is a necessity to make them correspond more closely with what the general public is used to. This means at least the ability to print both upper and lower case symbols. Seven bits can provide enough patterns for upper and lower case letters, the digits, and punctuation and still allow some room for expansion if we decide that a new symbol is used frequently enough to warrant its inclusion in the standard character set.

Once we have gone to seven bits, it is only a short step to eight. Now eight is a power to two and consequently easier to deal with in the binary system than either 6 or 7. In eight bits, one can store either one of 256 different symbols or a pair of BCD digits. In some cases, the eighth bit is not used to convey information directly, but is used to convey information about the other seven bits. When this is the case, the eighth bit is called a parity bit and is used to check the validity of the other seven bits.

### Parity Bits

The input output devices that are attached to a computer are generally less reliable than the internal parts of the machine. The paper tape readers, card readers, magnetic tape drives, etc. have moving parts that are subject to wear and misalignment. This means that they are prone to making errors, i.e., reading a hole for a no-hole and a one for a zero. Now it is quite obvious that no computer processing of information can be more meaningful than the data that is fed into the machine. We would like to be able to check up on these relatively unreliable devices and make sure that they are doing their jobs properly. This is what a parity bit is intended to do.

Suppose that of the 256 possible bit patterns provided by 8 bits, we decided to use only those that have an odd number of "ones" in them.

Either 1, 3, 5, or 7 ones. If then we were to read in a bit pattern and discover that it had an even number of ones, we would be certain that some mistake had been made and could either try to re-read the pattern or at worst stop the machine until the operator or the engineer corrected the flaw. If a malfunction causes an input-output device to misread a one for a zero or the other way around, and if we started with an odd number of ones, this single mistake will generate an even number of ones and, if there is appropriate checking circuitry, generate an error signal. If two mistakes are made in reading a particular bit pattern, we will end up again with an

TABLE 1.6   SIXTY-FOUR CHARACTERS FROM AN EVEN PARITY FORM OF THE ASCII CODE

| | | | |
|---|---|---|---|
| Space | 10100000 | @ | 11000000 |
| ! | 00100001 | A | 01000001 |
| " | 00100010 | B | 01000010 |
| # | 10100011 | C | 11000011 |
| $ | 00100100 | D | 01000100 |
| % | 10100101 | E | 11000101 |
| & | 10100110 | F | 11000110 |
| ' | 00100111 | G | 01000111 |
| ( | 00101000 | H | 01001000 |
| ) | 10101001 | I | 11001001 |
| * | 10101010 | J | 11001010 |
| + | 00101011 | K | 01001011 |
| , | 10101100 | L | 11001100 |
| - | 00101101 | M | 01001101 |
| . | 00101110 | N | 01001110 |
| / | 10101111 | O | 11001111 |
| 0 | 00110000 | P | 01010000 |
| 1 | 10110001 | Q | 11010001 |
| 2 | 10110010 | R | 11010010 |
| 3 | 00110011 | S | 01010011 |
| 4 | 10110100 | T | 11010100 |
| 5 | 00110101 | U | 01010101 |
| 6 | 00110110 | V | 01010110 |
| 7 | 10110111 | W | 11010111 |
| 8 | 10111000 | X | 11011000 |
| 9 | 00111001 | Y | 01011001 |
| : | 00111010 | Z | 01011010 |
| ; | 10111011 | [ | 11011011 |
| < | 00111100 | \ | 01011100 |
| = | 10111101 | ] | 11011101 |
| > | 10111110 | ↑ | 11011110 |
| ? | 00111111 | ← | 01011111 |

odd number of ones and will pass the check, even though the character is now grossly in error. What we are relying on with a parity check, as this is called, is that if a single error has a small probability, say 1 in 10,000, then a double error has a probability of only one in 100,000,000 and can for most purposes be ignored.

The designer of a code may choose to have either odd parity (described above) or even parity in which the machine expects an *even* number of ones and balks when it finds an odd number.

The American Standards Committee on Information Interchange (*ASCII*) (pronounced Asskey-2) has devised an eight bit, or as it is some-times called an eight level, code which has been quite widely accepted. Many competitors exist, and no single system has been accepted by every-one in the computer field. One version of the *ASCII* code is shown in Table 1.6.

## Residue Number Systems

Another way of representing numbers which has many useful properties is called the residue number system.[6,7] It is perhaps most easily described by giving an example. Take any set of integers that are all prime, say 5 and 3. Then the largest number which can be expressed is one less than the product of the members of the set. If the members are $p_1, p_2, \ldots p_n$ one discovers the representation of a particular number by taking its value modulo $p_1$ for the first space, modulo $p_2$ for the second, etc. Table 1.7 shows the representation of the numbers 0 through 14 in the (5,3) residue sys.

TABLE 1.7    A RESIDUE NUMBER
BASED ON 5 and 3

| Number | (5,3) |
|--------|-------|
| 0 | 0,0 |
| 1 | 1,1 |
| 2 | 2,2 |
| 3 | 3,0 |
| 4 | 4,1 |
| 5 | 0,2 |
| 6 | 1,0 |
| 7 | 2,1 |
| 8 | 3,2 |
| 9 | 4,0 |
| 10 | 0,1 |
| 11 | 1,2 |
| 12 | 2,0 |
| 13 | 3,1 |
| 14 | 4,2 |

system. (Note the value of a number modulo $n$ is called its "residue.") Now the first interesting property of this form of representation is that the sum of two numbers $N_1$ and $N_2$ can be found by taking the sum of the respective pairs of elements; each sum being computed modulo the prime corresponding to that position. For example, 4 is represented by (4,1) and 8 by (3,2). $4+3=7=2$ modulo 5 and $1+2=3=0$ modulo 3. We claim, therefore, that the sum of 4 and 8 should be represented by (2,0), which is indeed the representation of 12. Subtraction also works well.

What is particularly interesting is that multiplication works in the same fashion. Consider the product of 3 and 4. $3\times4=12=2$ modulo 5 and $0\times1=0$ modulo 3. The result is again (2,0), which indeed is the representation for 12. The interested reader may check for himself that the results of addition, subtraction, and multiplication are always correct modulo the product of the primes. Since this is true, negative numbers can be expressed by complementing each element of a representation relative to its prime.

The only operation which is difficult to perform is division.[8]

---

*Question 1.10:* Compare the density of information storage (assuming bistable devices) of binary and the residue number systems.

---

Once again, so far as this author knows, no machines have yet been constructed using a residue number system, but considerable theoretical work has been done and one day we may see one.

We have now examined a number of ways of representing information. Each way has its advantages and disadvantages. If one were forced to choose, one might well choose a binary, two's complement number system with other symbols represented in ASCII, but it is well to be aware of some of the possible alternatives, since who knows when a good cheap tristable device may come along and change all our thinking.

## REFERENCES

1. Brown, N. S., and Richman, P. L. "The Choice of Base." *CACM* **12**, 10, 560–562 (Oct. 1969).
2. Stein, M., and Munro, W. D. *Introduction to Machine Arithmetic.* Addison-Wesley, 1972.
3. Brent, R. P. "On the Precision Obtainable with Various Floating Point Number Systems." *IEEE Trans. on Comp.* C-22, 6, 601–607 (June 1973).
4. Cody, W. J. "Static and Dynamic Numerical Characteristics of Floating Point Addition." *IEEE Trans. on Comp.* C-22, 6, 598–601 (June 1973).
5. Scott, N. R. *Analog and Digital Computer Technology.* New York, McGraw-Hill, 1960.

6. Gilmore, P. A. *A Residue Number System, GER-12195.* Akron, Ohio, Good-year Aerospace Corp., 1965.
7. Garner, H. "The Residue Number System." *Proc. 1959 Western Joint Comput. Conf.,* 146–152.
8. Keir, Y. A., Cheney, P. W., and Tannenbaum, M. "Division and Overflow Detection in Residue Number Systems." *IRE Trans.* EC **11,** 4, 501–507 (Aug. 1962).

# 2 | GATES AND ELEMENTARY LOGIC

*A hair perhaps divides the False and True*
*Omar Khayyám*

In order to understand computer design, we must know a little bit about the circuits from which machines are constructed. In this chapter we will not examine how such circuits are designed. That is a course in itself. We will look instead at some simple circuit elements and discuss their external characteristics, that is, we will treat them as "black boxes." As we will see, only a small number of different types of circuits are used in computer design. Naturally, a designer will employ variations on these types, e.g., a high powered circuit capable of driving 20 or 30 other circuits, or a sensitive circuit that will respond to small currents or voltages. But we will not be concerned with these subtleties, only with the general cases.

In much of the literature you will find these simple circuits referred to as *gates.* This is because of their ability to "open" and "close" pathways for signals.

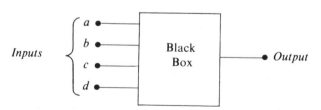

Fig. 2.1 A "black box" with four inputs and one output.

| $a$ | $b$ |
|-----|-----|
| 0 | 0 |
| 0 | 1 |
| 1 | 0 |
| 1 | 1 |

Fig. 2.2 Possible combinations of two inputs.

## BLACK BOXES

Consider the box shown in Fig. 2.1. Restricting ourselves to the binary system, we can say that each of the four inputs may be either ZERO or ONE, and that the output may also assume either of these values. There are two possible states for input $a$ and two for $b$. Considering only these two inputs for a moment, there are four possible combinations, namely, both ZERO, both ONE, $a$ ZERO and $b$ ONE, and $a$ ONE and $b$ ZERO. (See Fig. 2.2.)

Now consider input $c$. It may be either ZERO or ONE. For each case there are four combinations that $a$ and $b$ may assume, so taken all together the three inputs $a$, $b$, and $c$ may assume 8 different states, or combinations. (See Fig. 2.3.) When we add input $d$ which also has two possible values the four inputs can, between them all, attain 16 possible states. If there were $N$ inputs to the box, each assuming one of two states, there would be a total of $2^N$ possible input conditions.

Now for each possible input condition or combination or state we may, when we are "designing" the black box, choose to have the output either ZERO or ONE. Once we have made a choice for a particular black box, we will always observe that output, be it ZERO or ONE, whenever the corresponding input combination occurs. There is *no* random demon inside *our* black boxes. Figure 2.4 shows the output of one of the possible black boxes that we might design. It has been "designed" to produce a

| $a$ | $b$ | $c$ |
|-----|-----|-----|
| 0 | 0 | 0 |
| 0 | 0 | 1 |
| 0 | 1 | 0 |
| 0 | 1 | 1 |
| 1 | 0 | 0 |
| 1 | 0 | 1 |
| 1 | 1 | 0 |
| 1 | 1 | 1 |

Fig. 2.3 Possible combinations of three inputs.

|     | Input<br>a b c d | Output |
| --- | --- | --- |
| 0   | 0 0 0 0 | 0 |
| 1   | 0 0 0 1 | 1 |
| 2   | 0 0 1 0 | 1 |
| 3   | 0 0 1 1 | 0 |
| 4   | 0 1 0 0 | 1 |
| 5   | 0 1 0 1 | 0 |
| 6   | 0 1 1 0 | 0 |
| 7   | 0 1 1 1 | 1 |
| 8   | 1 0 0 0 | 1 |
| 9   | 1 0 0 1 | 0 |
| 10  | 1 0 1 0 | 0 |
| 11  | 1 0 1 1 | 1 |
| 12  | 1 1 0 0 | 0 |
| 13  | 1 1 0 1 | 1 |
| 14  | 1 1 1 0 | 1 |
| 15  | 1 1 1 1 | 0 |

Fig. 2.4 An example of one possible "black box" which shows the output that the box will generate for each of the sixteen possible input states.

ONE whenever the number of ONE's in the input is odd. If there are 0, 2, or 4 ONE's in the input, the box produces a ZERO output.

---

*Question 2.1:* Can you think of a place you might use the black box specified by Fig. 2.4?

---

Since we have specified what the box will produce for all possible combination of inputs, there is not much else interesting to say about it, except perhaps what is inside the box. We will not look inside the box just yet. First we must do a bit of preparation.

How many different black boxes could we construct with four inputs? If two boxes are to be considered to be different from each other, there must be at least one input combination which, when presented to the two boxes, will cause one of them to produce a ONE and the other a ZERO. How else could we tell them apart? To say this another way, when we design a black box we must specify a binary number which has as many bits in it as there are input combinations. If two boxes are "different," their binary numbers are different. Given a certain number of bits $C$, there are exactly $2^C$ different binary numbers that can be expressed, starting with zero, one, ..., $(2^C - 1)$.

| Input a b | Black Boxes | | | | | | | | | | | | | | | |
|---|---|---|---|---|---|---|---|---|---|---|---|---|---|---|---|---|
| | 0 | 1 | 2 | 3 | 4 | 5 | 6 | 7 | 8 | 9 | 10 | 11 | 12 | 13 | 14 | 15 |
| 0 0 | 0 | 1 | 0 | 1 | 0 | 1 | 0 | 1 | 0 | 1 | 0 | 1 | 0 | 1 | 0 | 1 |
| 0 1 | 0 | 0 | 1 | 1 | 0 | 0 | 1 | 1 | 0 | 0 | 1 | 1 | 0 | 0 | 1 | 1 |
| 1 0 | 0 | 0 | 0 | 0 | 1 | 1 | 1 | 1 | 0 | 0 | 0 | 0 | 1 | 1 | 1 | 1 |
| 1 1 | 0 | 0 | 0 | 0 | 0 | 0 | 0 | 0 | 1 | 1 | 1 | 1 | 1 | 1 | 1 | 1 |
| | NULL | NOR | NOT A | | NOT B | EQUAL | NAND | AND | EQUAL | | B | A⊃B | A | B⊃A | OR | UNITY |
| | | | | XOR—NOT | | | | | | | | | | | | |

Fig. 2.5 The sixteen possible black boxes with two inputs.

With 4 inputs there are 16 possible input combinations. For each of these input combinations we can choose one of two possible outputs. There are, therefore, $2 \times 2 \times \ldots 16$ times, or $2^{16}$ possible black boxes with 4 inputs. That is roughly 65,000 and would be rather many to enumerate. Instead, in Fig. 2.5 we show the 16 possible black boxes with two inputs. There are exactly 16 such boxes because two inputs can assume any one of four possible combination and $2^4$ is 16.

Whatever black box with two inputs you propose, you will find it already in Fig. 2.5.

Some of the boxes in Fig. 2.5 are rather silly. Box number 0 always produces a ZERO no matter what input combination is presented to it. Box 15 always produces a ONE. For Boxes 3 and 12, the value of the output is the same no matter what value input *b* assumes. Input *a* alone determines whether the output is ZERO or ONE. Boxes 5 and 10 similarly ignore input *a* and depend solely on *b*. For these boxes one might just as well disconnect the other input. That is what we have done in Fig. 2.6. There are four possible boxes with one input shown in Fig. 2.6.

| Input | | Output 0 1 2 3 |
|---|---|---|
| | | |
| 0 | | 0 1 0 1 |
| 1 | | 0 0 1 1 |

Fig. 2.6 A black box with only one input.

a in (3,12,
b in (5, 10 above w/o ignored inputs)

| $a$ | $\Theta$ |
|---|---|
| 0 | 1 |
| 1 | 0 |

Fig. 2.7 An inverter or NOT circuit and its truth table.

Ignoring boxes 0 and 3 in Fig 2.6, there are only two remaining. One of them (box 2) merely reproduces the input. We can replace this with a single wire connecting the input to the output. Box 1 of Fig. 2.6 is more interesting. It "inverts" or "complements" the input, interchanging ZERO's and ONE's. It is called an "inverter" or a NOT circuit. Whatever the input is, the output is NOT that. (See Fig. 2.7). A NOT is usually shown as a small open circle. This circle is usually "slid along" the line forward or backward until it meets another element. (See Fig. 2.9.)

Returning now to Fig. 2.5, let us look at box 8. It produces a ONE if and only if both input $a$ and input $b$ are ONE. It is called an AND element, and it is shown with a conventionalized symbol in Fig. 2.8. AND elements with $3, 4, \ldots,$ many inputs may be built. They will generate an output of ONE only if *all* their inputs are ONE simultaneously.

If we combine an AND and a NOT, we get black box 7, which is called a NAND element. (See Fig. 2.9.)

Another interesting black box in Fig. 2.5 is number 14. It is called an "inclusive or" (often just plain "OR"). If either $a$ or $b$ or both are ONE, the output is ONE. (See Fig. 2.10.)

Compare the inclusive OR of box 14 with the "exclusive or" (XOR) of Box 6 in which the joint case is *excluded*.

Figure 2.12 shows a simplified diagram of a transistor NOR circuit

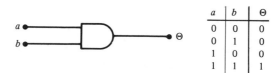

| $a$ | $b$ | $\Theta$ |
|---|---|---|
| 0 | 0 | 0 |
| 0 | 1 | 0 |
| 1 | 0 | 0 |
| 1 | 1 | 1 |

Fig. 2.8 An AND element with its truth table.

| $a$ | $b$ | $\Theta$ |
|---|---|---|
| 0 | 0 | 1 |
| 0 | 1 | 1 |
| 1 | 0 | 1 |
| 1 | 1 | 0 |

Fig. 2.9 A NAND element.

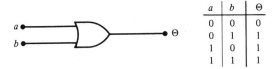

| a | b | Θ |
|---|---|---|
| 0 | 0 | 0 |
| 0 | 1 | 1 |
| 1 | 0 | 1 |
| 1 | 1 | 1 |

Fig. 2.10  An inclusive OR element.

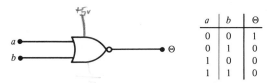

| a | b | Θ |
|---|---|---|
| 0 | 0 | 1 |
| 0 | 1 | 0 |
| 1 | 0 | 0 |
| 1 | 1 | 0 |

Fig. 2.11  A NOR element.

whose logical behavior is shown in Fig. 2.11.  It is a property of NPN transistors that if the base is more positive than the emitter, then current can pass between the collector and the emitter easily.

If the base is negative with respect to the emitter, then the resistance between collector and emitter will be high.  Let us adopt the convention that +5 volts is a logical ONE and 0 volts is a logical ZERO.  (See Fig. 2.13.)  Then if either *a* or *b* or both are ONE, the base will be positive with respect to the emitter, the transistor will be highly conductive, and the output node will be close to zero volts, representing a logical ZERO. Only if neither *a* or *b* are ONE (they are both ZERO) will the base be

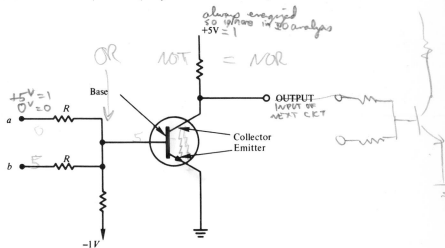

Fig. 2.12  A diagram of a two input NOR circuit.

| a | b | Output |
|---|---|---|
| $0^v$ | $0^v$ | $5^v$ |
| $0^v$ | $5^v$ | $0^v$ |
| $5^v$ | $0^v$ | $0^v$ |
| $5^v$ | $5^v$ | $0^v$ |

Fig. 2.13 The truth table of a NOR circuit.

$+5^v$ = logical ONE, $0^v$ = logical ZERO.

negative with respect to the emitter. Then the transistor will be "cut off" —will pass very little current—and the output node will be drawn up to $+5^v$—a logical ONE.

Now let us look at box 4 of Fig. 2.5. It has an output of ONE if b is ZERO and a is ONE. To say this another way, box 4 is the "AND of a with the NOT of b." Fig. 2.14 shows a way of representing this.

## SYNTHESIS OF BLACK BOXES

Even with only a handful of inputs, there are very many possible black boxes that can be designed. One would like some sort of guarantee that using only a few simple boxes (say AND, OR, and NOT) one could if one wished put together (synthesize) any box that could be dreamed up. We provide such a guarantee in the most helpful form of all: by showing how to construct any black box.

The table which specifies a particular black box is called its truth table. Figure 2.4 is an example of a truth table and one is included in each of Figs. 2.7 through 2.12. Now the output column of a truth table contains ONE's and ZERO's. If we could put together a circuit which produced an output of ONE where the truth table called for a ONE and ZERO under all other conditions then our job would be finished.

We proceed as follows. Consider a particular input combination which the truth table tells us should generate ONE in the ultimate output of the black box. Take an AND element with as many inputs as there are inputs to the black box, and connect each of the inputs to the AND circuit. If for this particular input combination a particular variable is ZERO, insert an inverter in the line before connecting it to the AND element. (See Fig. 2.14.) Then this AND element will have an output of

| a | b | Θ |
|---|---|---|
| 0 | 0 | 0 |
| 0 | 1 | 0 |
| 1 | 0 | 1 |
| 1 | 1 | 0 |

Fig. 2.14 A black box, number 4 from Fig. 2.5.

ONE whenever this particular input combination occurs and under no other circumstances. Repeat this procedure using an AND (and as many NOT's as are required) for each row of the truth table that should produce a ONE.

Now take the outputs of this set of AND elements and connect them all to the inputs of an OR element (one to each input). This OR must have as many inputs as there are ONE's in the output column of the truth table. Our job is done.

For any input combination that should produce an output of ONE, we have included an AND element to generate a ONE under just these very conditions. That AND is connected to the OR which passes the ONE on to the output of the black box.

For an input combination that should produce a ZERO output, at least one of the inputs is in the wrong state for producing a ONE at each of the AND elements we have. Under these conditions then, none of the AND's are producing ONE's so the OR circuit gives an output of ZERO, as required.

Figure 2.15 shows a three input truth table selected more or less at random and the circuit of NOT's, AND's, and OR's that will synthesise the required performance.

---

Question 2.2: How many black boxes are there with 3 inputs? With 5 inputs? With $N$ inputs?

*Question 2.3:* Suppose we were dealing with three-valued logic where each input or output could assume the values: 0, 1, and 2. What is the formula that will tell us how many different black boxes we could construct with $N$ three-valued inputs?

---

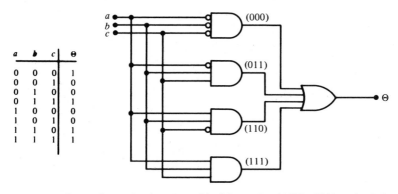

| a | b | c | θ |
|---|---|---|---|
| 0 | 0 | 0 | 1 |
| 0 | 0 | 1 | 0 |
| 0 | 1 | 0 | 0 |
| 0 | 1 | 1 | 1 |
| 1 | 0 | 0 | 0 |
| 1 | 0 | 1 | 0 |
| 1 | 1 | 0 | 1 |
| 1 | 1 | 1 | 1 |

Fig. 2.15  The synthesis of a three-input black box using AND's, OR's, and NOT's.

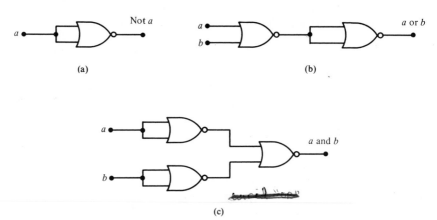

Fig. 2.16 The Synthesis of AND, OR, and NOT using only NOR elements.

The NOR circuit we have discussed previously is of interest because, using only NOR's, we can synthesise AND's, OR's, and NOT's, and we have just shown that using those three circuits we can build any black box. It follows then that all one needs to have is NOR's, from them we can construct whatever we like. Figure 2.16 shows how to generate AND's, OR's, and NOT's from NOR's.

---

*Question 2.4:* The NAND circuit can be used instead of the NOR. Reproduce Fig. 2.16 for NAND circuits.

*Question 2.5:* Synthesize all the black boxes of Fig. 2.5 using only NOR elements. Try to use as few as possible.

*Question 2.6:* Prove that the circuits of Fig. 2.16 behave as advertised by labeling intermediate wires where required and making truth tables for each circuit.

---

The synthesis of truth tables that we have been discussing does not usually yield the least expensive possible circuits, but it does always yield a circuit that will produce the desired behavior. That will be enough for us. The subject of minimal cost circuits is outside the scope of this book.

## THREE STATE CIRCUITS

Life is never as simple as authors would have you believe. Look back again at Fig. 2.12, the diagram of a two input NOR circuit. When one (or both) of the inputs is true, the transistor forms a good short circuit to ground and the output is tightly clamped to zero volts. It is said to have a low output impedance and hence is immune to stray signals inductively or capacitively coupled into the output line. It is relatively noise-free. But what happens when both inputs are zero? The transistor is cut off and acts like an open circuit—as if it weren't there at all. Now the only thing holding the output line at +5 volts is the resistor. If we don't want to have a lot of waste power flowing through the resistor when the transistor is turned on (is acting like a short circuit), that resistor is fairly large. It has a "high impedance." Then if this output line and some other output line run close to each other—as they are quite likely to do in a complex device like a computer—the high impedance will allow our output line to pick up stray signals from other lines; and when these stray signals (often called "cross talk") get to wherever the line is going, the circuit at that end will have trouble distinguishing the true signal from the false and irrelevant noise. To avoid this problem we must have a circuit that presents a low impedance under all conditions. (Well, under almost all conditions. It turns out that a high impedance state will be useful in just a few paragraphs.)

To provide this low impedance condition we arrange two transistors in series without any resistor as shown in Fig. 2.17.

We arrange that *either* the input to transistor $Q_1$ is high, in which case $Q_1$ turns on and the output is clamped to +5 volts, *or* the input to transistor $Q_2$ is high—which turns on $Q_2$ and clamps the output to ground (zero volts). An easy way to do this is shown in Fig. 2.18.

The circuit surrounding $Q_4$ is simply a reproduction of that of Fig. 2.12 and generates a signal that is the NOR of inputs $a$ and $b$. This signal is applied directly to $Q_1$ so the output is clamped to +5V when both inputs are low. Element $Q_3$ acts as an inverter (a NOT element); when $Q_4$ is high, the

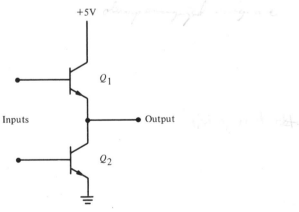

Fig. 2.17 A totem pole or series connection of transistors to provide low output impedance.

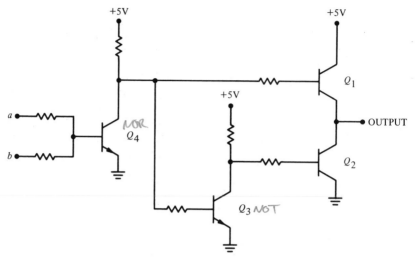

Fig. 2.18  A low impedance NOR circuit.

output of $Q_3$ is low, and when $Q_4$ is low, $Q_3$ is high. This signal is applied to $Q_2$, and when one or both of the inputs $(a, b)$ is high, $Q_2$ clamps the output to ground.

---

*Question 2.7:* What circuit would we get if we interchanged the inputs to $Q_1$ and $Q_2$?

---

Now about that parenthetical remark. Sometimes we like for other people to state their desires clearly and forcefully: "Yes! I want to go down-town," or "No! I want to stay home." But at other times a little diplomacy is called for: "What would you rather do?" So too with circuits we some-times desire a third or passive state. Suppose we have four circuit boxes, only one of which is active at any given time. Then it would be nice to con-nect their outputs together with a simple piece of wire and not have to use an OR element to connect them. This is called a "wired OR" and is sym-bolized as shown in Fig. 2.16c.

One way to make such three state circuits is, for example, to cut off the +5V power to $Q_3$ and $Q_4$ in Fig. 2.18 when we wish the circuit to assume the passive state. Then with both $Q_3$ and $Q_4$ outputs at ground, both $Q_1$ and $Q_2$ are open circuits and the output line is free to drift or be pulled high or low by some other circuit. The "select" lines of Fig. 2.19 when energized supply power to the appropriate $Q_3$ and $Q_4$, and that circuit takes over and drives the output.

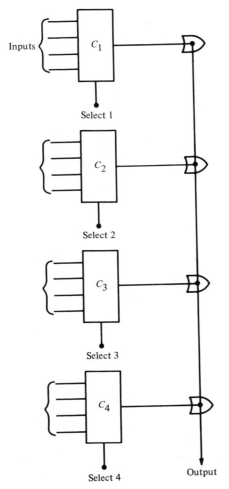

Fig. 2.19 Four circuits whose outputs are "Wire-ORed" together.

*Question 2.8:* What might happen if two circuits that are wire-ORed together are both selected at the same time?

## FLIP-FLOPS

So far we have discussed what are called logical circuits or gates. These gates reproduce the behavior of the classical operators of Boolean Algebra and mathematical logic. The output of these circuits depends entirely on

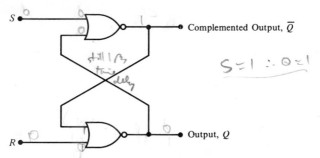

Fig. 2.20. A flip-flop constructed of two NOR circuits.

their present inputs. No memory or dependence upon the past is involved. But many times we wish to have a circuit that *will* depend upon past as well as present inputs. Consider a combination lock as only one example.

The next chapter will be devoted entirely to devices of this kind. Here we will consider one special device, made from circuits we have already covered, which possesses the property of "remembering." This circuit is special in the sense that it is used very often in computers where high speed is required.

Figure 2.20 shows a way of connecting two NOR elements together so that they will remember which input was ONE most recently. This circuit is called a flip-flop. The two wires on the left are the SET and RESET inputs to the flip-flop, and the wire labeled $Q$ is the normal output, while $\bar{Q}$ is the complement output. Let us study this circuit for a while.

Suppose that $S$ is ONE and $R$ is ZERO. Since $S$ is ONE the wire labeled $\bar{Q}$ must be ZERO. But now both the inputs $R$ and $Q$ to the lower NOR are ZERO so that $Q$ can, and will, become ONE. $Q$ and $\bar{Q}$ are the inverse (complement) of each other. If $S$ now goes to ZERO so that both $S$ and $R$ are ZERO, the circuit remains in the state described above with $\bar{Q}$ equal to ZERO and $Q$ equal to ONE.

---

*Question 2.9:* Why?

---

If $R$ now becomes a ONE, that will force $Q$ to ZERO, but now both inputs, $S$ and $Q$, to the upper NOR are ZERO so that $\bar{Q}$ becomes a ONE. This state will also persist.

So this flip-flop "remembers" which of its two input wires, $R$ and $S$, was a logical ONE most recently. shown by its output Gang remaining O

---

*Question 2.10:* What happens if both $R$ and $S$ become ONE? Then assume that $R$ goes to ZERO first, followed by $S$. What happens now?

---

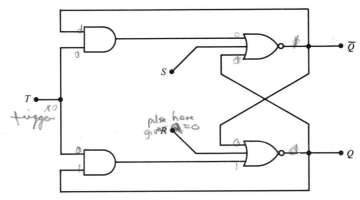

Fig. 2.21 A complementing flip-flop.

Sometimes we desire a circuit that will allow us to "complement" what a flip-flop is storing; that is replace, a zero by a one or a one by a zero. Figure 2.21 shows such a circuit.

The flip-flop is constructed from three-input NOR's. The $S$ and the $R$ inputs function as described above. Suppose that $Q$ is ONE and that a short pulse is applied to the $T$ (trigger) input. With $Q = 1$, the lower AND gate will pass the pulse to the input of the lower NOR. But since $\overline{Q}$ will be ZERO, the upper AND gate will be blocked, and the pulse on $T$ will not go the the upper NOR. Given this situation, $Q$ will be driven to ZERO, and this will allow $\overline{Q}$ to come to ONE. Provided the pulse applied to $T$ is back to ZERO by the time $\overline{Q}$ comes up to ONE, the circuit will remain in this state. The next pulse on $T$ will cause another complementation back to the original state and so on. These triggered flip-flops are sometimes called "divide by two" circuits. The usual symbol used for a flip-flop is shown in Fig. 2.22.

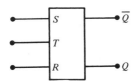

Fig. 2.22 A conventionalized symbol for the circuit of Fig. 2.21.

There are now several conventional types of flip-flops that are available in small packages at very low prices. We will describe some of the more common types shortly, but in order to understand how they work we need to explore first the phenomenon of delay.

When the input to a circuit changes state, the output does not change

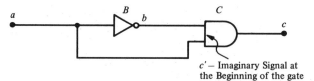

*c'* — Imaginary Signal at
the Beginning of the gate

**Fig. 2.23 A leading edge pulse generator.**

instantaneously. There is a brief delay called the "gate delay," during which the new input state must propagate through the circuit. The time required to pass a signal through a single gate determines how fast a circuit made of such gates can respond and hence how fast a computer constructed of such circuits can compute. Each different semiconductor technology—and there are many of them—has a characteristic gate delay. That and price and power consumption are the critical variables which are examined in selecting a technology to build a machine.

A discussion of the relative advantages and disadvantages of the available technologies is outside the scope of this book; besides they are changing too fast to belong in a textbook. But we can take advantage of the delay phenomenon to create short pulses out of level changes. Consider the circuit of Fig. 2.23.

Suppose *a* is ZERO. Then the output of the inverter *b* is ONE. Now let *a* change rapidly from ZERO to ONE. During the brief interval after *a* has changed and before the inverter responds to the change, both inputs to the AND circuit are ONE and its output will become ONE (after a brief delay, of course). But very soon the inverter responds and its output goes to ZERO, and the AND circuit is now unsatisfied and its output will go to ZERO (again after a delay). Figure 2.24 shows the timing of these events. This is sometimes called a "leading edge detector."

---

*Question 2.11:* Design a "trailing edge detector" that generates a pulse when the input signal changes from ONE to ZERO.

---

Now we are ready to examine a couple of standard packages.

### D-Type Flip-Flop

The *D*, or data, type flip-flop is an extremely versatile device. When the clock input goes from ZERO to ONE, it samples the information on the data input line and sets or resets the flip-flop according to whether the data value was ONE or ZERO. Figure 2.25 shows the effective circuit and the commonly used symbol for a *D*-type flip-flop.

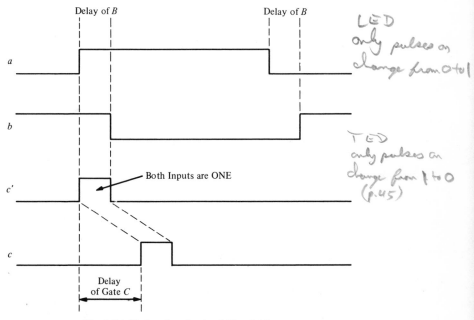

Fig. 2.24 Timing for circuit of Fig. 2.23.

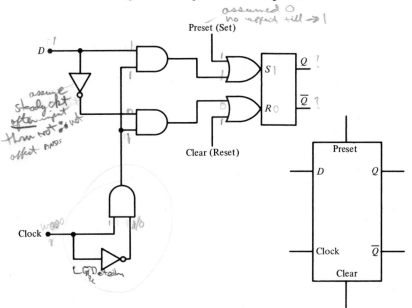

Fig. 2.25 A leading edge triggered D-type flip-flop.

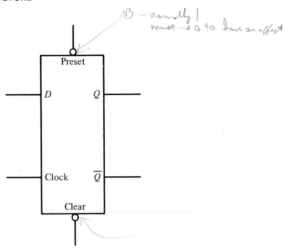

*B — normally 1*
*must → 0 to have an effect*

Fig. 2.26 A leading edge triggered *D*-type flip-flop with inverted PRESET and CLEAR inputs.

The PRESET and CLEAR inputs are available to set or reset, respectively, the flip-flop independently of the data and clock inputs. When either PRESET or CLEAR are energized, they override and take precedence over the data and clock signals. Often you will find that the PRESET and CLEAR and sometimes the CLOCK inputs are inverted. That is, they must go to ZERO to have an effect and are normally considered to be logical ONE's. Figure 2.26 shows a flip-flop with inverted PRESET and CLEAR. *D*-type flip-flops often come two or four to a package or "chip." A chip is a small piece of semiconductor material on which integrated circuits are made.

### J-K *Flip-Flop*

The next flip-flop we should examine is called a *J-K* flip-flop. Basically a *J-K* is just another *RS* flip-flop with input gates. A typical leading edge triggered *J-K* flip-flop is shown in Fig. 2.27.

If both *J* and *K* are energized when the clock goes to ONE, the flip-flop will complement.

### Master-Slave *Flip-Flop*

Perhaps the most useful flip-flop is the M-S or Master-Slave type. It actually consists of two flip-flops and a leading edge and a trailing edge detector. When the clock input goes from ZERO to ONE, the inputs are sampled and the first flip-flop is loaded (set or reset) correspondingly. But no change occurs in the output. Only when the clock goes from ONE to ZERO are the contents of the first flip-flop copied into the second or out-

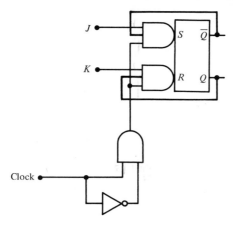

Fig. 2.27 A leading edge triggered J-K flip-flop.

put flip-flop. (See Fig. 2.28.) Using these devices, complicated circuits can be constructed with all kinds of feedback loops and interconnections. On the rising clock the present state of the circuit is sampled and the results are stored in the input halves of the M-S flip-flops. Since no change yet takes place in any output level, this loading may be done relatively leisurely without any race conditions to worry about. When everything is

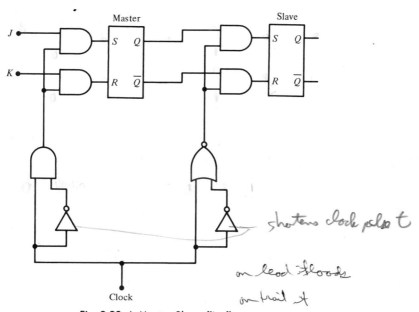

Fig. 2.28 A Master-Slave flip-flop.

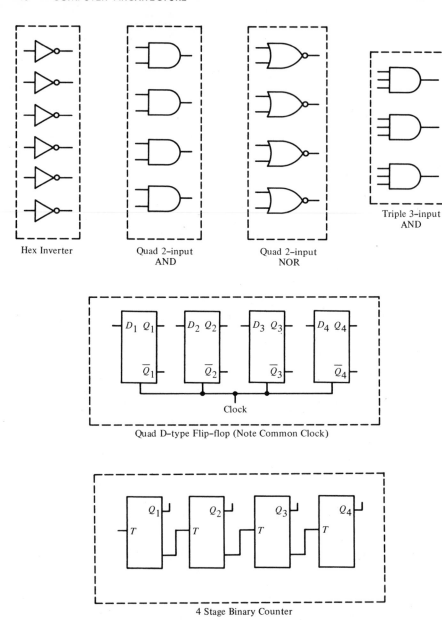

Fig. 2.29 Some few of the many circuit packages available.

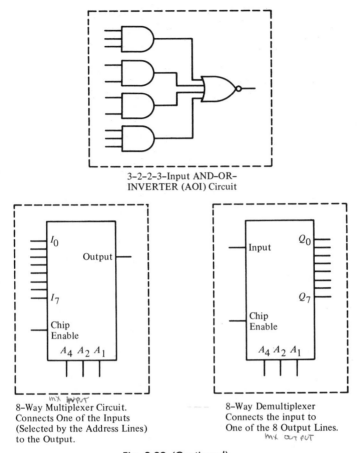

3–2–2–3–Input AND–OR–
INVERTER (AOI) Circuit

8–Way Multiplexer Circuit.
Connects One of the Inputs
(Selected by the Address Lines)
to the Output.

8–Way Demultiplexer
Connects the input to
One of the 8 Output Lines.

**Fig. 2.29 (Continued).**

ready, we drop the clock line, and on the falling clock all the flip-flops display their new states.

### Other Packaged Circuits

A bewildering variety of different circuits are currently available. We will leave their details and differences to the electrical engineers and solid-state physicists who specialize in this form of esoterica. Some of the most useful or most frequently met packages are shown in Fig. 2.29. The reader is urged to remember that the prices for these packages are now very low and still falling fast, so that if you need, say, four inverters and all you can find is a package with six, just go ahead and use it. Unless you are going to make 10,000 units it is undoubtedly cheaper to use a standard package and "waste" the extra gates than it would be to have special-purpose chips made to order. In fact, if you are going to make 10,000 units, you might profitably look into the possibilities of having the whole unit put on a single chip.

### TRANSFER OF INFORMATION

At various times we will have information stored in one flip-flop and may wish to have a copy of this information transferred to another flip-flop. For example, the instruction "enter accumulator with constant" requires the machine to copy information, presently in the instruction itself, into the accumulator. Both the accumulator and the instruction register (see Chapter 5) are usually constructed of flip-flops.

There are two methods in general use for copying information from one bank of flip-flops into another. These are called "jam" transfer and "clear and copy." Figure 2.30 shows a "jam" transfer circuit. A "clear and copy" circuit is shown in Fig. 2.31. In this circuit, first the CLEAR line is pulsed forcing $ff_2$ to ZERO (reset condition), and then the copy line is pulsed copying a ONE from $ff_1$ (if there is one) into $ff_2$.

The first circuit requires two gates per bit and the second only one.

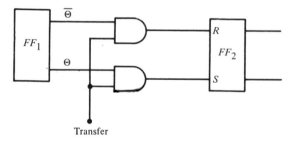

Transfer

Fig. 2.30 A "jam" transfer circuit. $FF_2$ is forced to agree with $FF_1$ whenever the TRANSFER line is energized.

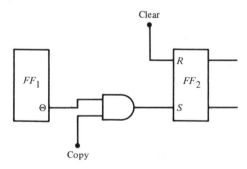

Fig. 2.31 A clear and copy circuit.

The second, however, takes two pulse periods to achieve the transfer and is thus only half as fast as the first. Both methods are used, depending on the relative virtues of economy and speed, but often $D$-type flip-flops surplant both methods.

## MULTIPLE PATHWAYS

Almost all present-day computers are bit-parallel. That is, all the bits of a word are processed at the same time. Twenty-five years ago some of the less expensive machines saved circuitry by processing bits one at a time, a method called bit-serial. This saving was at the expense of considerable slowdown of operation, generally $B$ times slower than parallel if there were $B$ bits in a word.

Given bit-parallel operation, there is naturally a tendency to replicate circuits—once for each bit of a word. In order to simplify diagrams a convention has been adopted to show this parallelism. This convention is to draw one circuit and put a slash across one of the lines and a number beside it indicating the number of replications. Figure 2.32 shows a four-bit-wide gate and the shorthand convention.

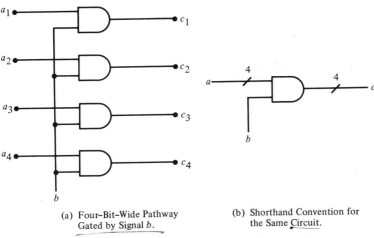

(a) Four–Bit–Wide Pathway
Gated by Signal $b$.

(b) Shorthand Convention for
the Same Circuit.

Fig. 2.32 Two ways of showing a circuit.

## SUMMARY

In this chapter we have looked at some elementary circuits and at a few ways of using these circuits to store information and to conduct it from one place to another. Our examination has concentrated on the logical behavior of these circuits.  We have ignored many things that are important to the engineers who must design or select the actual circuits that go into a computer.  How fast must the circuit operate? How many other circuits must it drive?  What variation in power supply voltage can be expected, and on, and on.  These subjects would consume not just other chapters, but other books, indeed other fields of study.

# 3 | STORAGE MECHANISMS

*"The Moving Finger writes; and, having writ, moves on..."*

*Omar Khayyam*

One of the most important parameters of any device used to hold information is its "access time." The access time of a storage device is defined to be the amount of time that will elapse between the issuing of a request for information stored in the device and the time at which that information will be available to the requestor. Access times range from a few nsec ($10^{-9}$ sec) up to a few tenths of a second. The other very important parameter of storage devices is their cost. This ranges from a few dollars per bit of storage down to less than one-hundredth of a cent a bit. Readers will not be surprised that the faster devices are the more expensive ones. A large part of the practice of computer engineering, as in all engineering fields, involves cost performance trade-offs, and storage speed versus price is an important consideration in any design.

Let us examine those devices which are passively stable. That is, they do not dissipate energy just holding the information. We will look first at those devices which employ magnetic fields.

## MAGNETIC CORES

Consider a number of small bar magnets pivoted at their centers and arranged in a circle as shown in Fig. 3.1. They are shown with an arrow head at the north seeking pole. Since north and south poles attract each other, there is a force tending to keep the magnets lined up as shown. If one were to twist one of the magnets so it pointed at the center of the

51

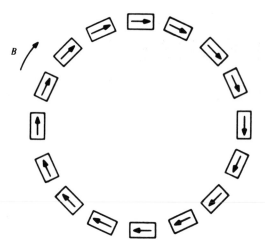

Fig. 3.1  A model of a magnetic core with the magnets pointing clockwise.

circle and then let it go, it would snap back into the alignment shown. This is what is meant by calling a situation "stable."

A system is said to be in a stable state if it requires the application of work or energy to cause the system to change to another state. That is, if small nudges don't cause a major alteration of the condition of the system. But suppose now that one were to twist each of the magnets through 180° (see Fig. 3.2) and let them all go at once. They remain still and do not

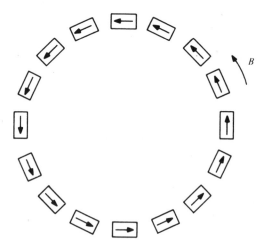

Fig. 3.2  Another picture of the model in its other stable state with the magnets pointing "counter clockwise."

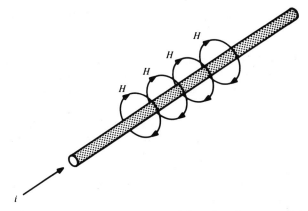

Fig. 3.3  A wire carrying a current and the induced magnetic field.

revert to the state of Fig. 3.1.  Indeed, one finds this second state is also stable against small perturbations.

Very much the same phenomenon takes place in a continuous ring of magnetic material (shown in Fig. 3.4), except that the sections of the core, as it is called, do not actually move.  The atoms of material merely change their alignment.  The direction of the magnetic flux is shown in each diagram by small arrows labeled *B*.

We have a device with two stable states and it is, therefore, a possible candidate for information storage.  It is well known that a wire carrying current is surrounded by a magnetic field.  The easiest way to remember which direction the field is pointing is to imagine a normal household

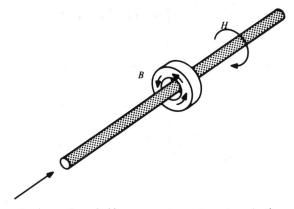

Fig. 3.4  A magnetized core threaded by a current-carrying wire.  As the current increases *H* will become large enough to cause the magnetic flux in the core to reverse.

screw (one with a right-hand thread) advancing in the direction of the current. (See Fig. 3.3.) The direction in which the screw must be rotated to cause this advance is the same as the direction of the magnetic field $H$.

Let us suppose that this current-carrying wire is threaded through a ferrite core as shown in Fig. 3.4. Assume that the core is originally magnetized in a counter clockwise sense as shown by the small arrows on the core.

Beginning with zero current, let us gradually increase it until, at some point called the "critical current" (symbolized by $i_{crit}$), the field generated by the current is great enough to cause the atoms of material to flip over and assume a clockwise orientation.

If the current is now reduced to zero, the core remains magnetized in this direction. This procedure is shown in the graph of Fig. 3.5.

This is half of what is known as a "rectangular hysteresis curve." If current is caused to flow in the opposite direction, the dotted half of the curve will be traced out. Two points should be made in reference to this curve. First, suppose that beginning at the point labeled "start," the current is increased to some value less than $i_{crit}$ and then reduced to zero. The core will not have changed its state, but will return to the same starting point. We will return to this point when we discuss selection circuits. Second, the square loop shown is a highly idealized version of what actually is found in an experiment. The actual hysteresis curve is much more rounded, and the "vertical" sides have a considerable slant to them. This is quite important from an engineering viewpoint, but need not concern us here.

So far we have seen that a ferrite core can be used to "remember" in

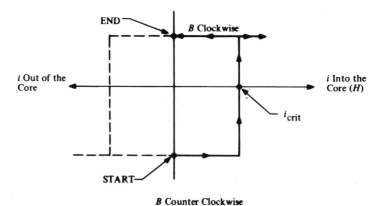

Fig. 3.5 The $B$ vs $H$ curve traced out by the circuit of Fig. 3.4 as $i$ is increased and then decreased.

which direction the last current greater than $i_{crit}$ passed through it. If a current greater than $i_{crit}$ is passed in the direction shown in Fig. 3.3, the core will be magnetized clockwise. A current in the opposite direction, provided it exceeds the critical current in magnitude, will leave the core magnetized counter clockwise. If we agree to call the first case ONE and the second ZERO, we have a storage element capable of holding one bit of information, and we have the means of making the bit either ONE or ZERO.

To determine whether a core is holding a ZERO or a ONE, we must destroy the information stored in it. This is because the only way we can detect a magnetic flux is by the fact that, when it is changing, it induces a voltage in a wire linking that flux. A steady, unchanging flux induces no such effect. In Fig. 3.6 we show a core threaded by two wires, with an initial magnetization in a clockwise direction. As the current $i$ increases,

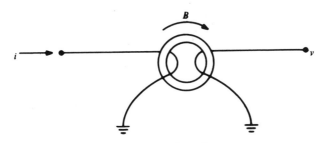

Fig. 3.6  A read circuit for a ferrite core.

it will eventually exceed $i_{crit}$ and cause the core to reverse its magnetic flux. This change in flux will induce a positive voltage in the right-hand wire due to the change in flux. But now we repeat the operation, again increasing $i$ from zero to some large value. The core will not change state again, since it is already in the counter clockwise state and that is where this current is urging it to be. Thus, no change in flux, no voltage on the right-hand wire. The read mechanism for cores uses this difference in response to detect the difference between a stored ONE and a stored ZERO. One inserts a current into the core such that it will "write a ZERO" in the core. If a voltage appears on the output wire, the core *was* holding a ONE. If no voltage appears, the core was already holding a ZERO. In either event, it is certainly ZERO after the reading operation. This is called "Destructive Read Out" and is abbreviated DRO. It is a considerable nuisance, because we must now make arrangements for re-writing a core after every read so that the information it held will be there if we want it again.

## PLATED WIRES   *lightly known*

A device which is similar to a core but which offers non-destructive read out (NDRO) is the plated wire.[1]

A more or less typical plated wire "bit" is shown in Fig. 3.7.

An ordinary copper wire is plated with a magnetic material which has a reasonably square hysteresis loop. If the copper wire is carrying a current during the plating process, the magnetic field due to this current will cause the atoms being plated to form anisotropic* crystals and hence have anisotropic magnetic properties. The result of this will be that the magnetic material "prefers" to be magnetized around the wire rather than along it. The direction around the wire is called the "easy" axis and the direction along the wire the "hard" axis. This anisotropy is what permits us to read out the stored information non-destructively.

Suppose that a small current $i$ is flowing through the drive strap of Fig. 3.7 in the direction shown. This will cause a magnetic field to be set up within the plating material which is back into the page.

Figure 3.8 shows the flux diagram of a small section of the wire. The current $i$ in the drive strap causes a field $H$ along the axis of the copper wire. Assuming the section is initially magnetized counter clockwise and is saturated (that is, it is as magnetized as it can get), then the combination of $B$ and $H$ will produce a resultant flux that will lie at an angle somewhere between $B$ and $H$ and will have *the same magnitude as B did originally*. It is as if in Fig. 3.2 we pushed the arrow heads into the page and pulled the

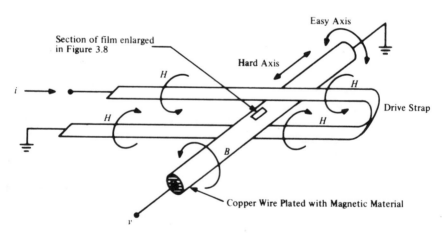

Fig. 3.7 One bit of plated-wire memory.

*Anisotropic means having properties which differ in different directions.

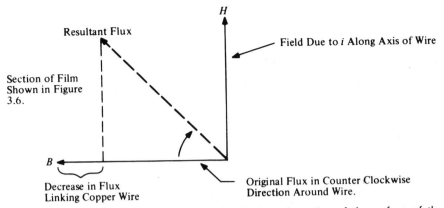

**Fig. 3.8** Flux diagram for read out from plated wire. A portion of the surface of the wire under the drive strap is shown.

tails up into the air. But the flux *around* the copper wire is the projection of the resultant flux on the original $B$ direction, and from Fig. 3.8, we see that this is less than the original magnitude of $B$. If we turn the current $i$ on and then off again, it is as if we had generated a small amount of clockwise flux around the wire and then removed it. But a positive change in the clockwise flux will cause a positive voltage $V$ to appear at the near end of the wire. When it is removed by allowing $i$ to go back to zero, a negative $V$ will be induced in the wire. Figure 3.9 shows the time relationships involved. When the original direction of magnetization is clockwise, we get first a negative voltage and then a positive one.

---

*Question 3.1:* Draw the diagram equivalent to Fig. 3.8 for a clockwise original magnetization and show why one gets a negative and then a positive pulse output.

---

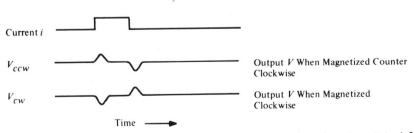

**Fig. 3.9** The output voltage V generated by a short current pulse when the original flux is counter clockwise and clockwise.

Circuits can easily be designed to distinguish between the two possible outputs. After the current pulse has died away, the device settles back into its original state; the information it contains has been read non-destructively. To write information into a plated-wire bit, we establish first a "tilting field" by passing a current through the drive strap. We then send a moderately large current in one direction or the other through the copper wire. This establishes a field either clockwise or counter clockwise that is large enough to "flip" the flux of the magnetic material in the desired direction. When both currents are removed, the information stored remains until changed.

The tilting field and the initial magnetization of the material combine to form a resultant flux whose projection on the easy axis (round the wire) is substantially less than what it would have been without the tilting field. Because of this, the flipping current in the copper wire may be made smaller than what is needed to flip an untilted flux. This means that one can store several bits on one plated wire, each under its own drive strap, and the only one that will flip when current is sent down the wire is the one whose drive strap is energized.

## CRYOTRONS skip

Another device which does not dissipate power, except when being read or written, is the cryotron.[2,3,4] This is a device with great potentialities. For the last 15 years it has been "just around the technological corner." Apparently the problems of making large arrays of cryotrons have been severe, and considerable development must still be made before they become practical, if indeed they ever do.

The cryotron is based on the phenomenon of super conductivity. At temperatures close to absolute zero ($-273°C$), certain materials have no electrical resistance whatsoever. Therefore, a current, once started, will flow in a closed loop forever. Some of the materials which exhibit this lack of resistance also display another property. When in the presence of a magnetic field, they become resistive again, even though they are cold enough to be super conductive in the absence of a field. Figure 3.10 shows $H$ versus $T$ curves for two materials $A$ and $B$. If the device is operating nearer the origin than the curve, it will be super conductive. Outside the curve it displays a normal resistance.

At the operating temperature, which normally is that of liquid helium (about $4°K$), there is a critical magnetic field below which both $A$ and $B$ are super conductive and above which $B$ has become resistive. The basic cryogenic circuit, or gate, is composed of two strips of material crossing each other at right angles as shown in Fig. 3.11. The vertical line is

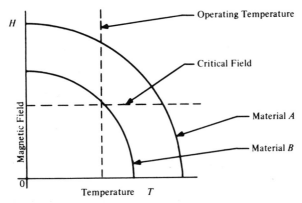

Fig. 3.10 The basis of the cryotron. At the operating temperature, a magnetic field, which slightly exceeds the critical field, will make material *B* resistive while material *A* is still super conductive.

partly composed of the easily switchable material *B* and is called the "gated line." Crossing the strip of material *B* and insulated from it is a strip of material *A* which forms the "control" line (*c-c*). As long as the control line carries no current, the gated line is super conductive throughout and presents no resistance between points *g-g*. Now let a current be passed through the control line *c-c* in either direction. As this current gradually increases, the magnetic field surrounding the control line will also increase. Eventually this will exceed the critical field of material *B* where the lines cross, and that section of line *g-g* will become resistive. The actual resistance that will appear between points *g-g* is quite small, a few tenths of an ohm; but if there exists an alternate path for the current that was flowing in *g-g*, and if that path is super conductive throughout,

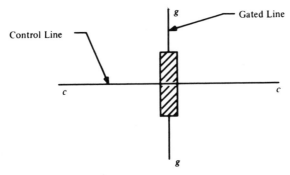

Fig. 3.11 A simple cryogenic gate of the crossed-film type. The wide hatched area is material *B*. The other lines represent material *A*.

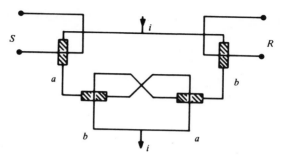

Fig. 3.12 A flip-flop constructed from cryotrons of the crossed-film type.

the ratio of the resistances will be infinite and hence the current in $g$-$g$ will go to zero, all of it being diverted to the alternate path.

Since the control line is made from material $A$, the magnetic field induced by the control current will not be great enough to make the control line go resistive. Using this fact, we can construct what is called a "flip-flop" as in Fig. 3.12. It is left to the reader to show that this device has two stable states (current flowing in the path $a$-$a$ or in the path $b$-$b$). Note that although there is current flowing in this device, the resistance is zero, and hence no power is dissipated. Passing a current through either $R$ or $S$ will allow us to RESET or SET the flip-flop. Read out will be discussed in the next chapter.

An interesting and important phenomenon in cryogenics is the fact that once current is flowing in one of two parallel paths and not the other, it requires some action to make it switch to the alternate path. Consider Fig. 3.13.

Suppose we pass a current through control line $a$-$a$ that is large enough to block the gate in the left-hand path. All of the bias current ($i$) will be forced into the right leg of the circuit. If the control current in $a$-$a$ is now

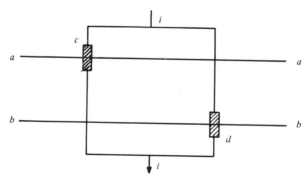

Fig. 3.13 A cryogenic circuit with two parallel paths.

turned off, one might expect the bias current to divide equally between the two legs. In fact, it does *not*. It requires a voltage to make a current flow between two points (*c* and *d*), and since the right-hand leg is super conductive, no voltage can exist between *c* and *d*. No voltage; no current, and so even after control current *a-a* is reduced to zero, all the bias current will flow down the right-hand leg. Only when a control current is applied to line *b-b* will the bias current flip over to the other leg. Thus, we have a flip-flop capable of remembering which control current was ON most recently.

## MAGNETIC BUBBLES

The present-day darling of the technological community is the magnetic bubble.[5] It has all the virtues of core and cryotrons combined and none of the drawbacks. Of course, it has drawbacks of its own that we will discuss in due time. First of all the magnetic bubble is non-volatile—it requires no power (or for that matter no special environment such as very low temperatures) to retain its information. Second, it is capable of batch fabrication. That is, one can make sheets of magnetic material capable of holding thousands of bits of information in a very few operations.

Consider a large thin sheet of magnetic material constructed with the easy axis of magnetization perpendicular to the page.* (See Fig. 3.14.)

Since the easy axis lies out of the page, the molecules will tend to line up with their own fields either up out of the page (shown hatched) or down into the page. Each molecule will influence its neighbors, and local regions are built up in which all (or most of) the molecules are in agreement: up

Fig. 3.14 A sheet of magnetic material showing domains.

*The reader should be warned that the explanation presented here is somewhat simplified.

or down. These are called "domains." They are irregularly shaped and irregularly spaced on the sheet. Now let us add an external magnetic field perpendicular to the sheet such that it urges all the molecules to point down into the page. Let us increase this field gradually. The first thing that happens is that the hatched domains (the ones pointing up out of the page) become more or less circular. This is a phenomenon similar to surface tension, which gets the maximum area with the minimum edge. Now as we increase the external field, the hatched domains shrink and become more circular. These "bubbles" of reverse magnetized material continue to shrink in size as the external field increases. Should it momentarily decrease, they would expand again rather like a soap bubble with the external pressure released. For a given field intensity the size of the bubbles is quite uniform and is stable. Of course, if the field becomes strong enough, the little bubbles "wink out" and disappear.

For quite moderate field intensities (achievable by inexpensive permanent magnets) the bubbles are of the order of a few microns in diameter. Now comes the interesting part: the bubbles are mobile—they can be made to move by applying magnetic fields parallel to the sheet. Furthermore, when brought close enough together they interact and repel each other. This latter phenomenon provides the possibility of magnetic bubble logic.

To see how the bubbles can be made to move in a controlled fashion we cause a magnetic vector in the plane of the sheet to rotate in a clockwise direction. (See Fig. 3.15.) This could be done by rotating a bar magnet above the sheet or (preferably) by placing the sheet between two pairs of coils and exciting one pair with a sine wave voltage and the other pair with a cosine wave. With 100 kilohertz sine and cosine waves we can complete a cycle in 10 microseconds. (See Fig. 3.16.)

On the top of the sheet (but not on its bottom) we imprint a pattern of alternating T's and I's in an easily magnetizable material with no preferred axis of magnetization. Suppose the external bias field is such as to generate bubbles with their south ends sticking up into the surface with the T's and I's. The north ends of the bubbles are buried at the other side of the sheet and are sufficiently far away to be ignored. So each bubble appears to be an

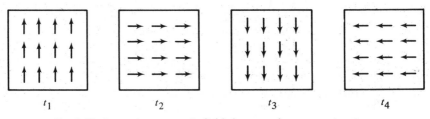

Fig. 3.15 A rotating magnetic field shown at four successive times.

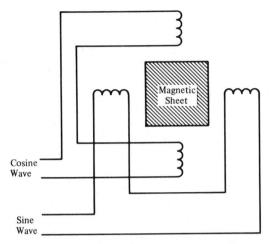

Fig. 3.16 Two pairs of Helmholz Coils used to generate a rotating magnetic vector in a sheet.

isolated south magnetic pole free to be attracted to or repelled from any poles induced in the T's and I's.

As the rotating field turns around it generates poles in the T's and I's as shown in Fig. 3.17. One magnetic bubble is shown as a shaded patch that moves in four steps from the leftmost T to the second T. Had there been another originally on the second T, it would have moved off to the right to a third T, and so forth.

At each stage the bubble moves to the nearest convenient north pole. Thus with a clockwise rotating field the bubbles move from left to right. (Left and right are defined locally with the T patterns in a upright position.)

---

*Question 3.2:* How would you make the bubbles move in the opposite direction?

---

We will not go into methods for making bubbles interact here. Suffice it to say that if a spot is occupied by a bubble and an approaching bubble has a choice of pathways to take, it will take the one farthest away from the occupying bubble.

Long chains of T's and I's can store a bubble (or no bubble) in each T-I pair, and hence we can have a string of ONE's (bubbles) and ZERO's (no bubbles) marching around on a sheet of material following the path we have laid down for them. This path can be closed, and the bubbles will circulate around the path forever—or at least as long as the rotating field rotates.

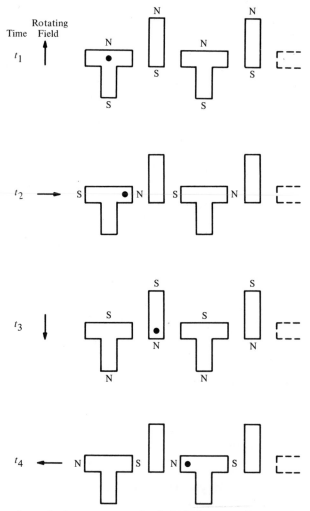

Fig. 3.17 Four stages in the movement of a bubble from one T to another. Time period 4 is followed by another time period 1.

While an interesting concept, this is not yet a useful storage device since we must be able to write into it and to read from it. To do this we need a "bubble generator/eater" and a detection device. It turns out that these can be identical devices: small coils of wire laid flat on the surface over one of the T's or I's. Suppose a bubble moves under one of these coils that previously had no bubble under it. There will be a change of flux linking the coil since now there is a south pole under it and previously there were only

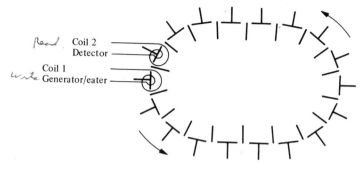

Fig. 3.18 A recirculating magnetic bubble storage loop.

north poles under it. This change of flux will generate a voltage in the coil and a sensitive amplifier can be used to detect this voltage, thus reading out the ONE's (passage of a bubble) and ZERO's (no bubble going past).

Let there be another coil also laid flat against the surface. Let there be a current flowing in this coil which generates a magnetic field opposed to the bias field. If this local field is strong enough, it will cause a bubble to "pop into existence" beneath it. Lo, we have a bubble generator and have written a ONE. If the current is flowing in the opposite direction, it will reinforce the bias field, making it stronger. Any bubble coming under the influence of this coil will be overwhelmed by the combined bias and local fields and will "wink out" of existence. Now we have a "bubble eater" and can write ZERO's. Figure 3.18 shows one possible arrangement of a storage loop. Bubbles are written (or erased) by coil 1 and detected by coil 2.

It has been estimated that within a few years, perhaps by the time this edition is out, one should be able to purchase a one-inch cube for $100 that would hold one million bubbles arranged as 32,000 words of 32 bits each—that is, there would be 32 planes each containing 32,000 T-I pairs.

But what of the disadvantages of magnetic bubbles? At .01¢ per bit, with zero standby power, and speeds predicted to reach one micro second per shift, why isn't everybody rushing to buy or build bubble storage devices? The answer is inherent in Fig. 3.18.

---

*Question 3.3:* Can you see what it is without reading the next paragraph?

---

It is quite simple. True, one can make bubbles transfer between adjacent T-I pairs in a few microseconds, but the write coil and the read coil aren't adjacent to each other in the direction the bubbles are traveling. They are as far apart as they can get. Of course, I can overwrite something I just read; but if I write something, it will have to travel all around the loop before I can read it. And if that loop contains some 32,000 T-I pairs it is going to take it 32,000 times a few microseconds to get back under the read heads—rather a long while for a computer that could be operating at sub-microsecond speeds if it only had the data available to operate on or the instructions necessary to tell it what to do. The obvious solution to this dilemma is to add more read heads. But in that direction lie escalating costs, since the *major* cost in a magnetic bubble memory is not the magnetic material—that might cost a few cents per square inch—but the number of read and write coils connected to sensitive amplifiers or to drive circuits. To put this another way, each loop has a fixed cost more or less independent of its length. To bring down the price per bit you make the loop longer—but then the access time gets longer as well. They do have the advantage that you can make an engineering trade-off of speed versus cost and pick any point on the curve you like.

Magnetic bubbles have one further advantage over other kinds of recirculating memories we will examine later in this chapter—they can be stopped!

Suppose you know that some time from now you are going to want to read out a particular word. Circulate the loop until that word is just about to come under the read coil and then turn off the rotating field. When you are ready—any time this week—turn back on the rotating field and out comes your word. Drums, discs, and delay lines just can't be stopped in this way. You have to wait for the information and take it when it flys by, not the other way around.

## MAGNETIC RECORDING

Yet another storage mechanism that employs magnetic fields relies on the fact that moving a magnet past a coil will induce a voltage in that coil and that the sense of that voltage will depend on whether the magnet is moving along north pole first or south pole first. Devices which employ this moving magnet principle include disks, drums, and magnetic tape.

Imagine that there is a strip of magnetizable material that may be moved under a fixed coil called the "head." If a pulse of current is passed through the head, a magnetic pattern will be created on the material as it goes by. Positive current pulses will induce one pattern, and negative pulses will induce its opposite. If some time later the material is passed again under the same or a similar head, a current pulse will be generated that will be of the same polarity as the original "writing" pulse.

Two recording techniques are in common use. These are called "return

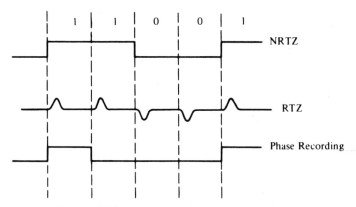

Fig. 3.19 Three methods of magnetic recording.

to zero" (RTZ) and "non-return to zero" (NRTZ). Several variations on these have been used.

Figure 3.19 gives a comparison of the two techniques. In non-return to zero, when a 1 follows a 1 or a 0 follows a 0, no change of state can be detected on output. In return to zero mode, each successive 1 generates a positive pulse and each successive 0 generates a negative pulse. There are advantages to both methods. RTZ is self synchronizing. That is, we know that the next item of information is passing under the head because we observe a pulse, positive or negative, when it does. With NRTZ, a string of bits of the same value generates only one pulse at the beginning. Consequently, we must have a separate timing track recorded in parallel with the information track to let us know when to look for a pulse—so we know when we don't get one. But RTZ requires magnetic patterns to be recorded that change polarity twice as often as NRTZ mode requires. Since we are limited by physical considerations (magnetic grain size and the size of the head gap) in how small a pattern we can record and detect, it is clear that with a given recorder we can pack twice as much information into an inch of magnetic material using NRTZ as using RTZ recording techniques.

One variation on NRTZ mode should be mentioned. As described above, we always use positive pulses to indicate a change from 0 to 1 and a negative pulse to indicate a change from 1 to 0. In this variation, we change the present state to its opposite when we wish to record a 1 and leave it the same when we wish to record a 0. This is sometimes called "phase recording." All three methods have been used, but phase recording at 200, 556, 800, or 1600 bits per inch has become the industry standard for magnetic tapes (see next chapter).

## ACTIVE STORAGE ELEMENTS

An active storage element is one which dissipates power in order to retain the information it is supposed to be storing. When power is cut off, even momentarily, information that was stored in an active element is lost. The most commonly used active storage element is the "flip-flop." We have already seen examples of these.

Flip-flops are used for the high-speed registers of most computers. They have the great advantage that the output voltage is sitting there waiting to be sampled (read). One doesn't need to disturb or destroy the contents in order to find out what they are. They are fast for both reading and writing (a few nanoseconds) but they used to be expensive relative to core storage. The advent of large-scale integrated circuits (LSI)* has provided greatly reduced prices so that at the present time semiconductor storage (using flip-flops) is at about the same price as core storage. Several present-day machines use large-scale integrated circuits for their main store.

A flip-flop has two disadvantages relative to magnetic cores. First, it consumes power to maintain its stable state, which a core does not. Second, if that power is cut off, the information stored is lost. With core you can turn off the computer, go away for a week, and if nobody else has been at the machine, come back and find your program and data still there, ready to run. With flip-flops, interrupt the supply of power, and all is lost. Some machines provide battery power supplies to tide you over a power failure.

### Parametrons

There are several other devices that have been used in the past or considered as possible storage elements. One of the most interesting of these is the parametric oscillator, or "parametron," which was apparently invented simultaneously by von Neumann in the U. S. and by Eilchi Goto of Tokyo University. Von Neumann's work was made public posthumously by Wigington,[6] and Goto's ideas resulted in the construction of an actual computer, the Musasino-1. The method of storing information in a parametron is called "phase script."

Figure 3.20 shows a resistor, a capacitor, and an inductor connected in a resonant circuit. The inductor and the capacitor are adjusted to resonate at frequency $f$, and if one of them is non-linear, they can absorb energy from the pump which oscillates at $2f$. Since there is only one positive peak of the output for every two positive peaks of the pump, the resonant circuit can assume one of two states: in synchrony with the

---

*LSI is a method of fabricating many circuits, transistors, diodes, etc., on a single chip of semiconductor material. It offers the possibility of high density, low cost per element, and good reliability.

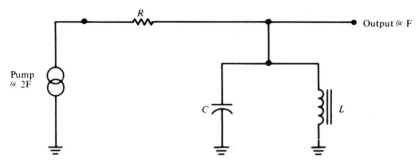

Fig. 3.20 An LC circuit resonant at frequency F being driven by a generator (the pump) at frequency 2F.

*even* peaks of the pump, or in synchrony with the *odd* peaks of the pump. (See Fig. 3.21.)   Clearly the two possible states are distinguishable and, moreover, they are stable as long as the pump continues to supply energy. To write into a parametron we first shut off the pump supplying it with energy. After the local oscillations have died down, we "inject" a small signal of the phase we wish to store (even or odd) and turn on the pump again. As the local oscillations build up, they will be "guided" by the injected signal and assume its phase. It takes about 20 cycles to establish an oscillation so that the operating speed of the computer gates will be one-twentieth of the resonant frequency.

To read out the contents of a parametron, we connect its output voltage of unknown phase to one leg of a summing circuit (see Fig. 3.22) and an equal amplitude signal of odd phase to the other leg. If the parametron is storing a ZERO (has *even* phase) the two signals will subtract and the voltage at the output will be zero. If, however, the parametron is storing

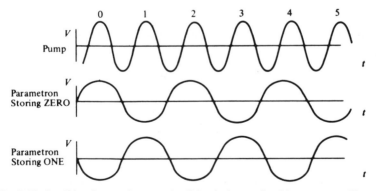

Fig. 3.21 Possible phase relations of a "divide by two" subharmonic oscillator.

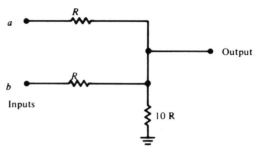

Fig. 3.22 A summing circuit for reading out the contents of a parametron.

a ONE (has *odd* phase), the two signals will add and a voltage will appear at the output.

Von Neumann proposed a resonant frequency in the range of 20 GHz ($20 \times 10^9$ cycles per sec) which would result in a speed of about $10^9$ operations per sec—allowing say 20 cycles of the resonant frequency for the build up and/or decay of local oscillations. In the Japanese design, a resonant frequency of 2 MHz was used, resulting in a computer that could perform about 10,000 additions per sec.

### Fluidic Devices

Another device[7-9] for storing information is the fluidic flip-flop. During the 1930's a Hungarian physicist named Henri Coanda discovered that a stream of air, or water, or indeed any fluid, would tend to cling to one wall of any channel it was flowing through. (See Fig. 3.23.) The reason

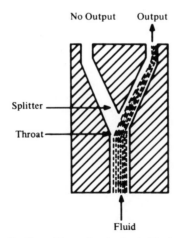

Fig. 3.23 A Coanda-effect flip-flop. The entire device is filled with fluid. Only the moving fluid is indicated.

for this is quite simple. A moving fluid exerts less sidewise pressure than the same fluid at rest. This is the Bernoulli effect. On the side of the stream away from the wall, surrounding fluid rushes into the reduced pressure area and joins the stream. This inrushing fluid brings the pressure back up close to that of the static fluid. But on the side nearest the wall, there is less surrounding fluid to rush in and, consequently, the pressure is not brought back up so much. This results in a net force pushing the stream towards the wall; and the closer it gets to the wall, the less surrounding fluid exists to be sucked into the stream, the less the pressure is restored, and the greater is the force pushing the stream toward the wall.

If the device is symmetric, the stream could just as easily "lock on" to the left-hand wall and exit through the left orifice. Thus once again we have a device with two stable states. One can easily "read" which state it is in by observing which orifice has the fluid coming out of it. By introducing two additional small channels, as in Fig. 3.24, one can "steer" the

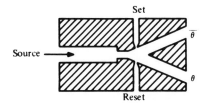

Fig. 3.24 A Coanda flip-flop with steering jets: S and R.

stream of fluid by "blowing" into one of them. This will "blow" the stream away from the wall and it will lock on to the other.

Another way of making a fluidic flip-flop would be by connecting two fluidic NOR gates together. To make a fluidic NOR, we deliberately design an assymetric device as shown in Fig. 3.25.

If fluid is being injected in neither a nor b, the source stream passes

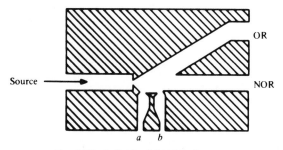

Fig. 3.25 A fluidic OR-NOR element.

straight through the device, emerging at the orifice labeled NOR. If fluid is being injected in either *a* or *b*, or both, the source stream will be deflected and exit through the orifice labeled OR. The switching speed of fluidic devices is of course limited by the speed of sound in the working fluid. A switching time of $10^{-3}$ to $10^{-4}$ sec is within the realm of possibilities. The great attraction of these devices is that they are relatively immune to heat, cold, and radiation. Thus, they have aroused considerable interest in the aerospace industry.

---

*Question 3.4:* It would have been possible for any ancient society that could make bricks to have constructed a fluidic computer, had they stumbled upon the secret. How do you imagine the Greeks or Romans or Egyptians might have used a computer?

---

### Delay Lines

When a wave or disturbance travels through a medium, it moves at a fixed speed called the "propagation velocity." This phenomenon has been used to store information. Figure 3.26 shows a typical delay-line unit.

A train of pulses (compression waves) generated by the transmitter travel "slowly" down the quartz rod and are picked up by the receiver. After being amplified and re-timed by the AND gate (to stay in synchonism with a master clock), the pulses are fed back into the transmitter and recirculate again. Let the delay between transmission and reception (the time it takes a sound wave to move from one end of the bar to the other) be $\tau$. Now consider the case when there is only one pulse in the line. Every $\tau$ seconds it will go once around the system and, if the point *a* were connected to a loud speaker, one would hear: pip, pip, pip, . . . .

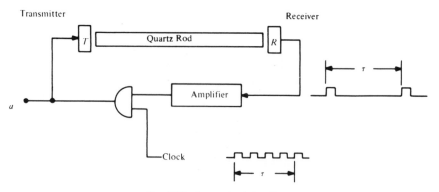

Fig. 3.26  A quartz delay line.

If now we were to open the circuit for a moment, the pulse would get lost and cease to recirculate. Then one would hear only silence. Let there be $N$ clock cycles in the circulation time. (The diagram shows 4.) At each clock pulse we could have either a *pulse* or the *absence of pulse*. Thus in this one delay line, we could store $N$ bits of information.

One can, at the present time, purchase such delay lines for under $250 that will store up to 1000 bits. The major disadvantage of this type of storage is inherent in its name: the delay that may ensue while waiting for a particular bit to come round.

---

*Question 3.5:* If the recirculation time of a delay line is $\tau$, what is the average wait that must be endured to obtain a particular bit?

---

### Charge Coupled Devices

Let us look at one more mechanism for storing information. It involves the storage of electric charge as a change from the usual magnetic field. These are called charge coupled devices (CCD's). A large number of CCD's have been invented and explored in the laboratory. Early in 1973 two semi-conductor houses even offered some for sale, so their eventual application to computers is not too far off, provided of course that their advantages outweigh their disadvantages in the minds of designers.

We will describe a three-phase CCD which may never be the one that catches on but which is relatively simple to understand. We have a metal plate which forms a ground plane, a layer of semiconductor material which is where the action takes place, an insulating layer, and a row of small conducting dots which do the steering and control. (See Fig. 3.27.) These dots are connected to three voltage sources ($A$, $B$, and $C$) as shown, every third dot being connected together.

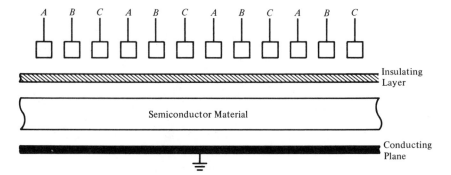

Fig. 3.27 A three-phase CCD.

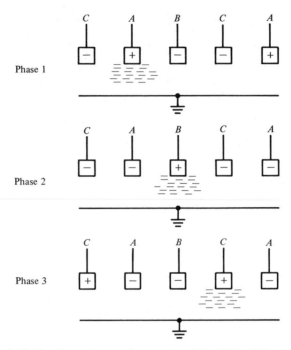

Fig. 3.28 The three phases of operation of the CCD of Fig. 3.27.

Let there be a cloud of electrons forming a negative charge under one of the A-type dots. If voltage A is plus with respect to the ground the A dot will attract the electrons, and if B and C are negative with respect to ground, the electrons will bunch up under the A dot (since opposite charges attract electrically and like charges repel each other). (See Fig. 3.28.) If the B dots become positive and A dots go negative, the cloud of electrons moves over one space, and as C becomes positive in its turn, the clouds shift again. One more shift and the cloud is under a new A dot ready to start over.

To inject electron clouds we place a contact on the semiconductor through the insulating layer. To detect them we connect a dot to a sensitive current amplifier and observe the "rush" of electrons leaving the dot when a cloud moves underneath it.

Two problems arise with CCD's. First, there is leakage. A cloud of electrons will dissipate, gradually leaking away. At present the lifetime of a cloud is around one second. This means that within, say, a half second of the time we put information into a CCD, we had better read it out and "refresh" it. Then if we like we can rewrite it and store it for another half second. The other problem has to do with the transfer of charges between dots. Not all of a charge will make an advance the way one would like to have it.  A little gets left behind.  This ghost then follows the "real" cloud around the circuit.  At each move a tiny bit more of the real cloud gets left behind and joins the ghost.  Of course the ghost has a ghost-ghost following it.  With each shift the ghost becomes stronger.  When it gets so large that it is difficult to tell if it is a ghost of the previous real cloud that passed by or another real cloud coming along, we have reached the limits of utility.

At present, laboratory elements are showing good reliability and ghost rejection with up to about 128 shifts.  This tells us how long a chain or loop we may have; but clever arrangements that we will explore in the next chapter allow us to overcome this last limitation to some extent.

## READ ONLY MEMORIES

So far in this chapter we have looked at mechanisms for storing information that permit reading or writing information electrically under control of a program within a computer.  In this section we will discuss the kinds of memory mechanisms which cannot be modified by a program.  These are called "read only memories," or ROM's.  The simplest example of this kind of memory might be a console switch set by the operator.  There exists no combination of instructions executable by the computer that will change the setting of such a switch.  Ten years or so ago there was a novelty item which consisted of a box with a switch on it.  When turned on the box would rumble and shake, and then a little hand would reach out and turn off the switch and snap back inside.  As far as I know, such a mechanism has never been incorporated in a commercially available computer.  If it were, then the console switches would be considered to be read-write storage and not read-only.

### Mask Programmable ROM

The last stage in the manufacture of a semiconductor chip before packaging is to put a layer of metal across the top of the chip to connect the various components.  Chips are made up as shown in Fig. 3.29; when the customer specifies the desired pattern of ONE's and ZERO's in his memory, metal is laid down across the contact points where he wants ONE's and omitted where he wants ZERO's.

The semiconductor house will charge one to two thousand dollars to make up the mask, but then the ROM's can be made in any quantity for a fraction (½, ¼) of a cent a bit.  Densities are high because of the simplicity of the cells, and 8192 bits per chip (organized as 1024 words by 8 bits) are common.  The diodes are present to prevent current passing down one column from "sneaking" back onto some other row and hence across and then down some second column.

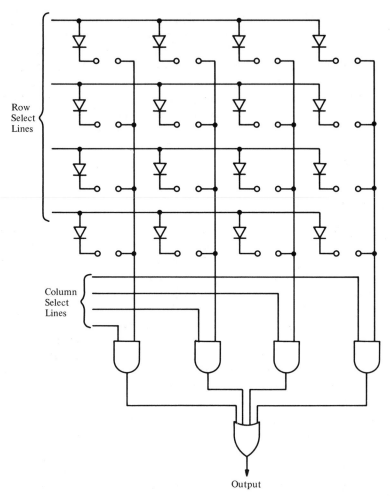

Row
Select
Lines

Column
Select
Lines

Output

Fig. 3.29 A 16 word by one bit mask programmable ROM.

*Electrically Programmable ROM's*

If we replace the diode-gap cell by the transistor-fuse cell of Fig. 3.30, we can selectively burn out the fuses to leave open circuits where we want to store zeros. This may be done on a special device which puts +5 volts on the desired row and a string of large negative pulses on the desired columns. The end user may buy such a device, and he can then program his own ROM's. Such electrically alterable ROM's are called "programmable read only memories" or PROM's.

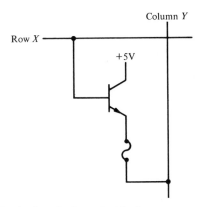

Fig. 3.30 The basic cell of an electrically programmable ROM.

### Reprogrammable ROM's

The ROM's we mentioned above can never be changed once they have been set up. Another device called FAMOS (floating avalanche metal oxide silicon) has the desirable property that it can be changed. Of course, this makes it not quite strictly "read only," but since erasure of information requires prying off a cap from the chip and exposing it to short ultraviolet light, most people keep on calling them PROM's. The semiconductor physics involved is reasonably formidable, but in principle what happens is that electrons are trapped on a floating control gate buried in the semiconductor. The potential field of this floating gate then controls the conductance between a conventional source and drain. Once charged, the floating gate is isolated by metal oxide and displays leakages of less than 20% per 100 years. This would not do for building time capsule computers but is just fine for most of us mortals. An avalanche breakdown of the metal oxide can be triggered by applying a large (30 volts) voltage across the device, thus charging the floating gate. The ultraviolet light results in a flow of photo current, neutralizing the charge and restoring the PROM to its initial unwritten state.

### SUMMARY

In this chapter we have examined a number of devices that may be used to store information. All our consideration has been directed toward binary devices, although the parametron could easily be adapted to store three stable states. Here we have concentrated on the physical phenomena involved. In the next chapter we will see how individual devices can be assembled into organized storage.

REFERENCES

1. McCallister, J. P., and Chong, C. F. "A 500-Nanosecond Main Computer Memory Utilizing Plated-Wire Elements." *Proc. AFIPS 1966 Fall Joint Comp. Conf.*, 305–314.
2. Buck, D. A. "The Cryotron—A Super-Conductive Computer Component." *Proc. IRE*, 482–493 (1956).
3. Slade, A. E., and McMahon, H. Q. "A Cryotron Catalog Memory System." *Proc. 1956 Eastern Joint Comp. Conf.*, 115–119.
4. Walker, P. A. "Cryotrons and Cryotron Circuits, A Review." *J. Brit. IRE*, **25**, No. 5, 387–397 (May 1963).
5. Bobeck, A. H., and Della Torre, E. *Magnetic Bubbles.* New York, American Elsevier, 1975.
6. Wigington, R. L. "A New Concept in Computing." *Proc. of IRE*, **47**, No. 4, 516–523 (April 1959).
7. Richards, E. F., and Depperman, W. B. "Fluidic Computer Technology." Nat. Symp. on the Impact of Batch Fabrication on Future Computers, 30–39 (April 1965).
8. Gray, W. E., and Stern, H. "Fluid Amplifiers—Capabilities and Applications." *Control Eng.* **11**, No. 2, 57–64 (Feb. 1964).
9. Gluskin, R. S., Jacoby, M., and Reader, T. D. "A Fluid Logic Digital Computer." *Computer Design*, **4**, No. 6, 26–36 (June 1965).

# 4 | PUTTING THE BITS TOGETHER

*"He shall have a noble memory"*
*William Shakespeare*

At the time of writing, there are three types of storage that can be purchased. These are co-ordinate addressed, content addressed, and push-down stacks. In this chapter we will examine each type. Most of the storage devices of the previous chapter can be adapted for any one of the types of memory organization.

We will use a different type of device for each type of storage so that as many different principles are displayed as possible.

## CO-ORDINATE ADDRESSED STORAGE

By far the most common type of storage is the co-ordinate addressed. These storage devices consist of a large number of cells, each capable of holding several bits of information. Typically we might have 16,384 cells each of 32 bits. Each cell has a number associated with it called its "address." Associated with this collection of cells we have two registers not normally available to the programmer. These are called the "memory address register" (abbreviated MAR) and the "memory buffer register" (MBR). Their use is best defined by example. Suppose we wish to know the content of cell 3456. We insert the cell's number (3456) into the Memory Address Register and request a READ operation. Some time later the information which was stored in cell 3456 will be available in the Memory Buffer Register. Suppose instead we wish to deposit some information in cell 3456. We put the data we wish to deposit into the MBR and the cell number in the MAR. Then we request a WRITE

79

operation.  Our purpose here is to discover how a particular cell is selected for reading or writing and how the information is conveyed between that cell and the Memory Buffer Register.

There are two different ways of organizing co-ordinate addressed memories and we will consider an example of each.  We will examine the conceptually simpler one first.

### Word Oriented Memories (2D)

Consider Fig. 4.1 which shows a 4 word memory of 5 bits per word arranged for reading.  It is constructed from plated-wire storage elements. The sequence of events required to read out a word is as follows:

1. The address of the word is placed in the Memory Address Register (MAR), suppose it is 01, meaning word 1.
2. The "clear" line is pulsed entering all ZEROS into the Memory Buffer Register (MBR).
3. The "drive strobe" line is pulsed.  The only AND gate that will be turned on by this pulse is the one associated with the desired word, namely word 1.

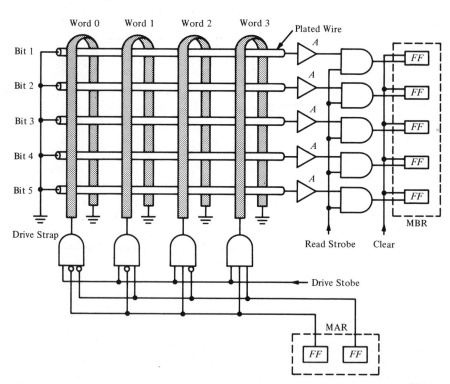

Fig. 4.1 A word-oriented memory of four words of 5 bits each constructed from plated wires. Each intersection of a drive strap and a bit line forms one "bit" of storage.

4. This causes a current to flow in the drive strap which "tilts" the fields of all five bit lines where the drive strap crosses them.

5. As explained in the previous chapter, this will generate a pair of voltage pulses on each bit line, first positive and then negative, or else vice versa. These voltage pulses are amplified by the triangular boxes marked $A$. These amplifiers are of the "integrating" type, so that when a positive pulse is presented to their input followed by a negative pulse, they give an output of $+1$ for the period between the pulses. When the negative pulse comes first, their output is $-1$. (See Fig. 4.2.)

6. At about the midpoint of the amplifier pulses, the READ STROBE line is pulsed, thus gating positive signals forward to set the respective flip-flop.

7. The AND gates treat any signal of zero volts or less as a logical ZERO and so stored ZERO's, which generate negative pulses from the amplifiers, are blocked by the AND gates and their flip-flops are *not* set.

At the end of the READing operation the information which was in word 1 is still there and a copy of it exists in the MBR.

This is in brief how we get information out of the memory. Had we wished to discover the contents of cell 2, we would have put 10 into the memory address register instead of what we did. If the memory address register contains $b$ bits, we can distinguish $2^b$ possible different addresses and hence may have $2^b$ cells in the memory.

Now we must show how to write information into the different cells. In addition to the circuitry of Fig. 4.2, we will need that of Fig. 4.3 connected to the bit lines.

The output side of each flip-flop in the Memory Buffer Register is connected to a drive amplifier (labeled "$D$" in Fig. 4.3.) The output of the driver is connected to the bit line.

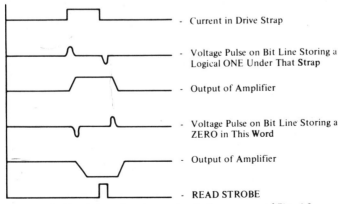

- Current in Drive Strap

- Voltage Pulse on Bit Line Storing a Logical ONE Under That Strap

- Output of Amplifier

- Voltage Pulse on Bit Line Storing a ZERO in This Word

- Output of Amplifier

- READ STROBE

Fig. 4.2 The timing of various pulses in the memory of Fig. 4.1.

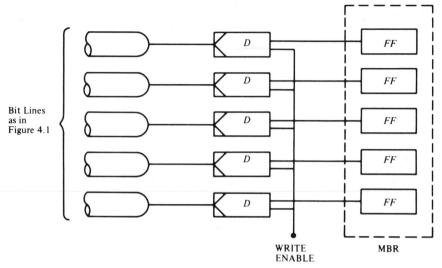

Fig. 4.3 Connections for WRITEing in a plated-wire memory.

The drivers are so constructed that when the WRITE ENABLE line is at ZERO, they have no output. When the WRITE ENABLE line goes to ONE, the drivers generate a positive current pulse if their other input (from the flip-flop) is ONE and a negative current pulse if their other input is ZERO.

First the drive strobe is brought to logical ONE, so that the drive strap selected by the number in the Memory Address Register is energized and the fields of the plated wires under that drive strap are "tilted" as described previously. Then the WRITE ENABLE line is pulsed and the appropriate positive or negative current pulses pass down the bit lines. These current pulses generate clockwise or counterclockwise fields, which are carefully adjusted in magnitude so that they will be too small to change "untilted" fluxes but large enough to enforce their own direction on a flux that has been "weakened" by "tilting." When the drive strobe and the WRITE ENABLE lines both go back to ZERO, the WRITE operation is over and the information which was in the Memory Buffer Register has been copied into the selected word of the memory. These then are the ways of reading from and writing into a plated wire, word oriented, coordinate addressed memory.

The plated-wire memory is reasonably easy to fabricate and the storage medium is inexpensive. The output signals on reading are rather small and require high-gain amplifiers, but no worse than an average home-type hi-fi set. Speeds are high, down to 200 nsec at present, and readout is nondestructive. The main disadvantage of this type of memory is the cost of the electronics required to select and energize a drive strap. There must be an AND gate for each word and it must be capable of producing enough power to drive its drive strap. With 16,384 words (14 bit address) we require 16,384 high-power AND gates, and even at only a few dollars each, that adds up rather rapidly.

One way of reducing the cost of such a memory is to make the memory "more square." A memory of 16,384 words each of 32 bits is considered *def* to be very "non-square," because there are many more words than there are bits. One might rearrange this to become a memory of 1024 words each consisting of 512 bits. If high-power AND gates and bit-sense amplifiers have the same cost, this latter arrangement will cost 512+1024=1536 units of cost as opposed to the original non-square arrangement that would cost 16,384+32 or 16,416 units of cost; a reduction by a factor of 10.

Unfortunately the rest of our computer will probably still want words of 32 bits, not 512.

One way around this is to group the bits of our big word into 16 groups of 32 bits each. All bits within a group have a common read strobe line and a common WRITE ENABLE line, but there are separate lines for each of the 16 groups. Now we can take the four low-order bits of the Memory Address Register and, instead of using them to help in the selection of a drive strap, we use them to select one each of both a READ STROBE and WRITE ENABLE line for connection to and from the Memory Buffer Register. Figure 4.4 shows a 32-word plated-wire memory of two bits per word. It is arranged as 4 groups of two bits each under 8 drive straps giving an 8×8 array. Only the reading circuits are shown. The two low-order bits of the MAR are used to select which of the four groups will be gated into the MBR. The three high-order bits of the MAR determine which drive strap will be energized.

*Bit Oriented Memories* (3D) coincident current memories

The other major form of co-ordinate addressed memory uses the shape of a magnetic core's hysteresis loop to help in selecting which word is being addressed. These are termed "coincident current" memories and are said to be bit oriented, because all the corresponding bits (one from each word) are collected together in one place.

A coincident current type of memory uses magnetic cores not only to store information, but to help in the selection of the word to be accessed. In Fig. 4.5 we show a two by two array of 4 bits. Suppose that we insert a current of three-quarters of $i_{crit}$ into the line labelled $Y_0$. This is not enough to cause either the core labelled (0,0) or the one labelled (0,1) to flip over, so nothing happens. Suppose now we put a similar current into

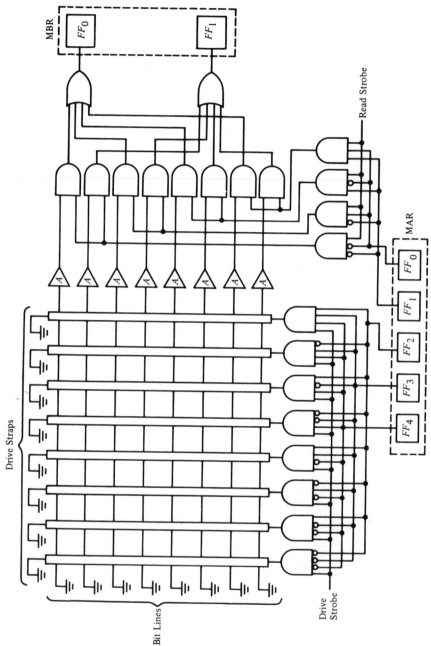

Fig. 4.4 A 32-word, 2-bit-per-word plated-wire memory arranged in an 8 × 8 square array.

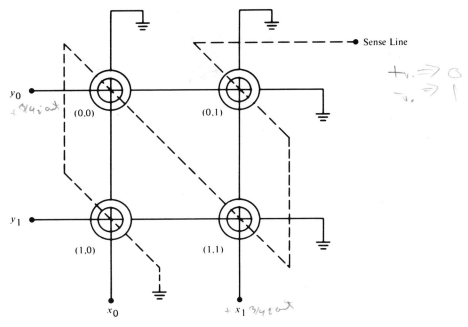

Fig. 4.5  A coincident current array of four bits.

the line called $X_1$.  Again the core (1,1) has only three-quarters of the current required to flip it over, but core (0,1) has three-quarters $i_{crit}$ from line $Y_0$ and three-quarters $i_{crit}$ from line $X_1$, or a total of one and one-half $i_{crit}$, which will force it into the "ZERO" state.  If core (0,1) was holding a ONE, the resulting change in flux will generate a voltage on the sense line and this can be detected by an appropriate amplifier.

The "memory" shown in Fig. 4.5 has four words of one bit each.  If we want, for example, a five bit word, we take five replicas of Fig. 4.5 and connect all the $Y_0$ lines together in series, all the $Y_1$ together, all the $X_0$ together, and all the $X_1$ together.  Each of the five sense lines comes out to a separate amplifier.  Now when we pulse the $Y_0$ and $X_1$ lines, we readout all five bits in parallel from word (0,1).  This will leave word (0,1) containing all ZERO's.  Generally, we do not want to destroy the contents of a memory cell when we read from that cell, in case we should want to read again.  Therefore, with this type of "destructive read-out" memory, we must have a "re-write" cycle following every read.  What is done is to put negative currents of three-quarters $i_{crit}$ on lines $Y_0$ and $X_1$ which will write a ONE in every bit of word (0,1).  Where we wish to leave a ZERO, we insert an inhibit current of plus three-quarters $i_{crit}$ into that sense line.  This will effectively reduce the net current passing through that particular core to less than the critical current, leaving a ZERO stored in that bit. This inhibiting current is often sent down a fourth wire (not shown) which, like the sense line, threads every core on a plane. Naturally enough, this is called the "inhibit line."

---

*Question 4.1:* During the "re-write" cycle, calculate the net current in each of the four cores of Fig. 4.5, assuming we have a 4 word × 5 bit memory, and,
1. we wish to end up with a ZERO in word (0,1) in this bit position,
2. with a ONE in word (0,1) in this bit position.

*give net in 1st core of front plane for all four words (0,0) (0,1) (1,0)(1,1)*

Coincident current arrays begin to come into their own as the size of the memory increases. Although they are more complicated to wire (4 lines instead of 2), the saving in electronics becomes considerable.

The number of drivers required in a coincident current memory increases with the square root of the size of the memory. Core memories have a slower operating speed than plated-wire memories, regardless of their organization, because of the necessity of restoring the information after every read operation.

Writing is accomplished by first reading out the information and throwing it away, thus leaving the word all ZERO's and then writing in the ONE's desired, as described above.

A number of variations on bit oriented (called 3D) and word oriented (called 2D) memories exist, some using external selection and some internal, but they are not significantly different from a system point of view. For that matter, a system designer is generally not too concerned with the difference between word and bit oriented arrays if he is specifying a co-ordinate addressed memory. Price and speed will determine choice, assuming other things to be equal.

## CONTENT ADDRESSABLE STORAGE

In a co-ordinate addressed memory, we ask for the "contents of cell *XXX*." In a content addressable memory (CAM),[1] we can ask "if there is a cell which contains the word *WWWW*." That is we select the cell with which we wish to communicate, not on the basis of *where* the cell is, but on the basis of *what* it holds. We can, in effect, say "will the *real* John Smith please stand up!" Given this ability, there are a number of interesting things that can be accomplished which we will explore in a later chapter. Here we are concerned with how such a memory might be constructed.

*The Comparison*

Suppose we have a memory which contains four words. Let these words be

$$W_1 = 10001$$
$$W_2 = 10100$$
$$W_3 = 11000$$
$$W_4 = 11100$$

Suppose further that we wish to discover if any of the words in the memory are identical with a particular bit pattern called the "comparand." Let us say that the comparand is

$$C = 11000$$

Examine the left most bit of each word and compare it with the left most bit of the comparand. If they are not equal, that word should be discard from the set of "responders"—the words which respond to the question "are you just like me?"

If we start out with all the memory words in this set and continue our winnowing process first on the left most bit, then on the second, then the third, and so forth, by the time we have examined all the bits, the only words left in the set of responders will be ones which match the comparand exactly.

Let us do this for the four words mentioned above. We start with $W_1$, $W_2$, $W_3$, and $W_4$ all being responders. When we compare the left most bit, all four agree with the comparand, so there is no change. Comparing the second bit, we are led to discard words $W_1$ and $W_2$ which leaves us with $W_3$ and $W_4$. Comparing now the bit third from the left we find that $W_2$ and $W_4$ are disqualified, because they have ONE in this position while the comparand has a ZERO. So we must discard them. $W_2$ is already crossed off the list so that leads to no change and all we have to do is cross off $W_4$. This leaves us with $W_3$ as a responder.

Since $W_3$ and the comparand agree in the fourth and fifth positions, the rest of the comparison produces no further change in the set of responders. We end up with $W_3$ as the only responder. Note that it is not necessary to do the comparison one bit at a time. It was described in that fashion for the sake of simplicity only.

Let us take another case. Suppose the comparand now is

$$C = 100\emptyset\emptyset$$

where the symbol $\emptyset$ means we "don't care" whether the word contains ZERO's or ONE's—either will do.

All words pass the test on the left most bit, but $W_3$ and $W_4$ have ONE's in the second position, so they are discarded. $W_2$ has a ONE in the third position, so it is rejected, leaving us with just $W_1$. Since we have said we didn't care about the last two bits, a word like

$$100\ 00$$

or

$$100\ 11$$

or

$$100\ 10$$

would have passed our test just as easily as $W_1$ did. Suppose instead we had been looking for "any old pattern" that ends with two ZERO's. That would imply a comparand of

$$C = \cancel{0}\cancel{0}\cancel{0}00$$

and words $W_2$, $W_3$, and $W_4$ would have ended up all being responders. When the situation occurs in which there are "multiple responders" (more than one member in a set), we can do one of two things: either narrow down the set by further searches or else agree to take the "first" responder —the one nearest the top of the memory. Multiple responses can occur even when we "care" about (specify) every bit position in the comparand; suppose that there are two words in the memory that match the comparand exactly.

### Organization of a Content Addressable Memory

Before we examine the details of a circuit, we must clear up a few points about the general organization of a content addressable memory.

First let us consider the "don't cares." These would seem to require a third state (not the same as either a ZERO or a ONE) in the comparand register. In actuality one uses two registers: A comparand register to specify what pattern is desired and a mask register to specify which parts of the word are to be compared with the comparand. We adopt the convention that a ZERO in the mask means "don't care" and a ONE means "yes we do." Thus,

$$C = 100\cancel{0}\cancel{0} \text{ implies comparand} = 100??$$
$$\text{mask} = 11100$$

while

$$C = \cancel{0}\cancel{0}\cancel{0}00 \text{ implies comparand} = ???00$$
$$\text{mask} = 00011$$

The places shown with a question mark could contain either ZERO's or ONE's, which ever is convenient. Since they are "masked out," we really *don't* care which.

Second we will compare all the words in the memory with the comparand simultaneously. This means that there must be a comparison

circuit for each word and also a flip-flop for each word in which to hold
the result of the comparison.

Third we can compare all the bits in parallel.  This will speed up the
operation, at the cost of additional circuitry.

Fourth we will need circuits to resolve (select the first of) multiple
responders and to report back to the rest of the computer whether or not
there *are* any responders to a search.

Finally we need some facility for READing out responders and for
writing into them.

Figure 4.6 shows the general layout of the memory.

The zeroth bit of every word is in the left most column.  The first
bit in the next column and so forth.  The bits of one word form a horizontal row.  Associated with each word there is some control circuitry.

The circuitry involved breaks up into four more or less independent
parts which we will consider one at a time.

We are going to construct this memory using conventional flip-flops.
If one were actually to contemplate building such a memory, one would
surely investigate the possibility of using large-scale integration with one

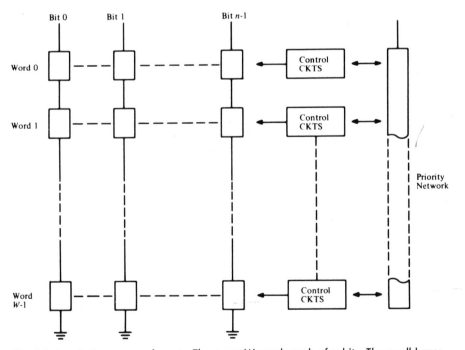

Fig. 4.6 Associative memory layout.  There are W words each of n bits. The small boxes
represent one bit of storage.

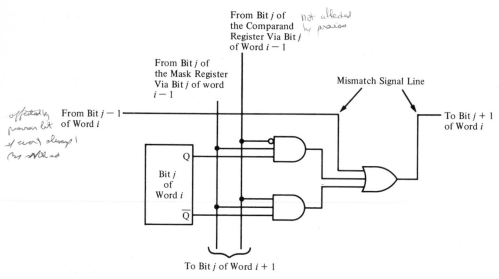

From Bit *j* of
the Comparand ~~not affected~~
Register Via Bit *j* ~~by previous~~
of Word *i* − 1

From Bit *j* of
the Mask Register
Via Bit *j* of word
*i* − 1

Mismatch Signal Line

*effectively*
*previous bit*
*of word always 1*
*(by NOR ed)*

From Bit *j* − 1
of Word *i*

To Bit *j* + 1
of Word *i*

Q

Bit *j*
of
Word *i*

$\overline{Q}$

To Bit *j* of Word *i* + 1

**Fig. 4.7 Match circuits for bit *j* of word *i*.**

or more words on each chip, but for our purposes we will deal with separate flip-flops and gates.

*Match Circuits*    Figure 4.7 shows the circuitry necessary at each bit of each word in order to do comparison of all bits of all words all in parallel. If the mask bit *j* is a ONE and if the *j*th bit of the comparand is ZERO while the *j*th bit of word *i* is ONE, or vice versa, then the mismatch signal line will have a ONE on it. If some one of the bits of word *i* doesn't match the masked comparand, then the *i*th mismatch signal line will be ONE by the time it has passed through the right-most bit of word *i*.

*Control Circuits*    To the right-hand side of each word in Fig. 4.6 we have a box labeled "control circuits." The most important function of this circuit is to store the information about whether this word is a responder or not. To do this we will use a flip-flop. (See Fig. 4.8.) The collection of these flip-flops (one per word) is called the "response store."

*Read-Write Circuits*    In this design we wish to be able to write into those bits of all responders where the mask has ONE's. We will write the value stored in the corresponding bits of the comparand. Figure 4.9 shows the circuits required to accomplish this. When the mask bit *j* is ONE, we energize $W_j$, and when the word *i* is a responder (the word enable line *i* is ONE), we store the value of the comparand bit *j* in flip-flop *i,j*.

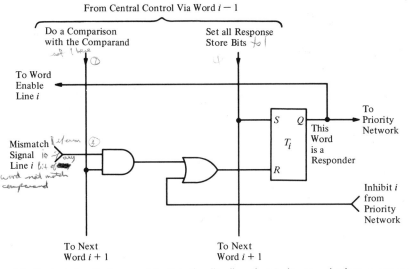

From Central Control Via Word $i-1$

Do a Comparison
with the Comparand

Set all Response
Store Bits

To Word
Enable
Line $i$

Mismatch
Signal
Line $i$

This
Word
is a
Responder

$T_i$

$S$    $Q$

$R$

To
Priority
Network

Inhibit $i$
from
Priority
Network

To Next
Word $i+1$

To Next
Word $i+1$

Fig. 4.8 Control circuits for word $i$. $T_i$ is the flip-flop that indicates whether or not word
$i$ is a responder.

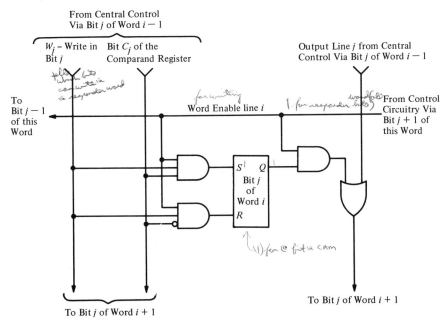

From Central Control
Via Bit $j$ of Word $i-1$

$W_j$ – Write in
Bit $j$

Bit $C_j$ of the
Comparand Register

Output Line $j$ from Central
Control Via Bit $j$ of Word $i-1$

To
Bit $j-1$
of this
Word

Word Enable line $i$

From Control
Circuitry Via
Bit $j+1$ of
this Word

$S$    $Q$

Bit $j$
of
Word $i$

$R$

To Bit $j$ of Word $i+1$

To Bit $j$ of Word $i+1$

Fig. 4.9 Read and Write circuitry of a content addressable memory.

*Question 4.2:* Redesign the write circuits using *D*-type edge triggered flip-flops. Assume that the lines $W_j$ go to ONE (where the mask stores a one) when you wish to write.

For reading, the *j*th bit of all responders are ORed together, and the outputs of these OR circuits are available at all times for reading by the central control unit. Obviously, if two or more responders to a search exist, what we read will be the bit by bit OR of all the responders.

*Priority Network*   The priority network (Fig. 4.10) is to provide two functions in this design. First, it will generate a signal that is available to the

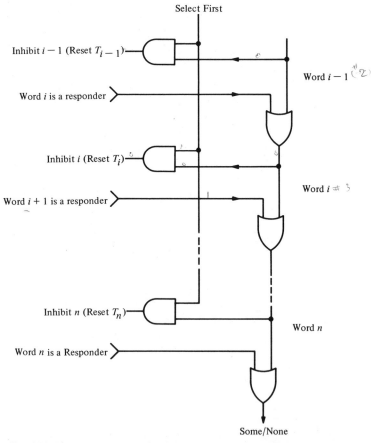

**Fig. 4.10 The priority network of the content addressable memory.**

*leaves 1 in only F♭ of 1ᵈ responder + ops. 1 so falls there is a responder*

central control unit of the computer which indicates whether or not there are any responders in the memory. This is called the SOME/NONE line in Fig. 4.10. Second, there are basically two situations in which we need to select one out of a group of responders. The first involves writing, the second reading.

Suppose that two cells in memory have identical contents and we wish to modify the contents of one, but not both. No possible search can distinguish one from the other—by hypothesis they are identical. Thus if we wish to write into only one of them, we must have some form of selection or priority circuit.

Suppose on the other hand that we have conducted a search on the bit patterns stored in the left-hand side of each cell and have ended up with several responders, perhaps many. In order to read these responders out of storage, we need to select one of the group, read it out, mark it processed, and then go back to search again for "unprocessed" responders. Since we want in both these cases to select one out of many, (we don't care which one) and since the way we have designed the SOME/NONE circuit makes it convenient, we will include a circuit to select the *first* (earliest) responder,[2,3,4] resetting all others. This consists of the *select first* line and an AND gate for each word. If, by the time it gets to this word, the SOME/NONE line already has a ONE on it, that means that some earlier word was a responder. When the *select first* line is energized, we send a reset signal called Inhibit $i$ to flip-flop $T_i$ of the response store. (See Figs. 4.8 and 4.10.)

## PUSHDOWN STACKS

The third general form of storage organization is called a "pushdown stack" or sometimes a "LIFO list." LIFO stands for "last in, first out."

Symbolically a pushdown stack can be represented by Fig. 4.11.

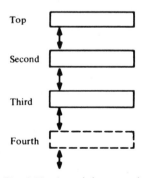

Fig. 4.11. A pushdown stack.

Given a memory of either of the two previously described forms (content and co-ordinate addressed), there are only two things that can be done with a memory cell. We can copy out its contents (READ) or we can change its contents (WRITE). With a pushdown stack, we have two more operations in addition to READ and WRITE. We will call these PLACE—for "place a new item on top of the old ones," and WITHDRAW—for "taking the top item off the stack."

Suppose we start off with an empty stack and we PLACE the words "SMITH," "BROWN," and "JONES" on the stack in that order. Figure 4.12a shows what the stack will look like. Figure 4.12b shows what the stack will look like if we PLACE the word "GREEN" on top of the stack. JONES will be pushed down into the second cell, which will push BROWN down to the third, which in turn pushes SMITH down to the fourth cell.

In Fig. 4.12c we carry out the other type of storing operation—namely, WRITING. This does not push down the stack, but overwrites the word in the top cell by the new word. The old contents of the top cell (JONES) are destroyed by a WRITE operation.

Now consider the WITHDRAW operation. It takes the item in the top cell of the stack and removes it, allowing the remaining items to "pop up." Figure 4.13 shows the effects of READing and of WITHDRAWing from a stack. In both cases, the word that is obtained for use elsewhere is the same—namely, "SMITH," but READ does not modify the stack and WITHDRAW does.

As a further example, consider three successive READS of the stack shown in Fig. 4.13a. The output will be "SMITH," "SMITH," and "SMITH." Three successive WITHDRAWals from the same stack will yield "SMITH," "JONES," and "BROWN." Obviously we can go on READing a stack forever, but what happens if we keep on issuing

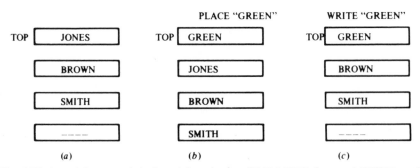

Fig. 4.12 A pushdown stack before (a) and after (b) PLACING the word GREEN on the stack. In (c) we WRITE the word GREEN on stack (a) instead.

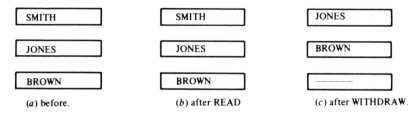

| SMITH | SMITH | JONES |
| JONES | JONES | BROWN |
| BROWN | BROWN | $---$ |
| (a) before. | (b) after READ | (c) after WITHDRAW. |

Fig. 4.13 A comparison of the two operations READ amd WITHDRAW.

WITHDRAWals to the same stack? The answer is that pushdown stacks are much like a local bank manager. Both frown on "overdrafts." Usually a computer with a pushdown stack will be arranged to give an "interrupt" (see Chapter 7) when there is an attempt to READ or WITHDRAW from an empty stack.

Although in theory a pushdown stack has unlimited capacity (has no bottom), in practice of course there will be a finite number of cells in any stack. Therefore, it is also possible to generate an interrupt if one attempts to place an item on a stack that is already full.

### A Notation for Stack Operations

Now consider two pushdown stacks called $S_1$ and $S_2$ and imagine that we wish to transfer an item of information from $S_2$ to $S_1$. If these were ordinary cells in a co-ordinate addressed memory, there would be only one thing to do—namely, copy the contents of $S_2$ into $S_1$. This can be shown symbolically as

$$S_1 \leftarrow (S_2).$$

But with pushdown stacks, there are four different ways in which this can be done. We have the option of preserving $S_1$ before the transfer (or not as we desire) (doing a PLACE operation) and of restoring (or not) $S_2$ after the transfer (doing a WITHDRAW operation). Suppose we start off with the following situation in all four cases

$$S_1\text{: ABLE} \qquad S_2\text{: YAK}$$
$$\text{BAKER} \qquad \text{ZEBRA}$$

The first type of transfer we will call *copy to* and denote by

$$\boxed{S_1 \longleftarrow (S_2).}$$

The result will be

$$S_1\text{: YAK} \qquad S_2\text{: YAK}$$
$$\text{BAKER} \qquad \text{ZEBRA}$$

The second type of transfer can be called *copy on* and requires a preservation of $S_1$ before the transfer. It will be symbolized as

$$\boxed{S_1 \curvearrowleft \!\!-\!\!-(S_2)}$$

and will result in

$S_1$: YAK      $S_2$: YAK
      ABLE             ZEBRA
      BAKER

The third we call *move to* and employs a restoration of $S_2$ after the transfer. Thus,

$$\boxed{S_1 \!\!-\!\!-\!\!-\curvearrowright(S_2)}$$

will give

$S_1$: YAK      $S_2$: ZEBRA
      BAKER

Finally we first preserve $S_1$, then transfer, and then restore $S_2$. This is called *move on* and in symbols

$$S_1 \curvearrowleft \qquad \curvearrowright(S_2)$$

produces

$S_1$: YAK      $S_2$: ZEBRA
      ABLE
      BAKER

The author has found these symbols for the different kinds of transfers a convenient way of denoting list and stack operations.

### Implementation of Pushdown Stacks

There are three principle methods of building pushdown stacks: shift registers; pointers; and linked lists. Strictly speaking, only the first of these is a real pushdown stack, but the other two methods are commonly used to make a co-ordinate addressed memory behave like a pushdown stack.[5]

*Shift Registers*    If we can demonstrate a one bit shift register, it is easy to see that by setting, for example, 32 of them side by side, we will have a **shift register capable of handling 32 bit words. Figure 4.14 shows one way** of constructing a shift register from flip-flops. Note in particular that there are two flip-flops per bit of storage, one in the "regular" bank and one in the "temporary" bank. This form is called a "two bank shift register."

The general principle is as follows. Information is copied from the left-hand, or regular, bank straight across to the right-hand, or temporary,

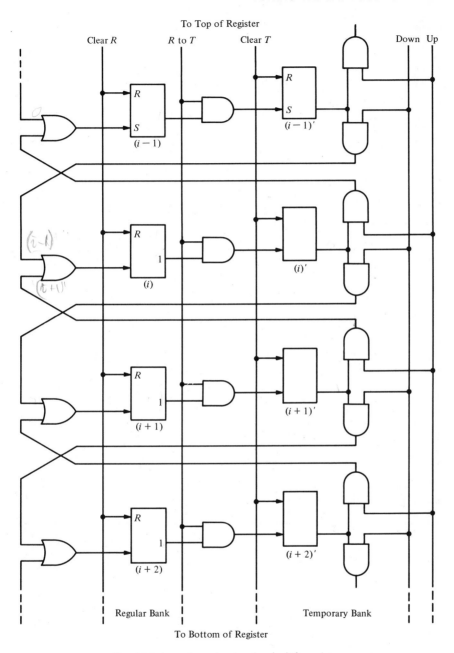

Fig. 4.14 A portion of a two-bank shift register.

bank. It is then copied back into the left-hand bank either down one position, or up one. The details of this procedure are:

1. Clear the temporary bank.
2. Energize the "*R* to *T*" line copying information from regular to temporary banks.
3. Clear the regular bank.
4. Energize either the UP or the DOWN line, thus causing the information in the temporary bank to be copied back to the regular bank either up one position or down one position.

For example, if the DOWN line is energized in step 4, the entire operation is called "Preserve" and the old contents of cell *i* go into cell *i*+1, the old contents of *i*+1 go into *i*+2 and so forth. On the other hand, if the UP line is energized, the operation is called "restore" and the old contents of cell *i* go into cell *i*−1 etc. These operations are sometimes called "PUSH" and "POP."

---

*Question 4.3:* Redesign Fig. 4.14 using *D*-type master/slave flip-flops.

*Question 4.4:* In the sequence described above, what would be put into cell *i* if *both* the UP and DOWN line are energized in step 4. Note: this is *not* a normal stack operation.

---

Now we are in a position to see how PLACE and WITHDRAW can be

implemented. PLACE consists of a preserve followed by a WRITE, WITHDRAW is a READ followed by a restore.

The PLACE operation occurs in two steps: a *preserve* to push down the stack (see Fig. 4.15), which moves all information down one cell; followed by a *write*, which copies the contents of the memory buffer register into the top cell.

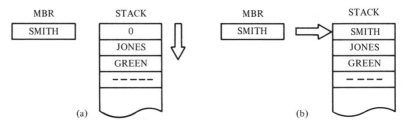

Fig. 4.15 The two-step execution of a PLACE command: (a) preserve the stack, (b) write from MBR into the stack.

Fig. 4.16 The two-step execution of a WITHDRAW command: (a) copy the top of the stack into the MBR, (b) restore the stack.

---

*Question 4.5:* Show the circuitry that must be added to a two-bank shift register similar to that of Fig. 4.14 in order to execute the PLACE command.

---

Similarly, the WITHDRAW command also consists of two phases: a *read* operation copies the contents of the top of the stack into the memory buffer register (Fig. 4.16a); and then a *restore* operation pops up the stack (Fig. 4.16b), eliminating the old top item.

---

*Question 4.6:* Using two stacks and an MBR, draw diagrams similar to these which illustrate the four inter-stack operations: copy to; copy on; move to; move on; described previously.

---

*Pointer Implemented Pushdown Stacks*    In the method described in the previous section, all the words in a stack are moved into the "next cell down the line" when a preserve operation is carried out. In this section, we will examine a type of construction that leaves the information stored in the stack stationery and moves instead the "top of the stack." This is done by having a "pointer" that points to the cell (contains the address of the cell), which is the current head of the stack. If, for example, the last three items placed on the stack were ABLE, BAKER, and CHARLIE, in that order, we would have the situation shown in Fig. 4.17.

To PLACE another item on the stack, we add one to the contents of the pointer, obtaining $(\alpha+1)$, and write the new item into that cell. To WITHDRAW an item, we read from the cell pointed at by the pointer and then subtract one from the pointer.

---

*Question 4.7:* Working with Fig. 4.17, construct a picture of each stage of the process of PLACING "DOG" and "EASY" on the stack and then doing three WITHDRAWALS.

---

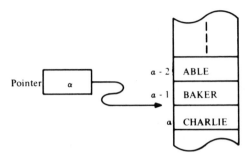

Fig. 4.17 A pointer-type pushdown stack.

So far the pointer type pushdown stack is identical with a co-ordinate addressed memory, except that on occasion we must add one to or subtract one from the contents of the memory address register (pointer). This may be accomplished either by using the regular arithmetic unit of the computer or by using the special circuit shown in Fig. 4.18.

This circuit consists of leading edge detectors and complementing flip-flops. Suppose the "add one" line is energized. The upper left LED puts a pulse into the first flip-flop causing it to complement. If the add one line is high and if the first flip-flop goes from ONE to ZERO its $\overline{Q}$ output will go from ZERO to ONE and a pulse will be passed to complement the second flip-flop. The reader should verify for himself that this indeed adds one to the contents of the register.

---

*Question 4.8:* Using 4 *D*-type leading edge triggered flip-flops, design a 4 stage binary counter that will count up to 15. Hint: you must rely on the fact that the output of a flip-flop doesn't change instantaneously.

---

Now we shall look at how a pointer-type stack should be connected to the central processing unit of the computer. Aside from the data lines connecting the memory buffer register to and from the rest of the machine, there must be command lines and certain signal lines to inform the CPU of the condition of the stack. We will assume that the CPU decodes the commands and, therefore, presents to the stack a signal on one of four wires: READ; WRITE; PRESERVE; RESTORE. We must choose under what conditions these signals should be obeyed. Clearly it will be impossible to PRESERVE a stack that is full. Equally clearly, we can neither READ nor RESTORE an empty stack. Should the CPU attempt

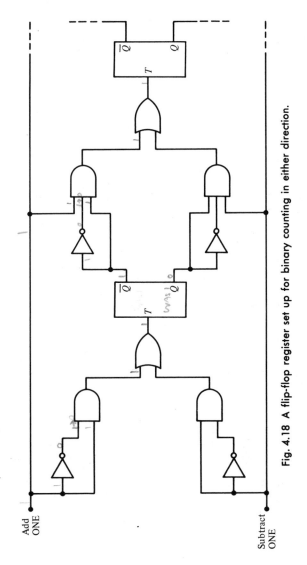

**Fig. 4.18 A flip-flop register set up for binary counting in either direction.**

any of these impossible operations, we should gently "slap its wrist" by raising what is called an "interrupt." We will discuss these more fully in a later chapter. Now we come to a less obvious situation. Should we permit WRITING in an empty stack? On the one hand, we might argue that writing is the same as placing in an empty stack. On the other hand, we might say that if a stack is empty it "contains no cells" and, hence, it is impossible to write into a cell that doesn't exist. This situation is typical of many that arise, in designing computers, where there is no obvious answer to a question. And yet, it is the answer that the designers choose in these cases that often make the difference between a "good" design and a "bad" one.

If there is truly no preferable choice, then one should select the one that is easiest to implement. But usually in conversation with one's colleagues —programmers in particular—or after careful consideration, or both, one can decide that $A$ is better than $B$, or vica versa. Sometimes when all else fails, one can consider the competition. If they have faced a similar problem and made a choice examine it carefully. Unless you have good reasons for differing, go along with the crowd. There is no point, in computer design at any rate, in being different just for the sake of being different. Let me urge you to remember, "decide in haste, repent at leisure."

How do these little bits of philosophy help us here? To begin with, most pushdown stacks currently implemented do not permit READ and WRITE as separate operations. They usually have PLACE and WITH-DRAW and sometimes permit PRESERVE (which duplicates the top cell) and RESTORE (which destroys the top cell).

For these designs, the question doesn't come up, so we find no help there. Certain list processing languages (see below) do allow reading and writing. In general, these languages treat empty lists as not containing any cells and, hence, as "unwritable" in. We will follow this approach.

To recapitulate—PRESERVING will be the only legal operation on an empty stack and the only illegal one on a full stack. An attempt to PRESERVE a full stack should cause a "stack overflow" signal to be raised. Attempts to READ or RESTORE an empty stack should cause a "stack underflow." An attempt to WRITE in an empty stack we will call an "illegal stack operation." A good programmer will want an opportunity to test for these conditions—stack empty or full *before* he gets into trouble. Since we must generate these signals for our own use, it costs next to nothing to pass them back to the CPU so that they can be tested there. Figure 4.19 shows a simplified block diagram of the stack controls we have described to date.

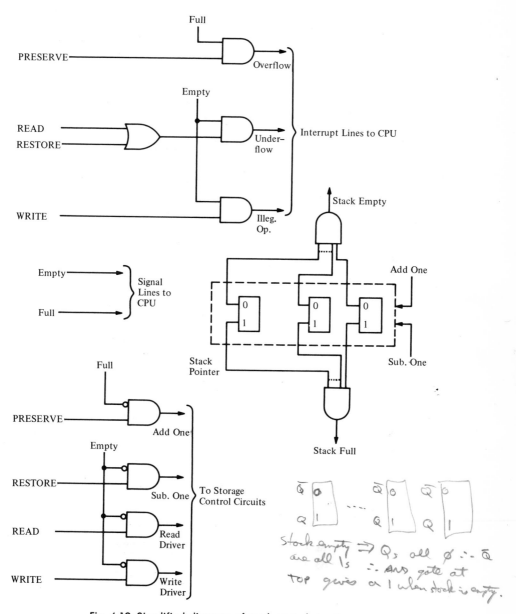

Fig. 4.19 Simplified diagram of stack control circuits.

*Question 4.9:* Using the design of Fig. 4.19, one cell of storage cannot be written into or used in any way. What is it? Can you re-design the circuit so that it could be used? Is it worth the extra hardware?

*Linked List Stacks*    There are many situations in which it would be convenient to have several pushdown stacks available for one's program to use.[6] One cannot predict in general how many stacks would be "enough" nor can one determine in advance how large each one should be. Worse, at one point in a problem one may need two large stacks and at a later point would prefer to have seventeen small ones. In this section, we present a scheme, based on the language IPL-V, which provides a great deal of flexibility at relatively low cost.

*Local Pointers*    In the previous scheme, we had a simple pointer which indicated which cell in storage was the current "top of the stack." Here, on the other hand, we store with each item a pointer (called the "link") to the next item on the stack. The link stored with item $\alpha$ is the address of the cell that *was* the top of the stack *before* $\alpha$ was added to the stack.

Figure 4.20 shows one way in which three stacks might be stored in a part of memory. There are several things to note about this figure. Cells 1, 2, and 3 are reserved to act as "head" cells. This is indicated by the *'s stored there. Cell 1 contains the address at which the top of stack 1 can be found. Cell 2 contains the address of the "top of stack 2" and cell 3 the address of the top of stack 3. If we had 5 stacks instead of 3, we would have reserved the first 5 cells to act as stack "heads." Next we note that the order in which items are stored in memory is irrelevant. The struc-

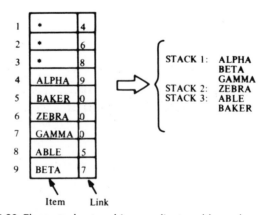

Fig. 4.20 Three stacks stored in co-ordinate addressed memory.

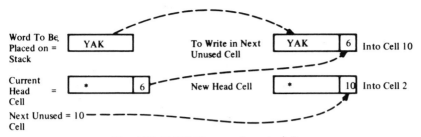

Fig. 4.21 PLACING a word on stack 2.

ture of the stacks is found by tracing down the links, beginning at the head cell and ending with a link of zero. An empty stack would have a head cell containing "*0."

Assume that cells 10 on are unused at present and that we wish to PLACE the word YAK in stack 2. Figure 4.21 shows how the word to be written into cell 10 is constructed and how the new head cell should look. What it does *not* show is how we know that cell 10 was empty, or what the next empty cell is now that 10 has been used. The method which is usually adopted to handle this problem is to take all the unused cells and link them together on a stack called the "available space list." In our present implementation, this could be stack "zero." The problems of stack manipulation can now be reduced to two relatively simple operations:

Given two registers $A$ and $B$,

1. Insert the cell named in $B$ after the cell named in $A$.
2. Delete the cell following the cell named in $A$ and put the name of the deleted cell into $B$.

Note that these are generalized "list operations" and none of the cells involved need to be head cells. For pushdown stacks, of course, only addresses of head cells may be put into register $A$.

*Insert and Delete*    Figures 4.22 and 4.23 show the action of the insert and delete operations on arbitrary cells. Figure 4.22 shows an initial stack holding the items SMITH, JONES, and BROWN. The cell (351) holding GREEN is "inserted" after cell 100, which is holding SMITH. This results in a stack containing: SMITH; GREEN; JONES; and BROWN. If cell 100 were the head cell of a stack, this would be equivalent to PLACING GREEN on the stack. Notice the way in which the links are manipulated. The old link of cell 100 (i.e., 210) is put into the link position of the new cell (351). This makes 351 point to the cell which used to follow cell 100. The address of the new cell (351) is put in the link position of cell 100, so that it points to the new cell.

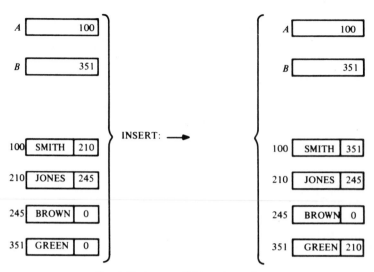

Fig. 4.22 *Insert* cell 351 *after* cell 100.

Figure 4.23 shows the process of deleting a cell. The initial stack contains: SMITH; JONES; and BROWN and we are requested to remove the cell following cell 100. This is done by putting the contents of the link portion of this cell into the link portion of cell 100. That is, the cell following 100 is initially cell 210. We discover this by looking at the link of cell 100. In cell 210 the link is 245, so we store 245 as the link of cell 100. This closes up the stack so it now contains: SMITH and

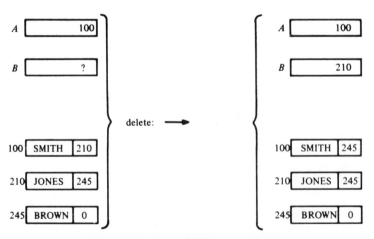

Fig. 4.23 Delete cell following cell 100.

BROWN. But we don't wish to "lose" cell 210 that was just removed from this stack, so we put its address in register *B*.

---

*Question 4.10:* Describe, using these two instructions, how one might RE-STORE a list whose head cell number is 1234.

---

### Implementation of a Linked List Stack

We are not yet ready to design a linked list stack in its entirety since there are several matters we have not yet covered. We can, however, layout a general plan of attack leaving some of the details to be filled in later.

In addition to the *A* and *B* registers discussed above, we will need a Memory Address Register, a Memory Buffer Register and one more short register, called *C*, for the temporary storage of a link.

Figure 4.24 shows the series of operations necessary to carry out an "insert" instruction. The left arrow means "replace the contents of" and L (MBR) refers to the link portion of the memory buffer register. Parentheses around a register name indicate the "contents of the register." Double parentheses mean the "contents of the contents of the register," or more simply "the contents of the cell pointed at by the register."

In step 1 the contents of the *A* register (100) are sent to the MAR and in step 2 a read is initiated. In step 3 the old link of 100 is saved in the *C* register and in step 4 the new cell address (the contents of *B*) are put into the MBR link position. Step 5 initiates the write operation. This is known as a "Read-Modify-Write" cycle and is quite often easy to implement in a co-ordinate addressed memory. In step 6 we send the name of the new cell (the contents of *B*) to the MAR and in step 7 initiate a read. In step 8 the saved old link is transferred from *C* to the MBR and in step 9 this information is written into the new cell.

1. MAR←(A)
2. Read: MBR←((MAR))
3. C←(L(MBR))
4. L(MBR)←(B)
5. Write: (MAR)←(MBR)
6. MAR←(B)
7. Read: MBR←((MAR))
8. L(MBR)←(C)
9. Write: (MAR)←(MBR)

Fig. 4.24 The sequence of steps necessary to carry out the "insert" operation of Fig. 4.22.

*Question 4.11:* Generate the equivalent of Fig. 4.24 for the delete process using the same registers: *A*, *B*, *C*, MAR and MBR.

From an examination of Fig. 4.24, we can construct at once an "information flow" diagram which will show us what information goes from where to where. Figure 4.25 is such a diagram for the insert process we

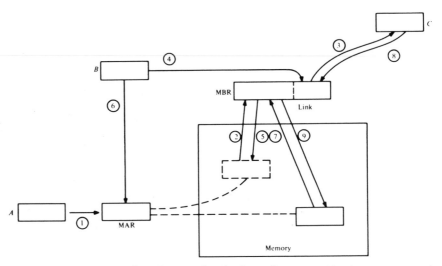

Fig. 4.25 An information flow diagram for the "insert" process. Numbers next to each arrow indicate the corresponding step of Fig. 4.24.

have been discussing. Quite often a preliminary design effort will leave things at this level, but we should have some practice in seeing what such a diagram implies at a more fundamental level.

To begin with, we note that registers *A*, *B*, *C*, the MAR, and the link of the MBR are all the same size—equal to the log to the base two of the number of words in the memory. Next let us look at the inputs to various registers. The MAR can be filled from both *A* and *B*. *C* can be filled only from the link of the MBR.

The left part of the MBR can, as far as we see here, be filled only from memory, but the link portion can be filled from memory, from *C*, and from *B*. Let us sketch the gates required to carry out these functions. We will show the MAR as having only one bit in order to simplify the diagram. (See Fig. 4.26.)

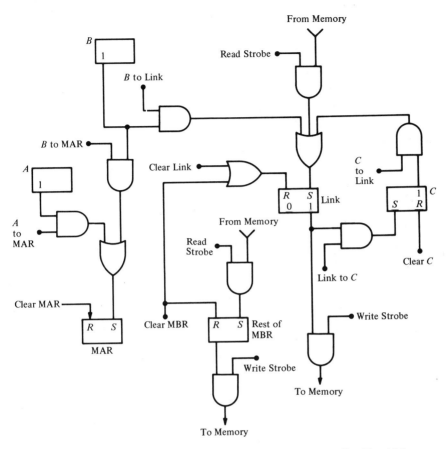

Fig. 4.26 One bit wide slice of the hardware necessary to realize Fig. 4.25.

*Question 4.12:* Add to Fig. 4.25 arrows which indicate the flow of information required to carry out the "delete" operation.

*Question 4.13:* Revise Fig. 4.26 so that all the information interchanges needed for both "insert" and "delete" can be carried out.

This figure is not to be taken too seriously at this stage. What we should note is that when two or more inputs come to a register, they are ORed together and that when a single register sends its contents to more than one place, there is an output AND gate for each such place. The way in which the various enabling lines to these AND gates are pulsed will be investigated in a later chapter.

Magnetic bubble memories can be arranged to shift in either direction by reversing the current to one of the driving coils (and hence causing the rotating magnetic vector to turn the other way). Given this bidirectionality they then make very good pushdown stacks.

## SEMICONDUCTOR CO-ORDINATE ADDRESSED STORAGE

As we saw in Chapter 3, flip-flops can be used to store information. It remains for us here to organize a collection of flip-flops into a memory of the coordinate address sort.

Let us begin by examining a reasonably inexpensive method of selecting one-out-$n$ lines. We will then use this method to address our memory. Suppose there are $2^{12} = 4096$ lines and we wish to select (energize) one of them. A straightforward but expensive method would be to purchase 4096 AND gates, each with 12 inputs. Each address line would be present as an assertion and as a negation (see Fig. 4.27), so both the value of the bits and their complements would be available.

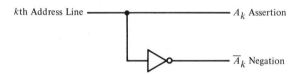

Fig. 4.27 Assertion and negation of address lines.

Then each AND is connected to the 12 address bits—either their assertion or their negation—in a pattern that is unique to that AND. Since there are 4096 ways of doing this (consider the binary numbers from 0–4095), each AND circuit is different from all the others, and when a bit pattern is presented on the address lines, exactly one of the AND's will be satisfied and its output brought to ONE. If we count up the total number of "gate inputs," this circuit will require we get: $4096 \times 12$ or 49,152.

A considerably less expensive (of inputs) method is called a "dual decoding tree." Recall that 4096 is $64^2$ and 64 is $8^2$. Suppose we have a circuit like Fig. 4.28. This circuit requires 12 two input AND's for an input count of 24. Now place two such 8-way decoding circuits at right angles so there are 8 horizontal wires and 8 vertical wires. At each intersection place a two input AND gate. (See Fig. 4.29.)

There are 64 such intersections, each requiring a two input AND plus the inputs required for each of the two 8-way circuits (24 each), so our total input count so far is $128 + 24 + 24 = 176$.

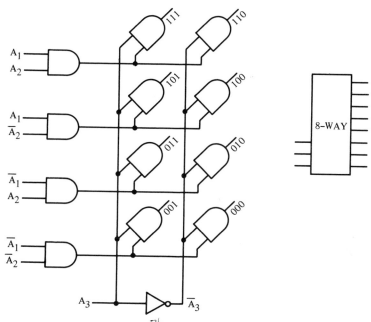

Fig. 4.28 An 8-way decoding circuit.

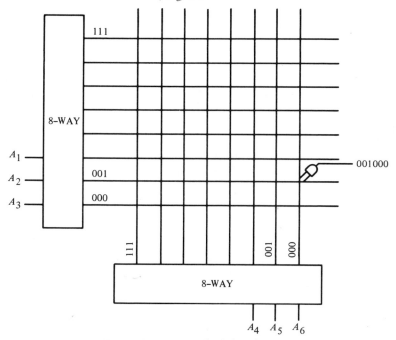

Fig. 4.29 A 64-way dual decoding tree.

It should come as no great surprise that we are going to take two 64-way decoders and at the $64^2 = 4096$ intersections place two input AND's. The total input count for this dual decoding tree is $4096 \times 2 + 176 + 176$ or 8544—considerably less than that required for the 4096 twelve input AND's above.

The only drawback to this scheme is that a signal must now pass through four gates—each with its inherent delay—instead of just one, so selection will be slower but much less expensive of inputs.

We will build our memory as 4096 words of one bit each. Longer words can be obtained by placing more of these memories side by side. The reason we do this is because today we can buy exactly such a memory including the complete address decoding on a single chip. Two years ago it was 2048 bits per chip—two years from now it will probably be 8192.

The circuit at each bit looks like Fig. 4.30. Note that since we have to have AND gates at each bit to enable the writing and the output we can eliminate the 4096 gates at the intersections of the two 64-way circuits.

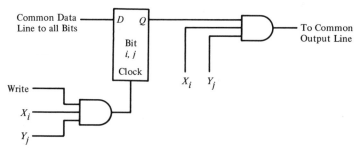

Fig. 4.30 One bit of the 4096 × 1 bit memory.

## DYNAMIC OR REFRESHING RAM'S

Some co-ordinate addressed random access memories (RAM's) are constructed in such a fashion that the information stored in the bits must be "refreshed" periodically. In order to save space on the chip the storage devices are made with only one transistor instead of two as in a flip-flop. These devices will hold information only for a finite time before it "decays" and a ZERO begins to look just like a ONE. When this is done we must stop using the memory every so often and read out each bit stored in it and rewrite them in clean easily distinguishable form. Memories designed this way are said to be "dynamic," and the periodic pauses for refreshment add complications to the computer that uses this type of memory. But the price is low, and so sometimes this is a worthwhile trade-off.

## MOVING MAGNETIC MEMORIES

We have already discussed briefly how a moving magnetic material can be used to store information. In this section, we will examine some of the properties of some of the devices that have been constructed using this principle. The four general classes these fall into are called drums, moving head discs, replaceable surface drums, and magnetic tape.

The first three of these are organized as co-ordinate addressed memories while the last, magnetic tape, may be considered to be a pair of pushdown stacks so arranged that whatever is WITHDRAWN from one is PLACED in the other.

We have lumped them together in a separate section for three reasons. First, they all employ moving magnetic media for the storage of information. Second, they are all much less expensive per bit of storage than other higher speed devices and finally, they are all usually used as secondary or tertiary storage. That is, they are used to hold data and programs that may be required soon by the main computer but are not currently being executed or processed. They form what is often called the "back up storage" of modern systems, as opposed to "main" or "on-line storage."

### Drums

Let there by a cylinder covered with magnetic material that is spinning around its axis. Near the surface of this cylinder (a few thousanths of an inch above it) let there be several read-write heads, each sweeping out a separate "track" around the surface as the drum spins. Suppose now that we have a certain bit pattern of ONE's and ZERO's written on the surface of the drum as a series of magnetized spots. Once on each revolution, this pattern will pass under one of the read write heads. When it is passing under a head, we can sense what has been stored there (read the pattern) or change what is there (write a new pattern). If we try to read the pattern when it is not under the head, we must wait for it to come by. This waiting time is called the "latency" and on the average we will have to wait for one-half of a revolution of the drum to take place before we can read out a pattern (word). This average latency is typically the order of 17 milliseconds.

---

*Question 4.14:* What rpm must the drum be turning for this to be so? What is the time required for one revolution?

---

With present day technology, we can conveniently read or write magnetic "spots" at a rate of about one million a second, so we can have as many as 32,000 "bits" around one track of a drum if we desire.

In a computer using 32-bit words, we can thus store 1024 ($2^{10}$) words per track. A typical drum may have as many as 512 tracks of data on it, giving a total storage capacity of about half a million words ($2^{19}$). Successive bits of a word are stored one after another along a track, and when the "proper" word comes under the read heads, these bits are fed into a shift register one after another until the whole word is assembled and is ready for transfer to the C.P.U. High-order bits of the desired address are used to select which read-write head is connected to the shift register. Figure 4.31 shows three "timing" tracks and one data track on a drum, together with a block diagram of the addressing circuitry that determines when the proper word is under the heads.

The master timing pulse is used to clear the 10-bit counter to all zeros, once a revolution, just so everything stays in sync. Just before each word comes under the heads, there is a pulse (on the word-timing track) which adds one to the contents of the counter. If the comparator decides that the current count is equal to the desired address, the desired word is just about to come up. The o.k. signal from the comparator and a slightly delayed word timing pulse (delayed to allow the comparator time to make its decision) together set the "present" flip-flop through gate 1. When this flip-flop is set to ONE, it allows the bit timing pulses to pass through gate 3 and begin making the shift register shift its contents to the left. The data pulses are thus taken by the shift register and stored.

The next word timing pulse signals the end of this word and, via gate 2, generates a "word complete signal" for the CPU; it also resets the "present" flip-flop, thus inhibiting any more changes in the shift register which now contains the complete desired word. Its contents can now be read out by the CPU at its leisure.

Writing takes place in a similar way, except that the left end of the shift register (which has been filled by the CPU) is connected to the write amplifier of the appropriate track, and successive shifts bring new bits into the left end to be written down.

As described here, this drum will take 32 $\mu$sec to read out a word. For some systems this is much too slow. One solution is to break a word of 32 bits up into 8 bit bytes and store each byte in parallel on 8 separate tracks. It then requires only four bit times or 4 $\mu$sec to recover a word once it comes up.

---

*Question 4.15:* How would you reorganize Fig. 4.31 to accomplish this? How many "groups" of 8 tracks would there be and how many words per track?

---

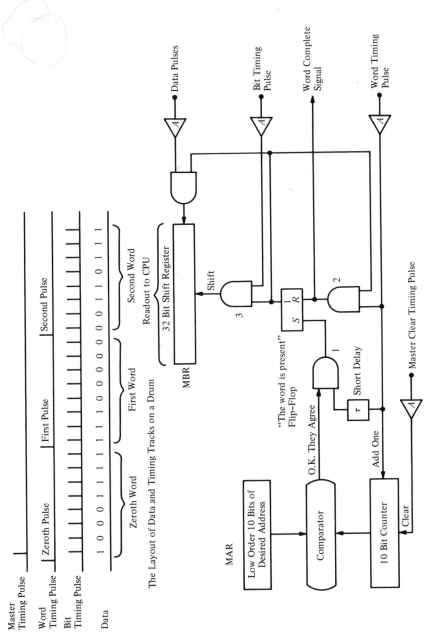

Fig. 4.31 The layout of data and some of the controls for a drum.

*Moving Head Disks*

Read-write heads are expensive and so are the amplifiers which are connected to them. One possible way of cutting down the cost of moving magnetic media memories is to use one set of heads to read-write from several sets of tracks. This is accomplished by physically moving the heads from one set of tracks on the magnetic surface to another. This type of storage is usually arranged to record information on the face of flat discs and hence is called "disc-storage." The movement involved is usually radial, that is toward or away from the spindle which rotates the discs. Often both top and bottom of a disc are used and several discs may be stacked up, about half an inch apart, on one spindle. Eight discs then provide 16 surfaces for recording. Each surface has its own set of heads. The radial motion may be of the order of 2 to 4 in. and with powerful positioning mechanisms, any position can be reached from any other in about 70 milliseconds. To read out a word, we must first position the heads, then select which head group is desired, and finally wait until the appropriate sector of the disc passes under the heads. Combining the times required to accomplish all these operations we find that about 90 milliseconds are needed to get to a given word.

In common with drums, once a given word has been found, the next word on the same track is available almost immediately and the one after that shortly thereafter. Thus, although it takes 90 msec to find and read (or write) one word, it takes only about 10 more msec to read (or write) the next 999. This has lead programmers to do "block" transfers to and from disc and drum. Blocks may be of any convenient size, but often run around 1000 words in length. We will see some of the consequences of this phenomenon in the section on paging.

Some disc units have replaceable discs so that information can be stored on a "disc pack" and removed and another disc pack with different data can be inserted in the drive mechanism in its place.

*Replaceable Surface Drums*

The actual magnetic surface of a drum is usually plated on and is quite thin. Several manufacturers have put this magnetic material on flexible plastic cards that can be removed from the drum. The trick is to have several hundred of these magnetically coated plastic cards in a bin. By means of some clever mechanical gadgetry, the desired card can be selected from the bin and blown down a chute where it is then wrapped around the rapidly spinning drum, ready to read from or write on. Selecting, blowing, and wrapping a card take between a quarter and a half of a second— quite slow by computer speeds—but in that time period you can bring into operating position a whole drum full of information.

Wrapping, unwrapping, blowing, and plucking a card all tend to cause wear and tear, and the cards must be thin and light and flexible to begin with. Reliability is thus a real problem with most of these units, but their low cost per bit stored makes them very attractive from an economic point of view. They are available from several places under names like RACE, CRAM, and DATACELL.

### Magnetic Tape

Almost everyone has seen a home tape recorder. A long, thin, narrow plastic ribbon coated on one side with iron oxide is pulled past a read-write head and information can be recorded or played back at will. The large, bulky tape drives connected to most computers are identical in practice, but built to more exacting standards. After all, one bit dropped out of a half hour symphony causes a single small "pop," but a bit dropped from a 2400-ft reel of data may turn the whole thing into useless trash.

Current technology permits us to record up to 1600-bits-per-in. along the tape and to run the tape past the heads at speeds up to 100-in.-per-sec or better. Looking across the tape we find either 7 or 9 tracks (new models have 9) which are used to store one byte (6 or 8 bits) of information and a parity bit.

---

*Question 4.16:* How many characters can I read off a magnetic tape in one sec?

*Question 4.17:* If a tape is 2400-ft long and is full of data, how far apart in time are the two ends of the tape?

---

Information is usually written on magnetic tape in blocks. Between blocks there are short (three-quarters in.) lengths of blank tape called inter-record gaps. These gaps are long enough so that once the end of a block has been detected, the tape drive can bring the tape to a halt before running out of the gap into the next block of information. When the next read command is given, the tape starts and gets up to speed before the beginning of the next block reaches the heads.

If information can be organized into more or less independent chunks that do not require much cross-referencing, then tape is a satisfactory and inexpensive means of storage. One reads a block, processes it, outputs the results, and then reads the next block. When however one needs to skip back and forth from one block to another, the linear nature of a magnetic tape and the time required to pass over presently irrelevant blocks of information make it an inefficient medium. In these cases, discs and drums come into their own and are used by all who can afford them.

## A CCD MEMORY

One of the obvious uses for charge coupled devices is to replace discs and drums. The appeal here is increased speed, reduced cost, and improved reliability. It has always been the goal of electronic engineers to eliminate all moving parts of any mechanism. Part of this is simple prejudice, but part of it has to do with friction and wear. Mechanical devices have historically been the least reliable parts of a computing system; so when charge coupled devices and magnetic bubbles came along with favorable cost performance ratios, they were eagerly explored. Building a one-for-one replacement for a drum using magnetic bubbles offers few challenges except for the speed of transfer that can be obtained. Using CCD's on the other hand is somewhat more interesting because of the limitation imposed by the "ghosting" phenomenon. After a couple of hundred transfers a logical ONE and its following "ghost" begin to be hard to tell apart. The question is: can we design a CCD shift register that holds, say, 4096 bits but requires only 128 shifts from end to end? The answer, surprisingly enough, is yes. Such a device might be called a "two-dimensional" shift register. (See Fig. 4.32.)

Bits are shifted into the top row and simultaneously out of the bottom row until the top is full and the bottom empty. Then all rows shift downward one, emptying the top row and refilling the bottom row. Each row holds 64 bits, and there are 64 rows. Consider the $N$th bit of a block of 64. It shifts in $N$ positions along the top row. Then downward 64 positions

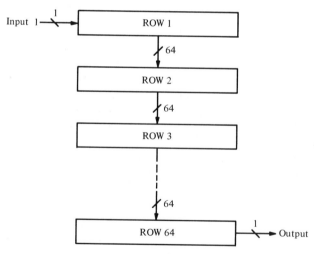

Fig. 4.32 A two-dimensional shift register for a CCD memory.

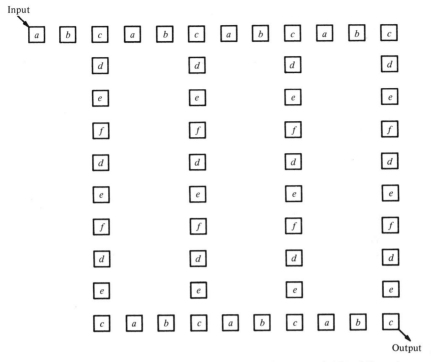

Fig. 4.33 The layout of pads for a three-phase two-dimensional CCD shift register.

and finally 64 − $N$ positions along the bottom row for a total of $(N) + (64) + (64 − N) = 128$ shifts.

The two-dimensional shift is accomplished as shown in Figs. 4.33 and 4.34. All pads with a given letter are connected together. Figure 4.33 shows a 4 × 4 two-dimensional shift register, and Fig. 4.34 shows the pattern of excitation of the six groups of pads. On the intermediate rows charge clouds are being held (or not held for ZERO's) under the $F$ group pads. Four cycles of $CA$, $A$, $AB$, $B$, $BC$, $C$ excitation occur, shifting information on the top and bottom row from one $C$ pad to its rightward $C$ pad neighbor on each cycle. Meanwhile $F$ has been high to hold information in the intermediate rows. Now we leave $A$ and $B$ at zero and perform one cycle of $CDF$, $D$ alone, $DE$, $E$ alone, $CEF$, and finally $CF$. Now we go back and have four more cycles of $CA$, $A$, etc., with $F$ held high. Information coming out of the output terminal can be amplified, squared up, and fed back into the input terminal to make this a circular buffer of 16 positions. Shifting rates of several tens of megahertz have been achieved in the lab. Fabrica-

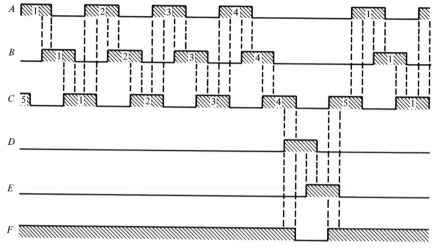

Fig. 4.34 The timing of the pulses on the pads of Fig. 4.33.

tion is simple and inexpensive, so very good cost performance ratios appear to be possible.

## REFERENCES

1. Fuller, R. H.  "Content Addressable Memory Systems," Report No. 63–25, Los Angeles, Calif., Dept. of Eng., U. of Calif. (June 1963).
2. Foster, C. C. "Determination of Priority in Associative Memories," *IEEE Trans. on Comp.* **C-17,** 8, 788–789 (Aug. 1968).
3. Rosin, R.  "An Organization of an Associative Cryogenic Computer," *Proc. AFIPS 1962 Spring Joint Comput. Conf.*, 203–212.
4. Seeber, R. R., and Lindquist, A. B.  "Associative Memory with Ordered Retrieval." *IBM Journal* 126–136 (Jan. 1962).
5. Knuth, D. C.  *The Art of Computer Programming*, Vol. 1, Reading, Mass., Addison-Wesley, 1968.
6. Newell, A., Tonge, F. M., Feigenbaum, E. A., Green, B. F., and Mealy, G. H. *Information Processing Language—V Manual*, 2nd Ed., Englewood Cliffs, N.J., Prentice-Hall, 1964.

# 5 | AN ELEMENTARY MACHINE

*"When you wish to produce a result by means of an instrument, do not allow yourself to complicate it."*

Leonardo da Vinci

In this chapter we are going to describe a very simple computer, one that might sell for about $1,000 or so. Eight years ago I estimated the cost of this machine at $10,000. Today if one were going to produce enough units to warrant the high initial cost of large-scale integration (LSI) one might easily produce a machine on three or four chips for about $100. We will describe first how this machine appears to a programmer, and then we will examine each of its parts and see how they are made. Readers who are familiar with the basic aspects of machine design will probably wish to skip over most of the details. Readers new to the subject are urged to study this chapter most carefully, as it will be the only place a complete design is presented.

## A PROGRAMMER'S DESCRIPTION

BLUE* is a binary, two's complement, stored program, fixed-word length, parallel, digital automatic computer. It has 4096 words of 1 μsec co-ordinate addressed core storage of 16 bits per word. When used to store data, these words are treated as 15-bit integers plus sign. When used to store instructions, they are treated as a four-bit op-code followed by a 12 bit address. (See Fig. 5.1.) There is a 16 bit accumulator, a 16 bit instruction register, and a 12 bit program counter, all of whose contents are displayed on the console by small lights that are ON for a ONE

*That's the color of the cabinet. I've grown weary of acronyms.

121

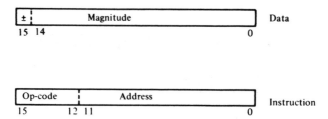

Fig. 5.1 Data and instruction formats.

and OFF for a ZERO. Also on the console, there is a 16-bit switch register that the operator may set, a START, a STOP, a LOAD PC, an EXAMINE, a DEPOSIT key, and a MASTER CLEAR button. The START and STOP buttons have their obvious significance. The LOAD PC button causes low-order 12 bits of the switch register to be copied into the program counter. When the EXAMINE switch is activated, the contents of the cell pointed at by the program counter are loaded into the instruction register for examination. The DEPOSIT switch causes the 16-bit number set into the switch register to be stored in the location pointed at

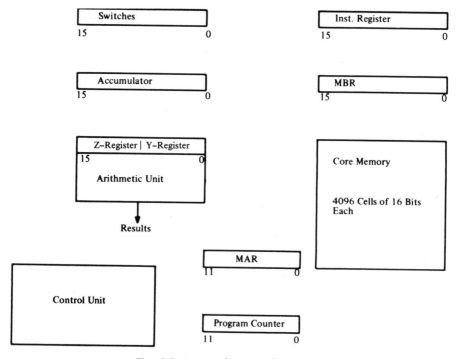

Fig. 5.2 A general picture of BLUE.

by the program counter. Both the EXAMINE and DEPOSIT switches cause the program counter to be incremented by ONE on completion of their cycle. The MASTER CLEAR button issues a signal that puts the entire machine and all its peripheral devices in a standard state ready to begin work. In addition to the three registers displayed on the console, there are a 12-bit Memory Address Register, a 16-bit Memory Buffer Register, and 16-bit $Y$ and $Z$ registers that are not accessible to the programmer.

The 4 bits of the op-code field provide 16 different instructions that may be programmed. We present them in order, giving first their octal equivalent, then a 3-letter mnemonic, and finally a brief description of their effects. Figure 5.2 shows the general layout of the machine.

## THE INSTRUCTION SET

The 16 instructions available in BLUE are presented below. In general, the assignment of the octal codes that represent the instruction were selected at random. The two exceptions to this statement are the HLT and the NOP instructions that were, respectively, assigned to the patterns: 0000 (00 octal) and 1111 (17 octal). This was done so that any attempt to execute a word containing all zeros would halt the machine. Thus, a random jump into an area that had been cleared to zero could be detected at once. Similarly, attempting to execute a data word of all ones (a common condition for flag words) would, if not stop, at least do no harm. The list of instructions follows:

| | | |
|---|---|---|
| 00-HLT | $XXXX$ | This instruction causes the computer to halt. Depressing the START button on the console will cause the computer to start going again, beginning with the instruction following the HLT. The address field ($XXXX$) is ignored. |
| 01-ADD | $XXXX$ | The contents of location $XXXX$ are added to the contents of the accumulator and the sum is put into the accumulator. If the resulting sum is greater than $2^{15} -1$ or less than $-2^{15}$, the machine stops. The contents of $XXXX$ are not changed. |
| 02-XOR | $XXXX$ | The bit by bit exclusive OR of the contents of location $XXXX$ with the contents of the accumulator replace the old |

|  |  |  |
|---|---|---|
| | | contents of the accumulator. The contents of *XXXX* are not changed. |
| 03-AND | *XXXX* | The contents of location *XXXX* are ANDed bit by bit with the contents of the accumulator and the result is put into the accumulator. The contents of *XXXX* are not changed. |
| 04-IOR | *XXXX* | The contents of location *XXXX* are ORed bit by bit with the contents of the accumulator and the result is put into the accumulator. The contents of *XXXX* are not changed. |
| 05-NOT | *XXXX* | Each bit of the contents of the accumulator is replaced by its logical complement. The address field (*XXXX*) is ignored. |
| 06-LDA | *XXXX* | The contents of location *XXXX* are copied into the accumulator. The old contents of the accumulator are lost. The contents of *XXXX* are not changed. |
| 07-STA | *XXXX* | The contents of the accumulator are copied into location *XXXX*. The old contents of *XXXX* are lost. The contents of the accumulator are not changed. |
| 10-SRJ | *XXXX* | The contents of the program counter (the present instruction location plus one) are copied into the low order 12 bits of the accumulator. The 4 high-order bits of the accumulator are cleared to ZERO. Then the number *XXXX* is copied into the program counter so that the next instruction will be taken from location *XXXX*. This instruction is used to jump to a subroutine. |
| 11-JMA | *XXXX* | If the sign bit of the accumulator is one (minus accumulator), the number *XXXX* is placed in the program counter and the next instruction is taken from location *XXXX*. If the |

sign bit of the accumulator is zero (positive or zero accumulator), this instruction does nothing and the next instruction is taken from the location of the present instruction plus one.

| | | |
|---|---|---|
| 12-JMP | $XXXX$ | The number $XXXX$ is copied into the program counter. The next instruction is, therefore, always taken from location $XXXX$. |
| 13-INP | $XXYY$ | The upper 8 bits of the accumulator are cleared to zero and the next 8-bit character from input device $YY$ is entered into the low order end of the accumulator. The $XX$ part of the address field is ignored. The next instruction is not executed until the data transfer is complete. |
| 14-OUT | $XXYY$ | The most significant 8 bits of the accumulator are sent to output device $YY$. The $XX$ part of the address field are ignored. If the output device cannot accept the data at this time the machine waits until the data is accepted before beginning execution of the next instruction. |
| 15-RAL | $XXXX$ | The contents of the accumulator are rotated left one place. The bit shifted out of $AC_{15}$ is entered into $AC_0$ so the shift is cyclic. The address field is ignored. |
| 16-CSA | $XXXX$ | The number set into the console switch register replaces the contents of the accumulator. The address field $XXXX$ is ignored. |
| 17-NOP | $XXXX$ | This instruction does nothing. The address field $XXXX$ is ignored. |

As the reader can easily see, the set of instructions available on this machine is limited, but complete. Up to 64 input and output devices may be connected, each capable of handling 8-bit characters. No index registers, no indirect addressing, and no interrupt facilities are provided. The resulting machine will be, however, quite complicated enough to analyze.

## THE BASIC MACHINE CYCLE

The BLUE computer, like most other machines of today, has a two part basic cycle. These are called the FETCH and the EXECUTE cycles. During the FETCH cycle, the instruction pointed at by the program counter is fetched from memory and placed in the Instruction Register (IR). Then the number stored in the Program Counter is increased by one so that it points at the "next" memory cell following the one containing the present instruction.

At the completion of the FETCH cycle, the instruction in the IR is analyzed, decoded, and executed. Quite often this task can be accomplished during the time in which the contents of the fetched location are being re-written. This is called "shadow time." An instruction which references memory (ADD, AND, LDA, etc.) must wait to begin its execution until the instruction itself has been rewritten and the memory is available.

## INFORMATION FLOW IN BLUE

Without analyzing the instructions in detail at this time, we can still get a picture of what information must be transferred from where to where within the machine. Considering first the transfer of addresses, we have the paths indicated in Fig. 5.3. Figure 5.4 shows the flow of operands and instructions, including those generated by the operation of the console controls. We note that the arithmetic unit has two inputs, the $Y$ and the $Z$ registers. Figure 5.5 shows the input and output data and device number transfers.

Counting up the paths shown in Figs. 5.3, 5.4, and 5.5, we find 5 possible address transfer paths, 8 paths for operands or instructions, and 3 paths

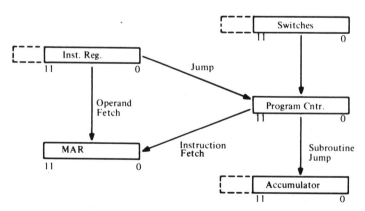

Fig. 5.3 The transmission of addresses in BLUE.

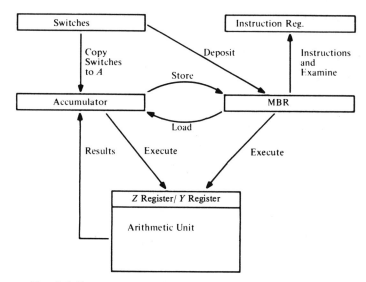

Fig. 5.4 The transmission of instructions and operands in BLUE.

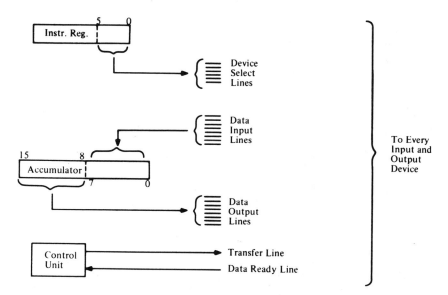

Fig. 5.5 The data input and output lines and the selection and control lines of BLUE.

(not counting control lines) for I/O operations, or a total of 16 distinct paths.

There are at least three different schemes that might be used to effect these transfers. They may be called: "the common bus," "the multiple bus," and "the point to point." This last method we have already described when discussing the control circuits for the preserve and restore operations on the pushdown stack.

The common bus scheme is illustrated in Fig. 5.6. There is one common highway. Any register can put its own information onto the highway and any register can copy off the highway. When many transfers must be accomplished, it is easy to see that the number of gates required by the common bus scheme will be much less than would be required for the point to point method.

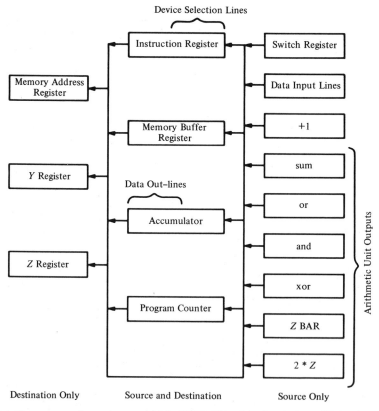

**Fig. 5.6 The common bus scheme used in BLUE. Note that the device selection lines from the instruction register and the data output lines from the accumulator are always energized. The six outputs of the arithmetic unit are shown separately.**

*Question 5.1:* Assume that a machine has *N* registers, each of which might be a source or a destination for an information transfer. What is the maximum number of gates that would be required to implement all possible transfers in a point to point scheme?—in common bus scheme?

The path from the instruction register to the device selection lines is external to the bus structure so that the bus may be used for data transmission while a device is being selected.

### Implementation of a Common Bus Scheme

In a common bus scheme, we have one "highway" or set of wires that connects all the registers together. One may, for example, connect the accumulator to the Memory Buffer Register. At another time, one might connect the Memory Buffer Register to the instruction register. But one can not make both connections at the same time, as there is only the one pathway for the flow of information.

In Fig. 5.7 we show three 2-bit registers and a common bus connecting them to each other. This bus is designed using *D*-type/leading edge triggered flip-flops. Whatever appears on the bus, we can obtain a copy of it in register *A* by briefly energizing the *load A* line which is connected to the clock input of all the flip-flops of the *A* register. To put something on the bus we energize one or another of the "send" lines.

*Question 5.2:* What happens if we energize two send lines at the same time?

Thus to copy information from register *C* to register *B* we raise the send-*B* line and while it is up raise the load-*B* line. Figure 5.8 shows the timing.

*Question 5.3:* Does it matter in which order they go down?

*Question 5.4:* What goes into *B* if we pulse *load B* when none of the send lines are energized?

*Question 5.5:* Design a circuit equivalent to Fig. 5.7 using *J-K* flip-flops instead of *D*-type.

### Circuit Elements for BLUE

BLUE will be constructed of conventional integrated circuits with one minor exception. The registers will be made of *D*-type flip-flops with each

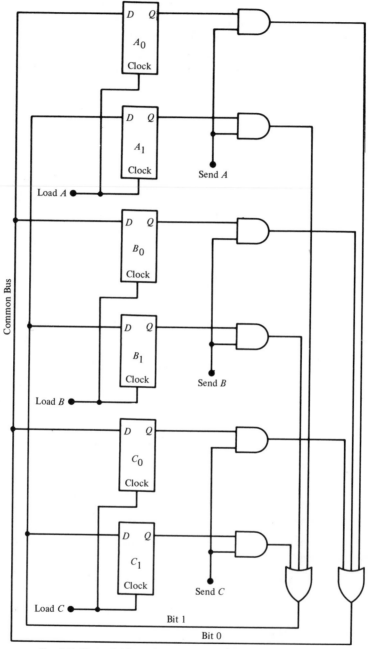

Fig. 5.7 Three 2-bit registers connected by a common bus.

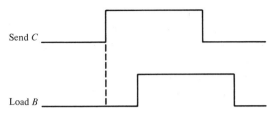

Fig. 5.8 The timing of the pulses required to copy information from register C to register B.

register having a common clock line (or "load register" line) which has a small (10–15 nanosec) delay built into it. The purpose of this delay is to allow us to present a signal to the inputs of the register and at the same time command a load of the register. The delay will give the input circuits time to stabilize and ensure accurate copying of the information.

When the program counter (PC) is transferred to the $A$ register, since the upper 4 bits of the PC ($PC_{15-12}$) don't exist, ZERO's will be loaded into $A_{15-12}$ because no signal is put on bus lines $B_{15}$ through $B_{12}$.

## CONTROL UNIT

Now we must consider how the various sequences of pulses and signals that we require are to be generated. This is the task of the control unit whose job it is to co-ordinate the actions of the machine.

Computers are categorized as being Synchronous or Asynchronous, depending upon how these sequences of pulses are generated. In an Asynchronous design, which we will not study here, each unit is charged with signaling its successor when it is safe for the successor to begin activity. This has the advantage that only as much time need be alloted to a task as is required to complete it. It has the disadvantage that each unit must have enough intelligence to know when it is through with its task. A "clocked" or synchronous design, on the other hand, breaks up time into discrete fixed periods, sometimes called "minor cycles." Events occur only when the clock emits a pulse. This has the advantage of keeping many diverse units in step with each other when that is required and has the further advantage that less logic is required of the individual devices. Of course, the obvious disadvantage to this approach is that nothing can take place in less than one complete minor cycle.

We have chosen to make BLUE a synchronous machine because it is easier to understand what is going on that way. Let us now begin to design the control unit of BLUE. First of all we will have three control unit flip-flops called the "RUN flip-flop" the "STATE flip-flop," and the "TRA" or transfer in progress flip-flop. The RUN flip-flop is turned ON by the START button. It is turned OFF by the STOP button, by the HLT command, and by the detection of an arithmetic overflow. The STATE flip-flop has two conditions to correspond to the "instruction fetch" and "execute" phases of carrying out an instruction. It is set to $F$ (*FETCH*) by the START button or at the conclusion of an execute cycle. Depending on what instruction is in the instruction register, it may or may not be set to $E$ (*EXECUTE*) at the conclusion of a fetch cycle.

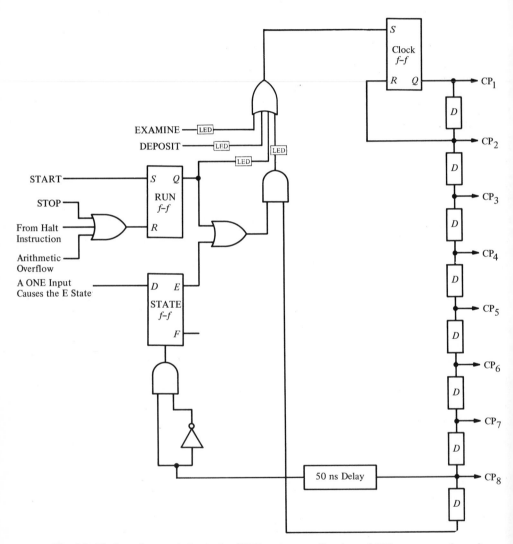

Fig. 5.9 Clock and control circuits for BLUE; generates 8 pulses of 125 nanoseconds each and repeats. $D$ represents a delay of 125 nanoseconds.

Each memory cycle of the machine will be divided into 8 equal 125 nsec time intervals (or minor cycles) by a master clock. The clock has 8 output lines, each of which will carry one pulse per memory cycle. Figure 5.9 shows one of the many ways of designing such a clock, and Fig. 5.10 shows the time relationship of the pulses on the CP lines as the 125 nsec pulse passes down the chain of delays. When the RUN flip-flop goes to ONE, a leading edge detector circuit generates a single positive pulse that turns on the flip-flop of Fig. 5.9. If the RUN flip-flop was ON, pressing START has no effect. This energizes the ONE output of the flip-flop, and this change in state propagates down the delay element $D$. 125 nsec later, the ONE state emerges from the output of the first delay element and is brought back around to turn off the flip-flop. The leading edge of this 125-nsec-wide pulse propagates down the chain of delay elements, followed in lock step by the trailing edge 125 nsec later. This generates uniform width pulses at the output points, $CP_1$ through $CP_8$, each one being delayed 125 nsec after the preceding one. Finally, the pulse comes out at the end of the chain and turns on the flip-flop again (provided the RUN signal is on or the state is Execute).

*Question 5.6:* There are several other ways in which we could have generated these clock pulses. How many can you think of?

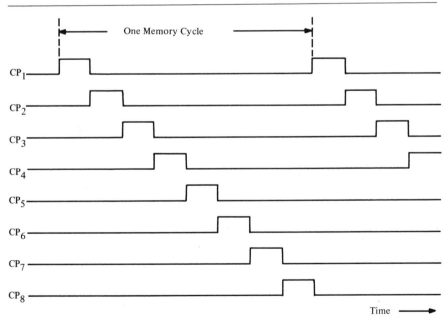

Fig. 5.10 The signals on the CP lines as a function of time.

## THE FETCH CYCLE

If the RUN flip-flop is set ON, it enables the clock (and starts it), and if the STATE flip-flop is set to FETCH, the action that the machine will carry out is to load the instruction register (IR) from the cell pointed at by the program counter (PC) and then add one to the contents of the program counter.

Figure 5.11 shows the sequence of events. With the onset of clock pulse 1 we copy the contents of the program counter to the memory address register and the $Z$ register, and we initiate the read cycle of the memory. At $CP_2$ put +1 in $Y$. During $CP_3$ we allow time for the sum to develop, and

| Clock Pulse | Action | Comment |
|---|---|---|
| 1. | Send PC, load MAR, load $Z$<br>Initiate read cycle | —copy (PC to MAR and to $Z$) and begin to read up the next instruction |
| 2. | Send 1, load $Y$ | —set $Y$ equal to plus 1 |
| 3. | — | |
| 4. | Send SUM, load PC | —add old (PC) plus 1 and replace in the PC. This increments the PC<br>—at the end of this cycle the new instruction will be ready to load into the MBR |
| 5. | Strobe data from memory to MBR<br>Initiate rewrite cycle | —load MBR from memory |
| 6. | Send MBR, load IR | —copy the new instruction into the instruction register and begin to decode it |
| 7.<br>8. | | —available for decoding and perhaps execution |

Fig. 5.11 The FETCH cycle.

in $CP_4$ we transfer the sum back to the program counter, thus using the otherwise idle arithmetic unit. By the end of $CP_4$, the next instruction will be ready to load into the MBR. This we do in $CP_5$. In $CP_6$ we copy it to the instruction register and begin to decode it. By the beginning of $CP_7$ then, we are ready to begin carrying out the new instruction. Since the storage device will not be finished restoring the cell it just read until the end of $CP_8$, we have $CP_7$ and $CP_8$ in which to do some execution. For some of the instructions of BLUE, this is enough time to complete all the necessary actions. These are shown in Fig. 5.12 with a breakdown of what actions they produce.

| Clock Period | HALT | NOP | JMP | JMA | SRJ | CSA | NOT | RAL |
|---|---|---|---|---|---|---|---|---|
| 7. | — | — | — | — | Send PC, load $A$ | — | Send $A$, load $Z$ | Send $A$, load $Z$ |
| 8. | Off→Run | — | Send IR, load PC | If $A_{15} = 1$, send IR, load PC | Send IR, load PC | Send SR, load $A$ | Send $Z$ bar, load $A$ | Send $2*Z$, load $A$ |

Fig. 5.12 The end of the FETCH cycle for the eight one-cycle instructions.

Since none of these instructions require an execute cycle, they do not change the STATE flip-flop, leaving it at FETCH. Thus the next cycle will be another fetch getting up a new instruction.

## INPUT/OUTPUT INSTRUCTIONS

There are two instructions which do not require memory references, but which do take more than one cycle. They are displayed in Fig. 5.13. To understand how the input and output instructions work, we must look at the peripheral devices that are to be connected to the computer. As typical examples, let us assume that device number 1 is a paper tape reader and device number 2 is a paper tape punch. The tape reader will be in the READY condition if and only if it is loaded with tape and a character (transverse row of punches) is sitting under the read head. This condition can be recognized by a photocell that "looks for" a sprocket hole on the tape. The tape reader will be NOT READY under all other conditions. When NOT READY, the clutch will engage to move the tape on to read the next character. When the next character comes under the head, the leading edge of the sprocket hole associated with that character will generate a pulse that will stop the tape and put the reader in a READY condition. (See Fig. 5.14.) From the computer to each I/O device, there are six lines called the Device Selection Lines. These lines are connected to the low order 6 bits of the instruction register and continuously "broadcast" the state of these bits to all I/O devices. In minor cycle 7 of the FETCH cycle of an input instruction, we turn on the transfer flip-flop (TRA). In the ON condition, this flip-flop indicates that an AND gate $A$ at each device will examine these lines to see if this device is the one being talked to. A device can only be "selected" during an input or an output command because only then will TRA be ONE. If the READY flip-flop is set to READY, gate $B$ will be activated and the 8 code-hole photo cells will be put onto the Data Input Lines at the same time as the $R$ line is driven to ONE. If the READY flip-flop was NOT set, nothing happens until a sprocket hole is detected. With the flip-flop reset to the NOT READY condition, the clutch will be energized, thus trying to make the tape advance to the next character. Meanwhile, back in minor cycle 8 of the FETCH cycle, the STATE flip-flop was set to execute. In minor cycle 7 of the execute phase of the input instruction, we sample the $R$ line. If it is ZERO, the computer waits one major cycle and tries again. When the I/O device is finally READY, the $R$ line becomes ONE and, in minor cycle 7 the Data Input Lines are gated into the low-order 8 bits of the accumulator. We have now "captured" the character and are ready: (1) to advance the reader (so it gets the

| | INP | OUT | Comment |
|---|---|---|---|
| 7. | $1 \rightarrow$ TRA | $1 \rightarrow$ TRA | —this causes $IR_{5-0}$ to be broadcast on the device selection lines (DSL) |
| 8. | $E \rightarrow$ STATE | $E \rightarrow$ STATE | —at end of period set state to EXECUTE |

Fetch cycle

Execute cycle

| | INP | OUT | |
|---|---|---|---|
| 1. | — | | |
| 2. | — | | |
| 3. | — | — | |
| 4. | — | — | |
| 5. | — | — | |
| 6. | — | — | |
| 7. | if R = 1, send data input lines, load $A$, $0 \rightarrow$ TRA | if R = 1, $0 \rightarrow$ TRA | —if response flag $R = 1$ then copy in data and clear TRA |
| 8. | if TRA = 0, $F \rightarrow$ STATE | if TRA = 0, $F \rightarrow$ STATE | —if I/O is complete fetch a new instruction. Else repeat the execute cycle |

Fig. 5.13 The input and the output instructions.

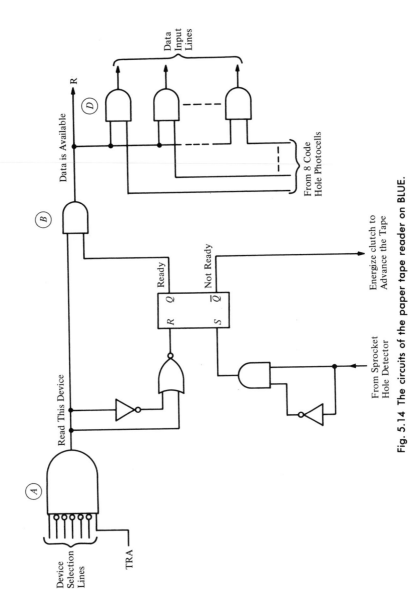

**Fig. 5.14 The circuits of the paper tape reader on BLUE.**

next character ready for the next input instruction, whenever that may come) and (2) to terminate this instruction.

So in minor cycle 7, if $R = 1$, we reset the TRA flip-flop to ZERO. This removes the device number from the device selection lines, causing the "read this device" line at the tape reader to go to ZERO. The trailing edge detector labeled $C$ in Fig. 5.14 generates a positive pulse when this happens, thus resetting the READY (flip-flop) to NOT READY. This in turn energizes the clutch and advances the tape.

Finally, in minor cycle 8 of the execution phase of the input instruction, if the TRA flip-flop is ZERO, we set the state to FETCH. The operation of the OUT instruction is very similar. The circuits associated with a paper tape punch are shown in Fig. 5.15. The reader is urged to follow the action as described in Figs. 5.13 and 5.15. Note that since the computer issues the OUT command (and terminates it) as soon as the punch goes IDLE, the punch itself must provide a storage buffer to hold the information that drives the punch magnets. This is done here by providing 8 flip-flops whose input is gated in from the data output lines.

---

*Question 5.7:* We could have eliminated the punch buffer by making the machine "hang" in the OUT instruction until the punch cycle was complete. Show the circuits and details of the instruction that would be required in this case. Can the punch be "busy" when an OUT instruction begins?

---

## TWO CYCLE INSTRUCTIONS

The next two instructions to be looked at will be LDA and STA, both non-arithmetic memory referencing instructions. Consider first the load $A$ instruction (see Fig. 5.16). In minor cycle 8 of the FETCH phase, we set the STATE flip-flop to execute. In minor cycle 1 of the execute phase we load the MAR from the IR and we initiate the read restore memory cycle. By the beginning of minor cycle 5, the read part of the memory cycle is complete and the data is strobed into the MBR. Then in minor cycle 6 the contents of the MBR are copied into the accumulator. While the shadow time of the restore half of the memory cycle is going on, we idle until minor cycle 8, when we set the STATE flip-flop to FETCH.

The store accumulator instruction is about the same except that we do *not* strobe the contents of the memory cell into the MBR but instead load the MBR from the accumulator in minor cycle 5.

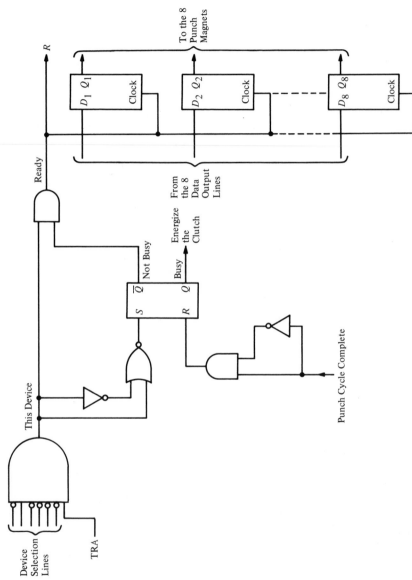

Fig. 5.15 Punch circuits for BLUE.

|  | LDA | STA |
|---|---|---|
| 6. | | |
| 7. | | |
| 8. | $E \rightarrow$ STATE | $E \rightarrow$ STATE |
| 1. | send IR, load MAR, initiate Read cycle | send IR, load MAR, initiate Read cycle |
| 2. | — | — |
| 3. | — | — |
| 4. | — | — |
| 5. | initiate Restore cycle, strobe data from memory to MBR | send $A$, load MBR, initiate Restore cycle |
| 6. | send MBR, load $A$ | — |
| 7. | — | — |
| 8. | $F \rightarrow$ STATE | $F \rightarrow$ STATE |

Fig. 5.16 The load and store accumulator instructions.

## THE ARITHMETIC UNIT

In order to describe the remaining four instructions, we must first describe the arithmetic unit of BLUE and how it works. Let us look first at the process of addition of two binary numbers. Consider one bit position within the word. There are the two inputs ($a$ and $b$) and possibly a "carry" from the next less significant place in the word (immediately to the right). At this position, we must generate a SUM bit and perhaps a CARRY bit which will go to the position on our left. Figure 5.17 shows such an ADDER in symbolic form. Note that there are three types of boxes shown here, $\alpha$, $\beta$, and $\gamma$. $\alpha$ is the circuit required in the sign position and must generate the resultant sign of the sum and an overflow signal if two positive signals give a negative result, or vice versa. Figure 5.18 shows the truth tables of $\alpha$, $\beta$, and $\gamma$, respectively.

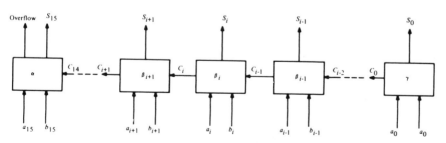

Fig. 5.17 A schematic of a parallel by bit adder.  $A + B$    $S$.

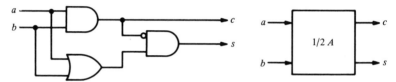

| $\alpha$ | | | | | $\beta$ | | | | | $\gamma$ | | | |
|---|---|---|---|---|---|---|---|---|---|---|---|---|---|
| | | | | Over- | | | | | | | | | |
| $a_{15}$ | $b_{15}$ | $c_{14}$ | $S_{15}$ | flow | $a_i$ | $b_i$ | $c_{i-1}$ | $s_i$ | $c_i$ | $a_0$ | $b_0$ | $s_0$ | $c_0$ |
| 0 | 0 | 0 | 0 | 0 | 0 | 0 | 0 | 0 | 0 | 0 | 0 | 0 | 0 |
| 0 | 0 | 1 | 1 | 1 | 0 | 0 | 1 | 1 | 0 | 0 | 1 | 1 | 0 |
| 0 | 1 | 0 | 1 | 0 | 0 | 1 | 0 | 1 | 0 | 1 | 0 | 1 | 0 |
| 0 | 1 | 1 | 0 | 0 | 0 | 1 | 1 | 0 | 1 | 1 | 1 | 0 | 1 |
| 1 | 0 | 0 | 1 | 0 | 1 | 0 | 0 | 1 | 0 | | | | |
| 1 | 0 | 1 | 0 | 0 | 1 | 0 | 1 | 0 | 1 | | | | |
| 1 | 1 | 0 | 0 | 1 | 1 | 1 | 0 | 0 | 1 | | | | |
| 1 | 1 | 1 | 1 | 0 | 1 | 1 | 1 | 1 | 1 | | | | |

Fig. 5.18 The truth tables of $\alpha$, $\beta$, and $\gamma$.

$\gamma$ is usually called a "half adder," for reasons we will see below, and can be constructed as shown in Fig. 5.19. Note that the $s$ output is the "exclusive OR" of the two inputs $a$ and $b$. We will utilize this fact later.

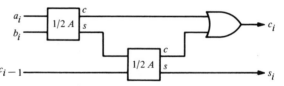

Fig. 5.19 A half adder and its symbolic representation.

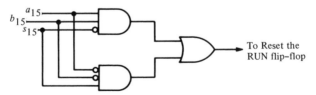

Fig. 5.20 A full adder constructed from two half adders.

A little careful thought will show that one can realize the truth table for $\beta$ by combining two half adders and an OR element as shown in Fig. 5.20. The circuit to generate $S_{15}$ for $X$ can be exactly the same as the full adder without the OR to generate the carry signal. To generate the overflow signal, we may use the circuit shown in Fig. 5.21.

Fig. 5.21 A circuit to generate an OVERFLOW signal.

*Question 5.8:* Making $\alpha$ as suggested above requires a total of 9 gates. Can you do it with less?

We are now ready to examine a typical bit of the arithmetic unit, remembering that the adders of the zeroth and fifteenth bits vary from the rest. The circuit is shown in Fig. 5.22. The $Y$ register and the $Z$ register together form the inputs to the arithmetic unit. They can be loaded from the bus. The left shifted ($2*Z$) contents of $Z$ and the complement of the contents of $Z$, can be gated onto the bus. In addition, the sum of ($Y$) and ($Z$) as well as the inclusive and exclusive or of their contents and the logical and of $Y$ and $Z$ can be put on the bus. Note in particular that the exclusive or function comes "for free." The *sum* output of the first half adder is generating this automatically, so all that is required is a gate onto the bus. This "for free"

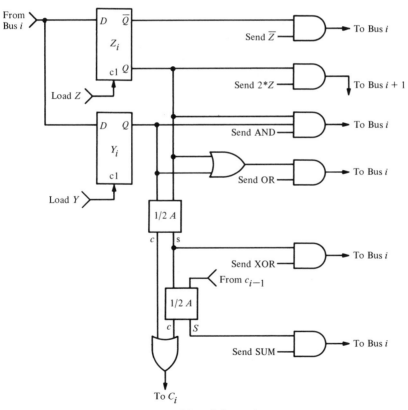

Fig. 5.22 A typical bit of the arithmetic unit.

| | ADD | XOR | AND | IOR |
|---|---|---|---|---|
| 6. | — | — | — | — |
| 7. | — | — | — | — |
| 8. | $E\rightarrow$STATE | $E\rightarrow$STATE | $E\rightarrow$STATE | $E\rightarrow$STATE |
| 1. | send IR, load MAR, initiate read cycle | send IR, load MAR, initiate read cycle | send IR, load MAR, initiate read cycle | send IR, load MAR, initiate read cycle |
| 2. | send A, load Z | send A, load Z | send A, load Z | send A, load Z |
| 3. | — | — | — | — |
| 4. | — | — | — | — |
| 5. | strobe data from memory to MBR, initiate restore cycle | strobe data from memory to MBR, initiate restore cycle | strobe data from memory to MBR, initiate restore | strobe data from memory to MBR, initiate restore |
| 6. | send MBR, load Y | send MBR, load Y | send MBR, load Y | send MBR, load Y |
| 7. | — | — | — | — |
| 8. | send SUM, load A, F→STATE | send XOR, load A, F→STATE | send AND, load A, F→STATE | send OR, load A, F→STATE |

Fig. 5.23 The execution of the four arithmetic memory referencing instructions in BLUE.

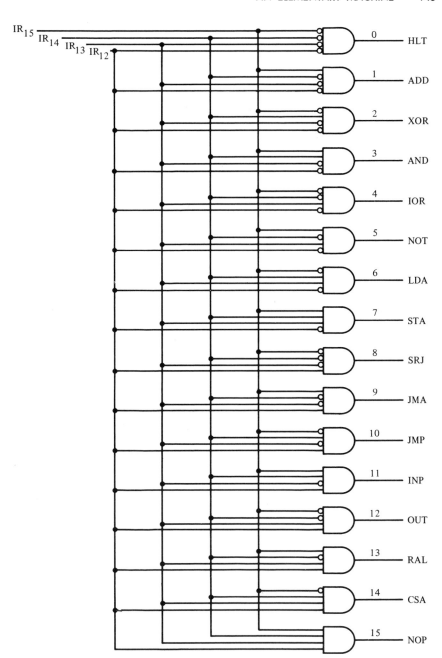

Fig. 5.24 A complete binary decoding tree for BLUE. Note that a circuit similar to these is now available on a single 24 pin DIP such as the 9311.

situation occurs quite often in computer design and the student is urged to look for and exploit it whenever he can.

The four remaining instructions are shown in Fig. 5.23. A detailed description of the operation of these four instructions should not be necessary.

## CIRCUITS OF THE CONTROL UNIT

So far we have given no indication of how the control unit decides what instruction is to be executed. The four high-order bits of the instruction register are lead to what is called a "complete decoding tree" (out of reverence for the old days when this operation was performed by a "tree" of electromechanical relays). Figure 5.24 shows such a tree with its outputs appropriately labeled. Such $1 \times 16$ "demultiplexors" are now available on a single chip. Circuit diagrams of the control logic required in BLUE are shown in Figs. 5.25 through 5.35. When more than one signal goes into a given place, for example, load $A$ is activated several different ways, it is understood that there must be an OR element merging these signals. Details of

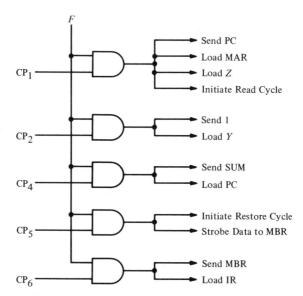

Fig. 5.25 Gates activated in the first part of the fetch cycle.

Fig. 5.26 Action of the Halt instruction.

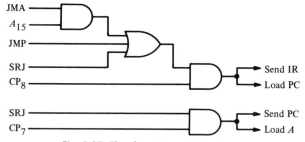

Fig. 5.27 The three jump instructions.

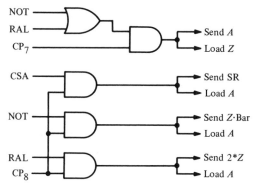

Fig. 5.28 The copy switches to A, the NOT, and the rotate A left instructions.

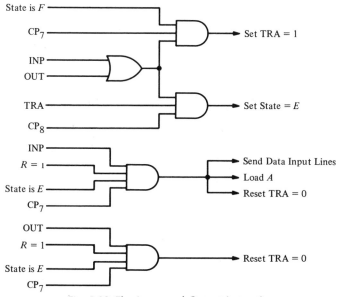

Fig. 5.29 The Input and Output instructions.

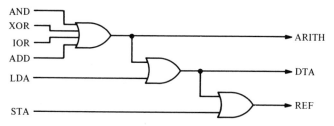

Fig. 5.30 Generation of the ARITH, DTA, and REF signals.

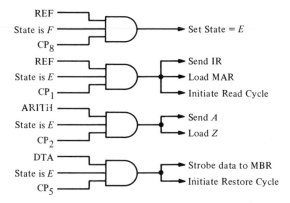

Fig. 5.31 Early steps of memory referencing instructions.

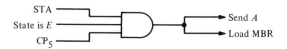

Fig. 5.32 The rest of the store accumulator instruction.

the memory have already been discussed, as well as the bus structure. Thus, this completes the description of BLUE.

---

*Question 5.9:* We have made some attempt to combine signals wherever we can. See, for example, the REF signal which is used in several instructions. Can you assign instructions to numeric opcodes in a way other than was done in BLUE so that even greater savings could be achieved?

*Question 5.10:* Draw the circuits required to implement Fig. 5.35.

---

Fig. 5.33 The rest of the load accumulator instruction.

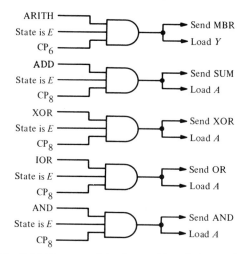

Fig. 5.34 The rest of the four arithmetic instructions.

|  | *Examine* | *Deposit* |
|---|---|---|
| CP 1 | send PC, load MAR, load $Z$, initiate read cycle | send PC, load MAR, load $Z$, initiate read cycle |
| CP 2 | send +1, load $Y$ | send +1, load $Y$ |
| CP 3 | — | — |
| CP 4 | send sum, load PC | send sum, load PC |
| CP 5 | strobe data into MBR, initiate restore cycle | send switch, load MBR, initiate restore cycle |
| CP 6 | send MBR, load IR | — |
| CP 7 | — | — |
| CP 8 | — | — |

Fig. 5.35 The operations generated by pressing the EXAMINE and the DEPOSIT switches on the front panel. It is assumed here and in Fig. 5.9 that these switches give a clean (debounced) signal lasting at least one microsecond.

## SUMMARY

In this chapter we have presented the design for a very simple computer; one so simple that probably nobody would actually want to buy one.

Then again, maybe someone might.   Several machines are presently on the market which are in about the same class as BLUE.

In BLUE, we have instructions to load, store, add, complement, and branch on minus. That is all that one really needs for internal computation.   In addition to these, we have a reasonable set of logic functions (OR, EXCLUSIVE-OR, AND) and an input and an output instruction capable of addressing up to 64 devices.

None of the "goody features" present on most current machines, e.g., indirect addressing, index registers, interrupt, etc., are present.   We will explore them in the chapters which follow.

# 6 | VARIATIONS IN ADDRESSING

*"Tell me to whom you are addressing yourself when you say that. I am addressing myself—I am addressing myself to my Cap."*

Jean Baptiste Molière

In BLUE we provided only one method of addressing information in storage. Under many circumstances, the user may wish for greater flexibility than that provided by one unmodifiable address stored as an integral part of the instruction itself. This chapter will concern itself with some of the many different mechanisms that have been dreamed up to give the user the flexibility he desires. These include multiaddress instructions, index registers, indirect addressing, paging, and segmentation.

## FOUR, THREE, TWO, ONE, ZERO

In a general sense, each dyadic instruction (those operations with two operands and a resultant) needs four pieces of data in addition to the op-code; namely, where to find the first operand, where to find the second operand, where to put the resultant, and where to locate the next instruction. In several of the early machines, all four addresses together with the op-code had to be specified by the programmer in every instruction. These were quite naturally called four-address computers. For example, an instruction might look like

$$\text{ADD}, A, B, C, D$$

and would be interpreted as meaning "add the contents of $A$ to the contents of $B$ and put the resulting sum in $C$. Find your next instruction in location $D$." This form of addressing has several advantages. First, there is no need for an unconditional jump instruction. Every instruction performs that function. Second, in a test instruction it is possible to specify the item to be tested and where to go for the next instruction if the specified item is negative, zero, or positive. Third, there is only one instruction FETCH per three operand memory references, as opposed to BLUE where they are one for one. There is, however, the great disadvantage that as the size of main memories grows larger, more bits are required in each address. Suppose we have $2^{15}$ cells in main store. Four addresses then require a minimum of 60 bits and, adding a few for the op-code and perhaps other features discussed below, we are faced with a very large word, larger in fact than we will need for most data. Thus, four-address machines ceased to be built. The first obvious place to cut down the word size is to eliminate the "next instruction address," since it is the usual practice (in non-drum machines) to place instructions in successive cells, except when a jump is required. This leaves a three-address machine of which the Honeywell 8200 is a present day example.[1]

In that machine there are 12 bits allotted for each address and 12 for the op-code and modifiers (see below). Since with 12 bits one can access only 4096 words directly, the designers were forced to invent several (actually 8) modes of addressing, via central registers, which serve to completely confuse a newcomer to the machine.

The next possible reduction is exemplified by the IBM 1620, which is a two-address machine.[2] An ADD instruction specifies "add $A$ to $B$ and put the result in $B$." A variant form of the two address scheme is called the "one plus one" and was used in the IBM 650.[3] The first address is the location of the operand and the second is the location of the next instruction. The 650 used a drum as main storage and there is always a problem of latency with a drum. The programmer therefore used the second address to specify a "good" location of the next instruction—one that will be under the read heads when the present instruction is completed. If any other location is specified the machine must wait, perhaps a full drum revolution time, until the next instruction can be read.

BLUE is a typical example of a single-address machine, which is the most common type available today. The ultimate reduction in the number of addresses is found in a zero address machine like the KDF.9[4] or the B5500.[5] Here, all addresses are implicit. The next instruction location is found in the program counter as in BLUE. The two operands are found in the top two cells of the pushdown-stack accumulator and the resultant is put into the top cell of the accumulator stack.

Occasionally it is necessary to reference main store (for more operands or to save partial results), and so some "long" instructions are provided which allow one to load the accumulator stack or to store its contents in main memory. These long instructions may take up two, three, or even four syllables (the space required to store a short instruction is called a syllable). Machines of this type are most economical of storage, but as can be readily imagined, they require relatively complex hardware to decide when the next syllable is a new instruction and when it is an address, or part of an address, for the current instruction.[6]

## INDEXING

Returning to a one address machine like BLUE, it was early discovered that a typical program has two housekeeping chores that occur very frequently in the course of computation. The first of these is address modification and the second is counting. For example, one might wish to add up 100 numbers lying in successive cells in storage. In BLUE the program would have to pick up the ADD instruction, increase the address field by one, lay it back down, and then go execute it. Further, one would wish to count how many cells were yet remaining to be added and exit from the summation loop when the number remaining to be processed fell to zero.

---

*Question 6.1:* Write a program for BLUE that will perform the example stated in the text above.

*Question 6.2:* Name some other examples of these two housekeeping chores.

---

Once machine designers realized how much time was being spent performing these two "housekeeping" operations, the so called *B*-box (as contrasted with the *A*-box, or accumulator) was invented. These "*b*-lines," or as they are now called "index registers," are available on all except the most inexpensive present day machines. Let us see how we might add such a feature to BLUE.

Since this addition will create a machine that will be quite different from BLUE, we call it INDIGO. We will have a 24-bit word which, for instructions, will consist of three fields

6 bits for the op-code
3 bits for the modifier field
15 bits for the address field

The 6-bit op-code will permit us to have up to 64 different instructions. Among these must be some to load, save, change, and test the contents of the index registers (see below). With a 15-bit address field, we can point to any one of $2^{15}$ or 32,768 different memory cells.

The modifier field is used to tell the machine what "mode" of addressing is desired. There are three modes that will be available in INDIGO

Direct        Use the number in the address field of the instruction as the address of the cell in which to find the operand, e.g., LDA 0 1000 will put the contents of cell 1000 into the accumulator.

Indexed       The modifier field will specify one of the available index registers. Add the contents of the specified index register to the number in the address field of the instruction to form an "effective address" at which the operand will be found.

Indirect      The effective address points to a cell which contains the actual address of the operand. (See the next section of this chapter.)

With three bits in the modifier field, the programmer can specify one of eight possible conditions. If he puts a ZERO (000) in this field, we will take this to mean that no indexing is required. The address in the address field is to be used without modification as the location of the operand. Suppose, however, he puts a ONE (001) in this field. This will mean that in order to discover the location of the operand he is really talking about, we will add the contents of index register number one ($B1$) to the contents of the address field to form an "effective address." Thus, if the address field contains 1000, the modifier field contains 001, and index register one holds 13, the effective address will be: $1000 + 13 = 1013$. Thus under these conditions, LDA 1 1000 will load the contents of cell 1013 into $A$. If, however, the programmer puts a TWO (010) in the index field, he means "add the contents of $B2$ to the address field to find the effective address." In general we may write

$$Y = y + (B_b)$$

where $Y$ is the effective address, $y$ is the contents of the address field of the instruction, and $B_b$ is the index register named in the modifier field. To make this equation true, even when no indexing is desired, we invent a fictitious index register $B0$ whose contents are identically ZERO at all times.

Usually a separate arithmetic unit is provided to perform the additions required to calculate the effective address. This unit alleviates the load on the normal arithmetic unit and can be made quite simply, since it is only required to perform addition. With a fast simple address-arithmetic-unit, one can have the effective address calculated long before the main store is ready to utilize it.

---

*Question 6.3:* Lay out the timing sequence of a LDA instruction in INDIGO with 7 index registers.

---

Index registers may be of any length, but in most machines, they are made the same size as the address field of an instruction. Thus in INDIGO, they would be 15 bits long. But sometimes (see the KDF.9 or the Honeywell 800),[1,4,7] they are made long enough to hold two or three fields of the size of the address field.

For example, in the KDF.9[4] the fifteen index registers (called $Q$-stores) are 48 bits long, consisting of 3 fields of 16 bits each. These fields are called the COUNTER, the INCREMENT, and the MODIFIER. Each field stores a signed number of TWO's complement mode. If indexing is specified by the programmer, the contents of the MODIFIER field of the designated $Q$-store is added to the address field of the instruction to form the effective address. If the programmer desires, he may also specify that the contents of the $Q$-store be "Incremented." When this option is declared, two things happen to the contents of the $Q$-store *after* the effective address is calculated.

1. The contents of the signed INCREMENT field is added to the contents of the signed MODIFIER field and the sum is stored in the MODIFIER field as a new modifier that will be used the next time this $Q$-store is referenced as an index register.
2. A ONE is subtracted from the signed integer in the COUNTER field.

Several things should be noted about this scheme. First, there are two instructions which can test the contents of the COUNTER field: jump on zero and jump on non-zero. This allows the programmer, by proper initialization of a $Q$-store and proper incrementing of it, to perform address modification and counting in one fell swoop. Further, since the INCREMENT field may contain integers other than ONE, he can if he wishes address every third or every $N$th cell in storage by inserting the proper value in the INCREMENT field.

For INDIGO and for many other machines, the index registers contain only one field. In these cases, a number of instructions must be added to the repertoire of the machine. These usually include at least the following:

| | |
|---|---|
| RXT R1, R2 | copy the contents of register $R1$ into register $R2$, where $R1$ and $R2$ may be $A, Q, B1, \ldots, BN$. |
| SIX $\alpha, b$ | store the contents of index register $b$ in location $\alpha$. |
| LIX $\alpha, b$ | load index register $b$ with the low-order bits from location $\alpha$. |
| ENI $\alpha, b$ | put the number $\alpha$ (considered to be an integer) into $b$. |

INI $\alpha,b$          add the number $\alpha$ to the contents of index register $b$.

IJP $\alpha,b$          if the contents of $b$ are not zero, subtract one from the contents and jump to $\alpha$. If the contents are zero, go on to the next instruction.

---

*Question 6.4:* Lay out the timing diagrams of these instructions as was done for the original instruction of BLUE. Which ones require one cycle (fetch only) and which require two?

---

As noted above, with 3 bits in the modifier field we can specify 7 "kinds" of modification in addition to no modification. One possible use of these bits would be to specify which of seven different index registers is to be used. Another use for one or more of these patterns is discussed below.

## INDIRECT ADDRESSING

In many of the machines available today, there is a third type of address modification available to the programmer in addition to "direct" and "indexing." This type of modification is called "indirect addressing" and there are at least two different ways of specifying it in an instruction and two different ways it can operate. Any one machine, of course, will have only one particular implementation available.

Let us first describe in words how the process works. If an indirect address is specified, we

1. Compute the effective address (say $\alpha$) and
2. Read out the contents of cell $\alpha$.
3. The integer in the address field of cell $\alpha$ is the name of the cell (say $\beta$) actually containing the data.

Thus, for example, if I specify a load accumulator indirectly from cell 1234 and if in cell 1234 there is a number like 7651, it is the contents of cell 7651, whatever they may be, that will end up in the accumulator. Such a mode of addressing would be very convenient if, for example, cell 1234 contained a pointer to a pushdown list. We will call the cell $\alpha$ the "nominator" cell, and we will call the cell $\beta$ (the one that actually contains the data) the "nominee."

Now in INDIGO we can treat the 3 bits of the modifier field either of two ways. One way is to say that there will be six index registers, numbered 1 to 6, and if the programmer puts a seven in the modifier field, he means indirect addressing. This is the way Control Data has designed their 3600 and 3800 machines.[8] The other way we could choose to treat these three bits is to say that the left most of the three will tell us whether or not there is indirect addressing, and the remaining two will be used to designate one of three index registers that can be used. Saying this another way, the two right most bits of the modifier field tell us how to compute the effective address, while the left most bit tells us whether the cell at that address is to be treated as a nominator or as the nominee.

Although this second treatment cuts down the number of index registers, we can have from 6 to 3, it permits us to index in the selection of a nominator, sometimes a very convenient facility. We will choose this latter alternative for INDIGO. Thus, we will have modifier field values of 0, 1, 2, and 3 mean: direct addressing with no indexing, indexed on $B1$, indexed on $B2$, and indexed on $B3$, respectively. Correspondingly fields of 4, 5, 6, and 7 will mean indirect addressing in which the nominator cell is selected with: no indexing, indexed on $B1$, indexed on $B2$, and finally indexed on $B3$.

We must now choose whether to index before or after indirect addressing. In what has gone before we have assumed "preindexing"—that is, that the effective address is computed first and that then indirect addressing (if any) takes place. But there is another alternative called "postindexing," in which the index value is added to the indirect address rather than to the address field of the instruction. We will choose preindexing for INDIGO but the reader should note that not every computer designer would concur.

---

*Question 6.5:* Suppose that the instruction is "LDA 1000, 1, indirect" and that $B1$ contains 5. Location 1000 contains 3. Make other necessary assumptions and describe what gets into the accumulator with preindexing; with postindexing.

*Question 6.6:* When would each kind of indexing be valuable?

---

We have still another choice to make before we can begin to design the address mechanism of INDIGO. That is: how much of the information stored in the nominator is to be considered as the address of the nominee? Shall we just pick up the address field and use that, or shall we get the modifier field stored in the nominator and allow another possible cycle of indexing and/or indirection? To put it more succinctly, in INDIGO do we pick up 15 or 18 bits? If we choose to pick up only 15 bits, we are limiting the programmer to one level of indirection. If we choose to pick up 18 bits, he can have as many levels as he chooses, but he can do silly things like

$$(500) = LDA \ 4 \ 1000$$
$$(1000) = NOP \ 4 \quad 500$$

which will never terminate, but will "indirect" back and forth between 500 and 1000 forever.

We will choose to pick up 18 bits. We will warn the programmers about this pitfall and, further, we will install a trap circuit as follows. The STATE flip-flop must now be expanded to have at least two bits in which to store at least 3 different states. We will call these FETCH, DEFER, and EXECUTE, where the DEFER state will be entered if there is indirect addressing specified in the just-fetched-instruction. When we enter the DEFER state, we will set to zero a timing mechanism that will run for 32 milliseconds. That is enough time to indirect address through every cell in storage—the maximum a programmer could legitimately specify. (After all, once every cell has been visited, there are only already visited cells left and they are bound to tie you in a loop.) If the computer is still in the DEFER state when the timer times out, we will generate an interrupt (see Chapter 7) and abort the program.

---

*Question 6.7:* Suppose the following instructions are about to be executed in INDIGO. Given the words stored in the locations specified, what will end up in the accumulator in each case?

| LDA | 1000 | when | (B1) = 3 |
| LDA 1 | 1000 | | (1000) = 1005 |
| LDA 4 | 1000 | | (1001) = 654 |
| LDA 5 | 1000 | | (1002) = 123 |
| LDA 5 | 1001 | | (1003) = 1001 |
| | | | (1004) = NOP 4 1002 |
| | | | (1005) = 321 |

---

## BASE REGISTERS

In the previous two sections, we have discussed devices (index registers and indirect addressing) that are designed to make a computer easier for a programmer to use. In this section and in those which follow in this chapter, we will discuss devices that make it easier for the computer system to serve the programmer. The first of these system-oriented devices is called a "base register."* A base register is like an index register in that its

---

*The reader should be aware of the fact that IBM uses the term Base Register in a different sense in their system 360. *They* mean a normal general purpose register (like an accumulator) that holds an address and is added to the "off set" in the instruction at the programmer's discretion.[9]

contents are added to the address field to help in forming the effective address. But it differs from an index register in two ways:

1. The casual programmer normally has no control over what is in the base register.
2. The contents of the base register are *always* added into the effective address before a memory reference is made.

One might well ask why such a device is desired. The answer is two fold. The first reason is that when a programmer is writing a program, it is most convenient to *assume* that the starting address of the program is in cell zero. That is admittedly an arbitrary choice, but it is hard to propose a better one offhand. Now any user of a large computer knows that there may be several reasons why a program cannot actually be loaded into memory beginning in location zero. First, the monitor probably occupies low core (the low-numbered addresses of storage). And second, even if there were no monitor (an unlikely situation nowadays) or even if it were located elsewhere, an average programmer may well want to have more than one program in store at the same time, and they can't *all* be located beginning with cell zero. There is, of course, a way around these problems without resorting to a base register. That is through the use of a "relocating loader." Such a loader can take a program which was assembled for location zero and, if proper care was taken in the assembly phase, move that program so that it can live happily anywhere in store. Such a loader can, with some extensions, also "link together" many subprograms which have public (or global) symbolic names as well as private (or local) ones. But there is a price that must be paid for these services. One of the earliest loaders for the IBM 7000 series was called the "one card loader" because the seven instructions that constituted the loader could all be punched on one Hollerith card. It is the author's understanding that current loaders may be several thousand times as long.

This is not meant to imply that given base registers we could duplicate a complex loader in only seven instructions. The demands made on loaders have increased immensely over the last 20 years. But it is obviously true that if we can push some of the functions (such as relocation) on to the hardware, then the software can be made simpler.

---

*Question 6.8:* With a base register in INDIGO write an equation that will indicate how to calculate an effective address.

---

The second, and perhaps more important, use of a relocation or base register is in the case of a multiprogrammed machine. In such a machine, where several programs may be resident in main storage awaiting their turn at CPU attention, one *cannot* know when writing or assembling a program what locations will be available in store when we come to load a particular program. Worse yet, once a program has been loaded, the monitor may need to *move* it in order to consolidate empty areas on either side of the program into one larger (and more useful) empty area. Now a regular relocating loader relies on clues laid down by the original assembler to distinguish between constants (which should not be modified) and relocatable addresses (which should). But once the program has been loaded into storage, these clues are lost. One is then faced with two alternatives. Either use a base register to modify the genuine memory references and leave the constants alone, or else reload the program from the assembled version on backup storage.

Consider for example the so-called literal instruction in which the address field is taken to be the operand.

ENI    1000, 1

which means put the number 1000 (not the contents of cell 1000) into index register 1. Suppose further that this instruction is followed by

LDA    1234, 1

If this program were located beginning at location zero, it is clear that the programmer means to get the contents of cell $1234 + 1000 = 2234$ and put them in the accumulator. A good assembler would flag the first of this pair as being "absolute" and the second as being "relocatable." Then if the program containing this pair was to be loaded, beginning at location 5000, the pair of instructions sitting in storage would read:

ENI    1000, 1<br>LDA    6234, 1

A reasonably sophisticated moving routine could distinguish a literal from an address as exemplified in the pair above, but what can it do about the constant that happens to "look like" an instruction with an address? A machine with a base register doesn't have these problems. The "offset" or base address is added into the effective address only when a memory reference is about to be made. A literal or a constant is thus immune to its influence, whereas a genuine attempt to reference storage is automatically modified to account for the starting location of the program, whatever it may currently be.

---

*Question 6.9:* Discuss subroutine calls in a machine with a base register. Should there be a relocating loader or not?

*Question 6.10:* Add a base register to INDIGO. Now show the calculation of effective address for an LDA instruction. What instructions must be included among the op-codes because of the base register?

*Question 6.11:* Would two (or more) base registers be helpful? What services could they provide?

---

## PURE PROCEDURES

A pure procedure is a sequence of instructions which does not modify itself. With the advent of large high-speed expensive computers, particularly those with autonomous input-output processors, there is an advantage to having several programs in store simultaneously waiting for execution, so that when one of the programs gets hung up waiting for I/O, there is another program there ready to utilize the CPU. This technique of trying to keep all parts of a machine busy by working on several programs at a time is called "multiprogramming." Suppose now that we have a subroutine which is in common use by two or more of the programs resident in the machine. In order for this to be possible, the subroutine must be written so that use by program $A$ does not change the way the subroutine behaves vis-a-vis program $B$. Technically, this subroutine would be called a "re-entrant procedure," and one of the easiest ways of achieving this is to make the subroutine a pure procedure. The reason for desiring such code is quite simple. If two or more programs require the use of a certain function, it would be of benefit to the system if only one copy of the function was required in core at a time. If the function is written as a pure procedure, the person now executing in that function can be interrupted and another user can use the function immediately without need for initializing the function. Naturally, the machine registers must be saved on interrupt, and any intermediate results must be stored in an area associated with the current user, not with the function itself. Providing one has a machine with an indexing capability and indirect addressing, this is not excessively hard to accomplish.

---

*Question 6.12:* Assume the users data area is in location 1000 and that a pure procedure is desired which will find the roots of a quadratic equation ($ax^2 + bx + c = 0$). Write the routine, assuming that a SQR instruction is available which takes the square root of the contents of the accumulator. How much overhead is incurred because of the necessity to keep the procedure pure?

---

The second advantage claimed for pure procedures is that there is no need to save them (roll them out) when a user is interrupted and temporarily demoted to backing store. Since the pure procedure is not modified in any way, the copy already on the backing store is as good as (and exactly the same as) the one in storage, so there is no need to save the in-storage version. This use of pure procedures allows the system to cut down on the size of transfers between main storage and backing store—a worthwhile thing to attempt.

One might imagine that a serious drawback to pure procedures would be the fact that it is impossible to generate an instruction, lay it down in storage, and then execute it. In actuality the number of times one wishes to do this is quite limited. Index registers and base registers have removed a good deal of the necessity for doing so, and finally there is the EXE-CUTE instruction which most machines have nowadays.

An EXECUTE instruction[10] tells the machine to load the instruction register with the contents of the cell pointed at by the address field of the EXECUTE instruction, and then actually execute what is put into the instruction register. No change to the contents of the program counter are made, except for the normal incrementation by one, unless the instruction fetched is itself a jump instruction. This allows the programmer to have an "indirect fetch" and execute one instruction not in the normal line of control. Thus, for example, if the current instruction is EXECUTE 1000 and the contents of cell 1000 are "LDA 1234," the effect is as if the LDA 1234 replaced the execute instruction. Since the address used in the EXECUTE instruction can be within the data area of the program, one can set up and store an instruction and then perform it using an EXECUTE, still keeping the procedure pure. Naturally enough, programs stored in ROM's must be purer than the driven snow.

## PAGING

The word page is used in several different ways in the computer field. Let us describe some of these ways.

### Short address Paging

In the PDP-8,[11] there are 4096 words of storage of 12 bits of length. In order to get an op-code into an instruction, we need to assign 3 bits to the op-code field to enable us to have 8 different instructions. This leaves 9 bits for the address field, which is only enough to address 512 different words of storage. Obviously, this won't do. What the designers did was to subdivide the remaining 9 bits of an instruction into three separate fields of 1, 1, and 7 bits each. The first of these is called the "indirect bit," and specifies whether direct or indirect addressing is to be used. To compute the effective address, we first determine what "page" is being referenced by examining the second field called the page bit. In the PDP-8, the 4096 cells of memory are divided up into 32 "pages" of 128 cells each, and obviously a 1 bit field won't allow us to select one of 32 different pages. So the programmer is restricted to declaring either of two possible "pages." These are "page ZERO" (the first 128 cells in the machine) and the "current page" (the page the instruction itself is located in).

An effective address is calculated as follows: first, the low order 7 bits of the instruction are sent to the Memory Address Register. They form the "line number" and indicate which word within the page is desired. Then if the "page" bit is ZERO, five ZERO's (00000) are put in the high-order end of the MAR, forcing a reference to page ZERO. If on the other hand the "page" bit is ONE, indicating the "current page," the five high-order bits of the program counter are copied into the high-order end of the MAR, forcing a reference to the page containing the instruction generating this address. Note that this must happen before the program counter is incremented. This scheme will *work* and allow one to address any part of core, but it throws an added burden on the programmer (of keeping track of where he is) that is a constant bother.

*Banking*

Another way of dealing with address fields that are too short to handle the available memory is called "banking." The CDC 3600[8] is a typical example of this approach. Storage units for this machine come in units of 32$K$ each called "core banks." Since the address fields have only 15 bits in them, this means that special arrangements must be made if one is going to use more than one bank of storage. This is done with two three-bit registers called the "operand bank register" and the "instruction bank register." These act as extensions to the address field and program counter, respectively. Special instructions allow the programmer to set either of the two registers, thus determining from which of the 8 possible banks he will draw (or store) his data and instructions.

*Paging in a Hierarchical Storage*

When writing a large program, the writer must consider how much memory is available in which to run the program. If the program is larger than the available space, he must break his program up into smaller parts, each of which will fit into the machine. Suppose, for example, his program breaks naturally into two parts. Part *A* does a calculation and passes its results to *B*. Then Part *B* analyzes these results and, if the analysis is not satisfactory, changes some initial conditions and gives control back to *A* for recalculation. This interchange of information and control may occur many times in the course of solving a problem. The trick that the programmer will employ in such a case is called "overlaying." He will store part *B* of his program on a magnetic tape or a drum or disk. When *A* finishes its portion of the task, its last action is to copy itself out onto, say, the drum and load part *B* into main storage so that it "lies over" the same cells that *A* itself was occupying. Then *A* transfers control to *B*. *B* in its turn will perform the same actions overlaying itself with *A* and so on back and forth.

Since these swaps take up time, the programmer has to be careful to keep them to a minimum. In the example we have just considered, the place at which to break the program apart was easily seen to be at the "joints" between *A* and *B*, but in more complicated problems, the decisions on how to fragment a program can become exceedingly complex.

Now consider the following problem: While one overlay of a program is being "rolled out" and its successor is being "rolled in," what will the CPU be doing? In a machine like BLUE or INDIGO, this is a rhetorical question. The CPU will of course be doing the transfer of information. But in more sophisticated machines (see Chapter 7), once a transfer has been initiated, it can continue by itself without further supervision or attention from the CPU. This then leaves the CPU idle in the situation we have described. But the CPU is an expensive thing and we are probably paying large rental for it, whether or not it is gainfully employed. This situation is not unique to overlaying, but will occur when cards are being read in or data is being printed out on the line printer.

Suppose it were true that we had another, independent program sitting in main store just waiting for such an eventuality. Then the obvious thing to do with our idle CPU is to put it to work on the second program while we are waiting for the I/O transfer (called for by the first program) to be completed. When this I/O transfer is complete, or perhaps when the second program requires some I/O of its own, we will look around again and see if there are any other programs that might be ready to execute and transfer control to one of them. So far, this sounds delightful. We put a "mix" of several different programs into main store and arrange to work on each in turn until it requires some I/O. We trigger off the I/O transfer and give control to the next program that is ready. We keep the CPU busy most of the time and the machine's throughput (programs processed per unit time) goes way up. This approach is called "multi-programming" and is being used quite extensively nowadays.[12-18]

There are, however, at least two problems which had to be solved before multiprogramming could become a practical reality.

The first of these is that with several users occupying the machine at the same time, a programmer can have no idea of how much space will be available to him when his turn at execution comes. Indeed, it may be different on two different days, or even from moment to moment. This is the programmer's dilemma. The system has a comparable one. When a program terminates, the space in storage that it was using is turned back to the system for assignment to someone else. It may occur that several small programs scattered through storage terminate about the same time. The total amount of released space may be large enough to accommodate the next program on the queue waiting to be run, but no single chunk of it is big enough to be useful as it stands. This is called "fragmentation" of storage.

One possible solution would be for the system to stop everything while it "cleans up" its store and moves resident programs around so that it gets all the available slots consolidated into one big empty area. This would add a good deal to your system overhead and must be avoided if at all possible. The Control Data 6600 operating system called KRONOS does just this kind of clean-up operation when it needs space. This is because no paging hardware is available on this machine. The ATLAS paging system solves both of the above problems and, in addition, eliminates the need for the programmer to worry about overlays.

This scheme was originally called a "one-level-store" by Kilburn[19] and his associates at the University of Manchester and has since been called a "virtual store" by others.

Let us suppose that we have a machine with $32K$ of core and several times that amount of drum storage. These storage units are logically divided into blocks each of a constant size (usually 1024 cells). The programmer writes his program as if he had a machine as large as he desires, one with an "unlimited" number of blocks. In actual practice, he will probably be limited by the size of his address field to something like a thousand pages of program,* but that's a million words of storage and it will take even a fast programmer some time to generate that much code.

Normally the programmer using such a system doesn't worry about page size or where the page boundaries fall. He just writes (and writes and writes) as if he had an infinite virtual memory. This then solves all the programmer's problems. He doesn't concern himself with other users, or overlays, or the actual size of the machine he will be working on.

Now let us look at what happens at execution time. The system will load the program in its entirety on to the drum and, eventually, a decision will be made that it is time to get a new program under way. So the first page of our program gets loaded into core in some convenient empty block, and the monitor makes a note of the fact that this block is now "in use" and by whom. Sooner or later this program begins to execute and all goes well until a reference is made to a page which is not now in residence. At this time, depending on the sophistication of the machine, either the hardware or the software monitor intervenes and the current program is "suspended," or "put to sleep" until the page containing the desired datum or instruction can be "rolled in." The name given to this approach

---

*One *page* of program fits into one *block* or "page frame" of storage.

is "demand paging." Once the new page is available the program can resume activity (be awakened). Meanwhile, control is passed to some other program.

At *least* five problems in the above description will be obvious to the experienced programmer.

1. When do we accept a new job into the system?
2. How do we keep track of what pages are in core?
3. How do we keep track of where non-resident pages are stored on the drum?
4. When a reference is made to a resident page, how do we translate the programmer's page name into a block name?
5. How do we decide what page to roll out so that we have space to roll in a new page?

There are as many ways of answering these questions as there are multi-programming systems. In this chapter, we will try to design a system for INDIGO which captures the best of these various approaches. The more the reader is familiar with other schemes than the one we have chosen, the more he will wish to argue with our choices. So be it. The not already prejudiced reader is referred to the literature in order to sharpen his literary claws before attacking.

First we will assume a drum is available on the computer to serve as backing store with a million words ($2^{20}$ words) or 1024 pages of 1024 lines each.* We limit the number of programs in the job stream (awaiting execution, partially executed, outputting results) to no more than 16. Each job in the stream will have a unique 4-bit number assigned to it when it is loaded on to the drum that will identify it and all its parts throughout its existence within the machine. We will permanently assign (lock down) one page of core to hold a Job Pointer Table and a drum directory. It will be organized as shown in Fig. 6.1.

Identified with each 1024 cell block in core, there will be a 14-bit register called the "block contents register." The upper 4 bits of the register will hold the job number of the current "owner" of this block and the lower 10 bits will hold the number of the page he is storing there. (His "name" for the page.) These 32 registers together form an associative memory. When interrogated with a combination of the current job number and the page that is being referenced, it will load the upper 5 bits of the MAR with a number corresponding to the block in which the page is stored. Finally, we need a 4-bit register to hold the job number of the program now in control. We will call this the "current job register." Now we are ready to see how an address is translated into a cell number. (See Fig. 6.2.)

*We are *not* describing the ATLAS system at this point but a fictitious design of our own.

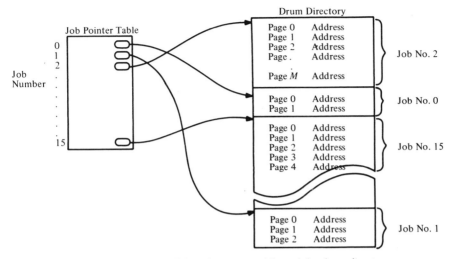

Fig. 6.1 The structure of the job pointer table and the drum directory.

After any indexing that the program may specify, the high-order ten bits of the address (which form the page number) are stripped off and combined with the contents of the current job register to form a 14-bit comparand with which to interrogate the Associative Memory. Let us assume that this page is in core. The *AM* will respond by setting the five high-order bits of the MAR. Meanwhile, the 10 low-order bits of the

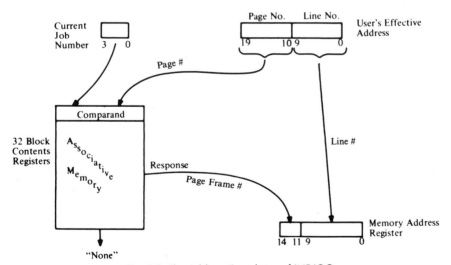

Fig. 6.2 The Address Translator of INDIGO.

users effective address (which are called the "line number") are sent directly to the low-order portion of the MAR, and the memory reference can proceed. This system is said to be "transparent" to the user because he does not see it. He thinks his pages are all in core and sequentially located. But as the reader can easily see, the user's pages can be located wherever it is convenient for the system, and the address translator just described takes care of the mapping from the users "virtual address space" into the real world of core addresses. This covers the case in which the desired page is in core. When this is not the case and the $AM$ responds "no such page" by raising the "none" line, a "page fault" is said to occur. What happens then is usually carried out by software rather than hardware, but we will discuss it here for the sake of completeness. Actually, the operations described could as easily be carried out by hardware and may well be in the next generation of machines.

When a page fault occurs, we will have to suspend the current job until we can fetch the desired page in off the drum. But first, we must find out where that page is stored on the drum. Suppose for example that job number 7 needs a reference to his page number 33. Using the contents of the current job register as an index, we access the job pointer table to find out where in the drum directory this job's "page table" is stored. (We will find this in the 7th entry of job pointer table.) Once we know where his page table begins (say location 345 in the drum directory), we use the page number that caused the fault as an index away from the start of this directory to get the entry for this page in the drum directory ($345_8 + 33_8 = 400_8$ is the location storing the drum address of this page). This entry will tell us where on the drum this page is stored.

Assuming we have an empty page (perhaps released by a program that no longer needs it) in core, we can immediately start loading, or "rolling in," the desired page. If this was the last free page and if we wish to ensure that we will have an empty page for roll in when the next page fault occurs, we had better start rolling out a current page before we give control to the next waiting job. Certainly one page we don't want to roll out is the one that caused the page fault, assuming that it was a memory referencing instruction and not a jump. The algorithm used to select a candidate for roll-out can be either very simple or very complex. It can range from "the page longest in residence" to the "page least likely to be needed again soon." No one has yet shown a *significant* difference in performance among the various choices that have been suggested, nor is this subject really within our area of interest.

In the design of the ATLAS,[19] an interesting algorithm was implemented and, because it uses some hardware features to aid it, we will discuss it here. In addition to the associative registers described above, there are two more bits identified with each block of core. The first of these is called the "USE" bit and is set to 1 whenever any cell within that particular block is accessed (for reading, writing, or execution). Periodically, the system pauses in its other activities and examines these USE bits. Among other items of information, the system stores (in some cells in core) how long it has been since a particular page was referred to. The one which has been inactive the longest is then the prime candidate for the roll-out. The other bit associated with each block is called the "WRITE" bit and is set to 1 if there is a write operation to any cell in the block. Since a page can't very well be modified without writing in it, if the WRITE bit of a particular block is ZERO, the page stored there is the same as the copy already (still) on the drum and there is no point in doing a roll-out. We merely declare the block to be "available" for use.

We will come back to the use of hierarchal stores that appear to the programmer to be of uniform level when we discuss cache memories in Chapter 10.

The above discussion of paging has concentrated on what is called a "page on demand" strategy. We load in a new page only when a program requires it. Although it seems a most attractive solution to many difficulties, there are still many problems associated with it that we have no room to discuss. These include the page turning algorithm (making the decision as to which page to roll out), the distinct possibility that one job will "hog" fast storage (leaving no room for others), the fact that only a very few programs will fit exactly into a block (and usually there will be unused space within many blocks), and last, but by no means least, the possibility (unfortunately realized with some of the 3rd generation time-sharing machines) that everybody ends up waiting for service by the drum. It is just because this paging mechanism is invisible to the user that some of these problems arise. Consider, as an example, a tight loop that iterates many times and is located, unwittingly, across a page boundary.

*Segmentation*

Although the paging system described above is supposed to be invisible to the user, another scheme called "segmentation," which has a very similar mechanism, is intended to be seen by and used by the programmer.[13] An address is broken up into three parts called "segment," "page," and "line." This scheme has been implemented on the GE 645,[20] the IBM 360/67,[13] and the English Electric System 4-75, in various forms.

Each user has a "segment table" and the starting address of the page table for the $n$th segment is found in the $n$th entry of the segment table. Once a page table is entered, action is as described above. The associative registers are expanded to hold both a segment name and a page name.

Many claims are made for segmentation. Their evaluation is beyond the scope of this book.

## PROTECTION IN A MULTI-USER ENVIRONMENT

With many users sharing storage and the control of a CPU, it is necessary to protect them from each other.[21-23] As any programmer will admit, it is all too easy for a program to run amuck and convert the entire contents of storage into meaningless trash. There must be some way to prevent one program from unintentionally influencing another.

The Control Data 3600[8] offers a typical second-generation approach to this problem. There are two aspects to this approach. First, there are two modes of operation called "master" and "slave," or "privileged" and "restricted." In the master-mode (usually reserved to the monitor system), all features built into the machine are available. In the slave mode, certain instructions become illegal and any attempt to execute them causes an interrupt (see Chapter 7) and a transfer of control to the system. Examples of these illegal instructions include all input and output instructions, all instructions which modify the interrupt response system (including the illegal instruction interrupt), and any attempt to change the contents of the "bounds register." The bounds register contains two 18 bit addresses. Each effective address, as soon as it has been calculated, is compared with the contents of the bounds register. If it is larger than the first and less than the second, it is said to be within bounds. Otherwise, a bounds interrupt occurs and control is given to the monitor.

In the 3600, you are forbidden to write out of bounds or to attempt to execute an instruction out of bounds. Reading is permitted, however, since it can do no direct harm to another program. Many other machines forbid reading out of bounds on the basis of privacy considerations.

Several other schemes exist. One of the better is used in the Honeywell 8200[1] where each block of storage has an additional register we shall call the access register. Part of this register contains a "lock code." Each program is assigned a unique key and, if the key does not match the lock, no access at all is allowed. This has the advantage that it can be used successfully in a paged environment, whereas a bounds register cannot.

---

*Question 6.13:* Why not?

---

The rest of the access register consists of three bits called the read, write, and execute bits. Only if a particular bit is set to ONE can the respective operation be performed even if the key matches.

*Question 6.14:* Must one write pure procedures for the H-8200?

Common subroutines provided by the system are stored with a lock of ZERO, which is treated as matching *any* key, and they are generally set to EXECUTE only mode.

Instructions which modify the access registers are available only in the privileged mode. An interesting problem arises in some of the large time-sharing systems when a common data base is to be referenced and possibly modified by several users, but not by every user. No general solution to this problem is known.

*Question 6.15:* Can you identify some of the difficulties involved? Can you suggest any hardware that might help? Software?

One final method of protection is provided by a virtual storage address-ing machine. Since all memory references in such a machine must be via segment and/or page tables that are set up by the system, we can simply "fail to mention" a certain page (make no entry for it) and then the user's program can't possibly get to it.

## CONCLUSIONS

In this chapter we have looked at several modifications to the hardware of BLUE that make it easier for the programmer to use (indexing, indirect addressing, base registers, and paging). In addition, we have mentioned briefly some of the problems that arise in multiprogramming machines and some of the hardware features that have been proposed to solve them.

## REFERENCES

1. *Honeywell Series 200, Model 8200, General Systems Description.* Wellesley Hills, Mass., Honeywell Elect. Data Processing, 1965.
2. *IBM Reference Manual 1620 Data Processing System.* White Plains, N.Y., IBM Corp., 1960.
3. *S.O.A.P. Symbolic Optimal Assembly Program, Programmer's Guide and Summary of IBM Type 650 Operations.* Ann Arbor, Mich., Statistical Research Lab., U of Mich., 1955.
4. *KDF.9 Programming Manual.* Kidsgrove, England, English Electric-Leo Computers Ltd., 1963.
5. *Burroughs B-5500 Information Processing Systems Reference Manual.* Detroit, Mich., Burroughs Corp., 1964.

6. McGovern, P. J. "The Computer Field and the IBM-360—A 1966 Progress Report." *Computers and Automation* **16**, 1, 16–20 (Jan. 1967).
7. *Honeywell 1800 Programmers Reference Manual*, Wellesley Hills, Mass., Honeywell Elect. Data Processing, 1964.
8. *CDC-3600 Computer System Reference Manual.* St. Paul, Minn., Control Data Corp., 1966.
9. Amdahl, G. M., Blaauw, G. A., and Brooks, F. P. "Architecture of the IBM System/360." *IBM Journal of R&D* **8**, 2, 87–101 (April 1964).
10. Brooks, F. P. "The EXECUTE Operation: A Fourth Mode of Instruction Sequencing." *CACM* **3**, 3, 168–170 (March 1960).
11. *Small Computer Handbook.* Maynard, Mass., Digital Equipment Corp., 1966.
12. Critchlow, A. J. "Generalized Multi-processing and Multiprogramming Systems." *Proc. AFIPS 1963 Fall Joint Comp. Conf.*, 107–126.
13. Arden, B. W., Galler, B. A., O'Brien, T. C., and Westervelt, F. H. "Programmed Addressing Structure in a Time-Sharing Environment." *J. ACM* **13**, 1, 1–16 (Jan. 1966).
14. Belady, L. A. "A Study of Replacement Algorithms for a Virtual Storage Computer." *IBM Systems Journal* **5**, 2, 78–101 (1966).
15. Brawn, B., and Gustavson, F. "Program Behavior in a Paging Environment." *AFIPS Proc. FJCC* **33**, 1019–1032 (1968).
16. Coffman, E. G., and Varian, L. C. "Further Experimental Data on the Behavior of Programs in a Paging Environment." *CACM* **11**, 7, 471–475 (July 1968).
17. Joseph, M. "An Analysis of Paging and Program Behavior." *The Computer Journal* **13**, 1, 48–54 (Feb. 1970).
18. Randell, B. "A Note on Storage Fragmentation and Program Segmentation." *CACM* **12**, 7, 365–370 (July 1969).
19. Kilburn, T., Edwards, D. B. G., Lanigan, M. J., and Sumner, F. H. "One-Level Storage System." *IRE Trans. on Electronic Computers* **EC-11**, 223–235 (April 1962).
20. *GE 625/635 System Manual.* Phoenix, Ariz., General Electric Computer Dept., 1965.
21. Lampson, B. W. "Dynamic Protection Structures." *AFIPS Proc. FJCC* **35**, 27–38 (1969).
22. Needham, R. M. "Protection Systems and Protection Implementations." *AFIPS Proc. FJCC* **41**, 572–578 (1972).
23. Schroeder, M. D., and Saltzer, J. H. "A Hardware Architecture for Implementing Protection Rings." *CACM* **15**, 3, 157–170 (March 1972).

# 7 | VARIATIONS IN INPUT/OUTPUT

*"Noise is the most impertinent of all forms of interruption."*
*—Schopenhauer*

In BLUE all input and output takes place via the accumulator. This is not unusual. The IBM 701 operated this way and, even as late as the CDC 3600, messages from the operator via the console typewriter entered as an "input to *A*." However, it was soon realized that, finances permitting, better methods could be devised that did not immobilize the expensive CPU while a data transfer was taking place. In this chapter we will explore some of these methods and what is required to implement them. Before looking at these methods, however, we shall investigate the subject of interrupts and how they are treated.

## INTERRUPTS

As we have noted, there are certain events which are rare enough so that they would be cumbersome to program for and yet important enough so that they must be attended to when they do arise. The most convenient way to handle this sort of problem is to arrange the hardware so, that when these events do occur, there is an automatic way of "suspending" (interrupting) the ongoing program and transferring control temporarily to a special routine designed to handle these events.

Let us consider a primitive interrupt system as it might be incorporated into INDIGO. First of all, there is an "interrupt system state" flip-flop which may be turned on and off by two instructions we will designate as ION and IOF. If this flip-flop is turned off (reset), the interrupt system

173

is said to be "disabled" and no interrupts can occur. If, however, it is turned on, then the interrupt system is "enabled."

Whenever an interrupting condition occurs, a flip-flop assigned to that condition and called the "condition flag" is turned on. Whenever a flag bit goes to ONE (assuming the interrupt system is enabled), an interruption of the currently executing program occurs just before beginning the next FETCH cycle. That is, the instruction being executed is allowed to finish, but no new ones will be begun until the interrupt has been dealt with. Three events occur when an interrupt arises:

1. The interrupt system is turned off so that no further interrupts can disturb our handling this present one.
2. The contents of the program counter are stored in location ZERO so that we can return to the main program when we are done.
3. A ONE is inserted in the program counter and a FETCH cycle is entered so that the next instruction will be taken from location ONE.

Beginning in location ONE, there must be a routine which decides what caused the interrupt and does whatever is necessary about it. To decide what caused an interrupt, we make use of another special instruction called "skip on flag." Since there may be many possible interrupt generating conditions, we need to use the address field of this instruction to specify which flag is to be tested. This means we don't have enough room to put a regular storage address and make this a normal conditional jump. A "skip on condition" does nothing if the condition is not met (the flag is ZERO in our case). If the condition is true (the flag is ONE), the contents of the program counter are increased by an extra one, causing the program to skip over one instruction. A typical instruction sequence might look like:

```
SKF 1            Skip if flag 1 is set.
JMP NOTONE       It wasn't, go check some other flags.
  .
  .              Begin processing, interrupt 1.
  .
```

A group of routines will be set up, each beginning as shown, and linked together by the jump instructions. These routines taken collectively will determine what the condition was and process it accordingly.

The interrupt handling software must make arrangements for storing the contents of all the registers it uses so that they can be restored to their original state before going back to the main or interrupted program, assuming of course that the condition was not fatal, and the main program can continue. More sophisticated machines sometimes save all the machine registers automatically when they save the program counter.

After the interrupting condition has been processed, the interrupt program still has some things to do before giving up control. First, it must clear the flag which caused this interrupt. Otherwise, once the interrupt system is turned on again, the flag will still be set and we will start the process all over again. This can be done by a "clear flag" (CLF) instruction. Sometimes the instruction which tests a flag simultaneously clears it. Next we must restore all registers we have used. Then we execute an instruction called "IRT-interrupt return." This instruction does two things. First, it loads the program counter with the contents of cell ZERO, and second, it enables the interrupt system by turning on the interrupt system flip-flop. These actions must be carried out in the order stated. Suppose instead we enabled the interrupt system first, and suppose that another flag was set (another interrupting condition had arisen while we were processing the first one); thus with a flag set and the interrupt system enabled, an interrupt will occur. After this second interrupt takes place, the contents of the program counter will be the address of the cell following the cell holding the IRT instruction. The original contents of cell ZERO will be wiped out when this address is stored in ZERO and we will have no way of getting back to the main program. By ordering the way in which he tests the flags, the programmer of the interrupt system has control over which one he will process first. This can become important in some of the more complicated systems.

---

*Question 7.1:* Design a complete interrupt system for INDIGO, including the necessary instruction timing charts, as described above.

---

The system we have described above works and several computers employ it. A slightly more complicated version of the above allows us to select which conditions will be allowed to interrupt the course of the main program. To do this, we imagine all the flags to be collected into a "flag register." We add a "mask register" that has as many bits as the flag register. There must be instructions that allow us to load the mask register from storage. Now, a condition which sets a flag in the flag register has no effect whatsoever unless the corresponding bit in the mask register is ONE. If the mask bit is ONE *and* the flag comes up *and* the interrupt system is active, *then*, and only then, does an interrupt occur. Any mask bit set to ZERO inhibits the corresponding condition from affecting the machine.

---

*Question 7.2:* Add a mask register to INDIGO.

---

A somewhat faster method of deciding what caused an interrupt is exemplified by the "main product register jump" (MPJ) in the CDC-3600.[1] The 3600 has a 48 bit word, and consequently the designers arranged to have a 48 bit flag register and a 48 bit interrupt mask register. The bit by bit AND of the flag and interrupt mask registers is called the "main product register." Suppose the main product register jump is located in cell 100. Scanning of the main product register begins at the left end (bit 47) and proceeds to the right (toward bit 0). As soon as the first ONE is detected (say in bit $i$), the scan ends and the next instruction is taken from the present location plus $(i + 1)$. Thus, in our example if bit 23 of the main product register is ONE, the next instruction will be taken from location $100 + 23 + 1 = 124$. If no bit of the product register is ONE, the next instruction is taken from the lower half of the present location (the 3600 has a number of 24 bit instructions including MPJ and jump, which allows us to pack two instructions in one word). Execution time for this instruction is 1.3 microseconds, which is considerably faster than a skip chain of 48 tests. The disadvantage of this instruction is that the assignment of interrupts to the flag register is fixed and the scan is predetermined, so that interrupt $i$ will always take precedence over $j$ $(i > j)$ and the priority of various interrupts cannot be conveniently modified by the programmer.

Another method of determining what condition generated the interrupt is that used in the PDP-11 made by the Digital Equipment Corporation.[2,3] A similar scheme was used in the IBM 7000 series.

Each interrupting condition is assigned a unique address, sometimes called the "trap vector address." This address is supplied by the interrupting device. At the trap vector address the programmer stores the location of the beginning of the routine that is intended to handle this condition; so in effect what takes place is an indirect jump through the trap vector to the interrupt handlers.

In the PDP-11 the old contents of the program counter are stored on a pushdown stack that is pointed at by general register 6—the "stack pointer" register. Actually, in the PDP-11 the trap vector for each condition is two words long, and two words are stored on the stack. The second word to go on the stack is the contents of the machine's "status register" (see below), and the second word in the trap vector is a new set of values for the status register. The advantage of using a pushdown stack is that many different interrupts can be allowed to happen, and if each ends by popping the two top words from the stack back into the PC and the status register, these interrupts can be "nested" to any desirable depth. When each interrupt stores its return address in location zero, each interrupt handler must take care to save this return address somewhere before it dares to turn on the interrupt system again to allow other, perhaps more important, interrupts to occur.

Now a word about the status register. The machines we have considered above have only two states for their interrupt systems: off and on. Either we get no interrupts or all unmasked interrupts.

In the PDP-11, and in many other current machines, there are several states of the interrupt system called "levels." When the processor is running at a given level (say 5), no interrupts at that level or below (1, 2, 3, 4, or 5) are honored, but interrupts at higher levels (6 and 7) can interrupt the current program and take command of the CPU. When an I/O device sends its trap vector address, it also sends a wired-in interrupt request level. This request level is compared with the current level (stored in the processor status register), and if the request is at a level greater than the current level, an interrupt takes place. As part of this interrupt a new status word is loaded into the processor status register and a new current level is established— whatever level seems good to the programmer who sets up the trap vector. This gives the user the ability conveniently to establish whatever interrupt priority structure he desires—subject only to the constraint of the level of request wired into the I/O devices.

It is possible to get the same effect using an on-off interrupt system and a mask, but, having tried it, I can say that this multilevel scheme is considerably simpler.

Writing and, worse, debugging interrupt programs is not a pleasant task, and there are only a few who profess proficiency at it. Perhaps the following observations might be of help if you ever find yourself in this unenviable position. If one were rich enough, one would buy a CPU for each desired interrupt level and set it waiting for this level of events, which it could then handle in a presumably intelligent fashion. If indeed we had such a set of CPU's, there wouldn't actually be any interrupts necessary, except for such things as bounds violations. CPU 1 would, for example, take care of running user programs, CPU 2 would take care of paper tape I/O, and CPU 3 could devote all its energies to doing disk transfers. Of course, most of these CPU's would be sitting around idle most of the time because I/O events are relatively rare, and, as everyone knows, *the devil finds work for idle CPU's.* Up until very recently this work ethic made a great deal of sense, for CPU's were large and expensive.

Since we were not rich or sinful enough to use this method of handling I/O interrupts, what was done was to *pretend* that we had many CPU's by use of an interrupt system. When an I/O event occurs, the one real CPU stops pretending to be the user's CPU and starts to pretend to be one of the I/O CPU's. It accomplishes this switch of persona by storing away the PC and the other user CPU registers in core and donning the cloak of values for its registers that the I/O CPU persona left behind just in case such an event should occur.

If one is as stupid as the residents of Metropolis, one never notices that

Superman and Clarke Kent are somehow never there at the same time, and one can *believe* in these virtual computers.

The machines we have described above store (and reload) one or at most two control registers when an interrupt occurs, and it is up to the programmer to take care of saving the rest of the CPU registers. The set of values that reside in the registers of the CPU are called the "context" of a program. In order to return to a program after an interrupt, we must restore the context of the program to what it was just before the interrupt occurred. Some of the larger machines of today provide a "swap context" instruction that gets executed when an interrupt occurs (for example, the CDC 6600 has an Exchange Jump instruction). This takes care of preserving the context in one step, and to return we execute another "swap context" to replace the old values.

## SEMI-AUTONOMOUS DATA CHANNELS

Suppose that we wished to free the central processing unit from the necessity to intervene in the transmission of every character in or out of main storage. Suppose indeed that we decide to include another small simple processor that is dedicated to just this task of controlling I/O. Let us call this second processor a "data channel."[4] What information must the CPU tell the data channel in order to accomplish an input or output? Consider first an output. We must tell the data channel to do an output, on what device, where to find the first word of information in main storage, and the address of the last word to be output.* So we must pass to the data channel "direction," a "first word address" (FWA) a "last word address" (LWA), and a device name or number. The data channel itself must be able to select a device, it must be able to fetch words out of main storage (and deposit them there) and it must be able to hold its instruction (so it doesn't forget what it is supposed to be doing). Finally it must be able to give certain signals about its status (busy, idle, etc.) to the CPU when requested.

---

*Question 7.3:* Without reading further, discuss how you might modify and simplify BLUE to act as a data channel for INDIGO.

---

To be able to incorporate a data channel into INDIGO, we have to add several instructions to its repertoire. First we need to be able to check the status of the channel, whether it is busy or idle. A "jump on channel busy"

*Some systems pass a word count instead of a last word address.

(JCB) instruction will accomplish this task most conveniently. Next we need to be able to give the channel the information it requires to carry out a transfer. There are several different ways to perform this function. We will choose to have a pair of instructions called:

LC1  $\alpha$    -load register 1 of the data channel from cell $\alpha$. $\alpha$ will contain the number of the device to be read or written and the "first word address" (in main storage) at which to begin the read or write.

LC2  $\alpha$    -load register 2 of the data channel from cell $\alpha$. $\alpha$ contains one bit signifying the direction of transfer and the address of the last word to be filled or emptied. The action of loading register 2 will initiate the transfer.

Within the data channel we have several operations to perform. These can be summarized as a program for the data channel. This program is of course "wired in." The action is as follows for an output instruction:

1. Make the channel "busy."
2. FETCH the word stored at FWA.
3. Separate word into parts that can be accepted by the peripheral device (12, 8, or 6 bits depending on the device).
4. Add ONE to the FWA.
5. Send the first byte of information to the desired device.
6. When the device has absorbed that byte, send another.
7. Repeat step 6 until this word has all been sent.
8. If the FWA is not greater than the LWA, go to step 2. Otherwise go to step 9.
9. Mark the channel as not busy and set the "channel not busy" flag in the interrupt register.

---

*Question 7.4:* Sketch the hardware required to perform the above.

*Question 7.5:* Describe how an input instruction would operate and sketch its hardware.

---

Note that in step 9 we do two things. First we make the channel "not busy" so a status check will show it to be idle. Second we raise the interrupt flag. If the programmer has enabled this interrupt on "end of operation" the program can now initiate another I/O transfer. This latter method of programming will leave the channel idle as little as possible.

Most modern machines have at least one data channel. Many have two or three, each of which can be carrying out a transfer at the same time. Some have as many as 10 so-called peripheral processors.

## CYCLE STEALING

If more than one processor is attempting to access memory at the same time, a race condition can result. This is usually resolved by putting a "scanner" on the storage module. This acts just like a rotary switch, scanning around among the possible requestors for one desiring service.

Suppose, for example, we have a storage device which is to work with one CPU and three data channels. Such a storage device is said to have four "spigots," or ports. Operation is cyclic. The scanner examines the first port. If there is a request for service, the scanner stops and services the request. If not, or when the service (read or write) has been provided, the scanner advances to the next position where the process is repeated. Each port is examined in turn 1, 2, 3, 4, 1, 2, ... and so on. The rate of advancing the scanner is usually one minor cycle, or for BLUE or INDIGO about 100 nsec.

---

*Question 7.6:* Design a 4-spigot storage for INDIGO.

---

This method of handling I/O often is called "cycle stealing." The CPU doesn't really know that the data channel is active. It is just that occasionally the data channel steals a memory cycle that might otherwise have gone to the CPU.

### Variations

One, reasonably common, variation on the above scheme is to give the data channel only an address called the CWA (control word address). The channel's first action is then to FETCH the word at the CWA and also possibly its immediate successors to load its control registers with. This variation permits one to "chain" input output commands. One bit of the control word tells the channel what it should do when it has finished the present transfer. Whether it should cease activity or go to CWA + 1 to find information about another transfer. Another variation is to use a "resetting scanner." After servicing a request, a resetting scanner goes back to look at port 1 to see if it needs service. It then goes to ports 2, 3, and 4. This design allows one to put a high-speed device on port 1 and be certain that it never needs to wait more than one memory cycle before being serviced. This is particularly useful for "impatient" devices like drums, disks, and tapes that are moving and will possibly lose data if it cannot be accepted when necessary.

Some contemporary designs allow peripheral devices to be connected to two or more data channels. If a particular channel is busy, there exists an alternate path to the device that may be available. In this type of design, one must be able to test if the device as well as the channel is busy. Sometimes a "connect" instruction is provided which allows the programmer to specify a channel number as well as a device number. If both the channel and the device are idle, the instruction can be executed. They are both marked "busy" and further instructions sent to that channel will be directed to the device "connected" to it. If either is busy, the request is "rejected." Either skip on accept, or skip on reject, or, if there is room in the word, an address to transfer to on rejection of a request is usually provided. Some machines automatically disconnect all other devices from the channel when a connect instruction is accepted. Others provide a "clear channel" instruction to do this and reject a connect if there is already a device connected to the indicated channel.

---

*Question 7.7:* What are the relative advantages and disadvantages of these methods?

---

## PERIPHERAL COMPUTERS

As can be seen from the discussion above, a data channel is almost an independent computer with one wired-in program. In several contemporary machines, designers have taken the obvious step and converted the data channel into a complete autonomous stored program computer that works with rather than for the main central computer.

Various degrees of integration between the two machines are possible. One of the earliest such system was the IBM 1401/7090 combination. The 1401[5] is a computer that is character oriented and capable of handling I/O with dispatch, but weak on computational abilities. The 7090,[6] on the other hand, had so much computational ability that it seemed a shame to tie it down to the speed of a card reader or line printer. The complementary attributes of the two machines made them a natural pair. Cards were read by the 1401 and copied onto magnetic tape. When a "batch" of jobs had been collected on a tape, that tape was transferred to a drive unit associated with the 7090. Later, physical transfer of the tape from one drive to another was eliminated by using "switchable" drives. The 7090 then read in the jobs one by one from the tape, this being many times faster than reading them from a card reader.

Each job was executed and any generated output was written onto another mag tape. When the batch was finished or the output tape full, that tape would be given back to the 1401 to list on the line printer and/or punch on the card punch.

This procedure resulted in a considerable speed up of operations in computer centers with more jobs processed per hour than could have been handled by a 7090 alone. Sometimes as many as three or four 1401's were used with one 7090, thus improving even further the utilization of the hardware. Although it improved things from the center's point of view, there were drawbacks on the users side. No job, no matter how short, could get back to the user until an entire batch has been processed. This "turnaround" time became a matter of great concern and in some installations often exceeded 24 hrs.

A somewhat closer integration is achieved by using a magnetic drum as the communication device between the two processors, instead of mag tape. The CDC 3600[1] operating system, called Drum Scope, utilizes this technique as does the GE 265,[7] which is composed of a 235 computer and a Data Net 30 I/O multiplexor.

This approach offers two advantages over tape I/O. First the communication medium is considerably faster, and second jobs can, if desired, be processed out of order. That is, there can be a priority system which allows short jobs, for instance, to get through the system without waiting for the long ones. This can, if properly used, reduce the average turnaround time considerably.

Even closer integration can result if both units can address the same high-speed storage. One example of this is the Honeywell 8200,[8] which consists of a H-4200 character processor and a H-1800 central computer. Another example is the CDC 6600,[9,10] which has one central computer and 10 so called peripheral processing units (PPU). All eleven computers can address central store, which may consist of up to a quarter million 60-bit cells, and in addition, each PPU has its own private store of 4096 cells (12 bits per word). A PPU might typically read a program from a card reader and deposit the program in central core. The central processor will translate and/or execute the program, leaving any generated output in central core to be picked up and written out on a line printer (or punch) by whichever one of the PPU's becomes available next.

One gets the picture of the PPU's scuttling around storage doing housekeeping tasks (loading, unloading, cleaning up) while the great "number cruncher" gobbles up programs as fast as they are presented.

The design of the PPU's is quite unusual, and we will discuss it further in Chapter 10.

## HANDSHAKING

When two or more computers are competing for the same equipment—for example the PPU's of the 6600 can each request assignment of any of the I/O devices connected to the system—it is possible for simultaneous requests to be generated. The resolution of such "races" is sometimes called "handshaking," I assume, because it involves a gentleman's agreement between the two machines. The procedure, whether it be implemented in hardware or software, involves something like the following steps:

1. Examine the status of the desired device (perhaps the contents of a "reservation word"). If it is busy, go do something else.
2. If it is free, mark it as reserved. In software this could be done by a "replace add one"* to the reservation word.
3. Now examine the reservation word and see if any other machine grabbed the device since you last tested it. If not, the device is yours —go use it.
4. If yes, remove your reservation (by a "replace subtract one").
5. Wait a few cycles and then go to step 1.

The reason for this complicated way of taking control of a device is that with two independent machines they may both execute step one at the same time and, both finding the device unassigned, think they own it. This is the reason for the check in step three. In step five we wait a few cycles (a different number for each possible competing computer) before trying again. This varying wait breaks the deadlock so the next time through one machine will get in first and win the race.

---

*Question 7.8:* Lay out the replace add one (RAO) and replace subtract one (RSO) instructions for INDIGO.

*Question 7.9:* If the reservation word is kept in main storage that both machines can access, explain how you might program a dual INDIGO to carry out this function. Could you combine steps 1 and 2?

*Question 7.10:* Discuss how these actions might be carried out in hardware.

---

If we wish to designate one of the computers as the "master" we can design a somewhat simpler system. A slave computer desiring the use of device *n*, will put the number of the device in a cell (postbox) unique to

---

*This instruction adds one to the contents of a word and puts the results back in the word and in the accumulator.

that slave, but readable by the master, and then issue an interrupt to the master. Now the master can examine the assignment status of the device at its leisure and either assign it to that slave, or not. No races develop here, because only one machine is doing the assignment, and even simultaneous interrupts by two or more slaves will be resolved by the order in which they are scanned or processed.

In the design of BLUE we saw a primitive type of handshaking involving the TRA line and the *R* line. A much more sophisticated version is to be found in the PDP-11. In the PDP-11 all communication takes place over one bus called the "Unibus." This Unibus constitutes a one-dimensional string of devices connected by pieces of wire (the actual *bus*). The CPU is at one end of the bus and a bus terminator (some resistors) is at the other end. At any instant in time there is one bus master, and the master may be trying to talk with one slave. Usually, but not always, the CPU is the bus master. I/O devices of all sorts are usually acting as slaves, and blocks of memory are always slaves.

Three problems are solved by the PDP-11 unibus control mechanisms:

1. Who is the present bus master.
2. Synchronization of master and slave for data transfer.
3. Deskewing the data and address signals.

A set of signals can become skewed if the physical lines carrying the signals are not identical. Light travels only one foot per nanosecond, and electrical signals on wires may move two or five times more slowly than this. So a set of signals traveling down wires of slightly different length or of different physical characteristics may get out of step with each other, and some may arrive at the destination before the rest. This is called "skew." To deskew a set of signals, we wait after transmitting the signals for a period of time that is great enough so that the slowest pulse will have a chance to catch up with the fastest. Now suppose that the CPU wishes to read a word from memory block *M*. The following set of steps is taken from the *PDP-11 Peripherals Handbook 1975*, pp. 5–14.[11]

Transfer of information:

1. The bus master puts the address and a "request to read" on the address and control lines of the unibus.
2. Each device on the bus receives this information and decides if it pertains to that device. Memory block *M* will recognize its name on the high-order bits of the address lines.
3. After 75 nanoseconds for address deskew plus 75 nanoseconds for device decoding, the master asserts a line called "Master Sync"— provided that the line "Slave Sync" is negated, indicating that the previous transfer is complete.

4. Memory block *M* recognizes its name and sees the Master Sync signal. It gets the requested data from its store (this may take some time—up to a microsecond or more) and puts the data on the Data lines of the Unibus. Then when valid data are on the Data lines, the slave asserts Slave Sync.
5. When the master sees an asserted Slave Sync, it knows that valid data are on the Data lines. The master waits 75 nanoseconds for deskewing and then strobes in the data.
6. The master drops Master Sync.
7. Seventy-five nanoseconds after dropping Master Sync, the master drops the address and control lines. This delay ensures that these lines will not change while Master Sync is asserted and possibly confuse the slave—or some other device.
8. When the slave receives the negation of Master Sync, it removes the data from the Data lines (lets go of its end of the bus) and then drops Slave Sync. This ensures that when Slave Sync drops the entire bus is free, since the master let go of its end of the bus (except for the sync lines) back in step 7.
9. If the master is willing to relinquish control of the bus, it drops Bus Busy. Otherwise it keeps Bus Busy high and goes back to step 1.

This completes a single data transfer from memory to CPU, and shows how deskewing and synchronization are done. Now we must examine how the bus master is determined. Twelve of the Unibus lines are reserved for the priority arbitration operation. There are five bus request lines, five bus grant lines, one selection acknowledge, and one bus busy line.

Arbitration begins when the present bus master negates the selection acknowledge line (SACK).

Arbitration sequence:

1. A device requests mastery of the bus at one of five levels by raising one of the five bus request lines. The level is wired into the device.
2. An arbitration unit, which is active only when SACK is negated, selects the highest request outstanding and asserts the corresponding bus grant line. The device nearest the CPU (along the bus) that is making a request at this level "grabs" the grant off the bus and does not pass it along to devices further downstream.
3. The device acknowledges receipt of the grant by asserting the SACK (selection acknowledge) line. The device then drops the bus request.
4. The arbitrator acknowledges receipt of the assertion of SACK by dropping the bus grant line.
5. The device in question is now the acknowledged "next bus master." As soon as Bus Busy, Bus Grant, and Slave Sync go to zero and are

sensed as such by the next bus master, the next bus master asserts Bus Busy and thus takes over active control of the bus and drops SACK.

6. The bus master does whatever it wants to over the bus.

7. At the completion of the use of the bus, the bus master drops Bus Busy.

Note that we have overlap here of the selection of the "next bus master" (steps 1–4) with the use of the bus by the "present master" (steps 5–7). Thus no apparent time is required by the arbitration unit. Step 6 of course involves all of steps 1–9 of the transfer of information sequence.

The CPU drops Bus Busy at the completion of each instruction so that other devices have a chance to gain control of the bus. Since the CPU always has a request for the bus being sent to the arbitration unit, it gets all cycles that are not otherwise used. Once a device has become a bus master, it may issue an interrupt to the CPU (via the bus) causing transfer to the interrupt handling program.

---

*Question 7.11:* Design circuits that accomplish these sequences for a machine like the PDP-11.

---

One final point should be made about the 11. The high order 4096 words of addressing space are reserved for I/O devices. Each device has one or more registers (typically two) which it uses to hold data and status information. To the device these are its own private registers, but to the CPU these are just more words of memory. It can read or write in the device status register to find out if the device is idle (transfer complete) or to tell the device to issue an interrupt when it goes idle. The CPU can read from the data word of input devices (when the device is idle, indicating that valid data are present) and write in the data buffer of output devices. Block transfer devices like disks and drums have registers to hold main storage addresses and word counts and peripheral addresses. Such devices operate asynchronously doing a complete block transfer by periodically requesting the bus (usually with highest priority) and depositing or reading a word in main store. Only when the block transfer is over will the drum interrupt the CPU to tell it that all is well or that an error has occurred. This form of bus organization does away with the need for any I/O instructions in the CPU.

## SUMMARY

In this chapter we have looked at the problems involved in I/O and in the co-ordination of one machine with another. We have perforce looked into the handling of asynchronous interrupts. Our emphasis has been on hardware approaches to handling these problems. We have ignored, as being beyond the scope of this book, several interesting software techniques for working on the same problems.

## REFERENCES

1. *3600 Computer System Drum Scope Reference Manual.* Palo Alto, Calif., Control Data Corp., 1965.
2. Bell, C. G., Cady, R., McFarland, H., Delagi, B., O'Laughlin, J., Noonan, R., and Wulf, W. "A New Architecture for Minicomputers—the DEC PDP-11." *AFIPS Proc. SJCC* **36,** 657–675 (1970).
3. *PDP-11/05/10/35/40 Processor Handbook.* Maynard, Mass., Digital Equipment Corp. (1973).
4. Brown, D., Eibsen, R., and Thorn, C. "Channel and Direct Device Architecture." *IBM Systems Journal* **11,** 3, 186–200 (1972).
5. *IBM Reference Manual 1401 Data Processing System.* White Plains, N.Y., IBM Corp., 1958.
6. *IBM 7094 Principles of Operation,* Form A22-6703-3. Poughkeepsie, New York, IBM Corp. (1962).
7. *GE-225 System Manual.* Phoenix, Ariz., General Electric Computer Dept., 1961.
8. *Honeywell Series 200, Model 8200 General Systems Description.* Wellesley Hills, Mass., Honeywell Elect. Data Processing, 1965.
9. *Control Data 6400/6500/6600 Reference Manual, Pub. No. 60100000.* Palo Alto, Calif., Control Data Corp., 1966.
10. Thorton, J. E. *Design of a Computer—The Control Data 6600.* Glenview, Ill. Scott Foresman, 1970.
11. *PDP-11 Peripherals Handbook.* Maynard, Mass., Digital Equipment Corp., 1975.

# 8 | OTHER INSTRUCTIONS

*"That we but teach bloody instructions, which, being taught, return to plague their inventor...."*

William Shakespeare

So far we have discussed some two dozen or so instructions that might appear in a machine like INDIGO. It can be shown that a "replace subtract and branch on minus" with two addresses, one for the operand and one for the branch address, is sufficient to duplicate the behavior of a Turing machine, and as is well known, that machine can compute any computable number.[1] Provided we make some of the addressable cells represent input and output devices as is done in the PDP-11, a machine with that single instruction is all powerful—it can do, perhaps a bit more slowly, everything that a most modern and expensive device can perform. Extra instructions then are just gilding on the lily, but that gilt may determine whether or not we can get a program written, debugged, and executed within the decade. Extra instructions are, therefore, added for speed of execution and for the programmer's convenience.

Once one moves out of the class of BLUE, certain groups of instructions are almost always found. These include ADD, SUBTRACT, MULTIPLY (integer and fractional), DIVIDE (the same), FLOATING add, subtract, multiply, divide, AND, OR, NOT, shift left and right, end off or end around, with or without sign extension and in varying amounts up to a full double register length at one time. Jumps on assorted conditions (zero, non-zero, plus, minus) are also included, often for several different registers. So much is reasonably standard. Other groups of instructions are more idiosyncratic, sometimes present, sometimes not.

## BYTE MANIPULATING INSTRUCTIONS

A byte is defined as a collection of bits treated as a unit. Through usage, this word has come to be associated with the size of a character (6 or 8 bits depending on the machine), but this is not necessarily the case.

Many machines include part word instructions in their repertoire. The KDF-9 already mentioned allows third-word instructions to operate on the $Q$-stores (index registers) and half word operations elsewhere.[2] The Univac 1108 allows full-, half-, third-, and quarter-word arithmetic operation. Most machines permit address substitution in several different forms in which the address field of a storage cell can be replaced or modified without changing the other contents of cell.

The IBM 1620[3] is a character-oriented machine, as opposed to BLUE which is said to be word oriented. A field storing, say a number, is pointed at by giving the address of its least significant character (it is a decimal machine) and the left-hand end of the field is defined to be at the first "record mark." (A special character.) Addition of two fields is character serial and proceeds until one or the other field runs out of characters to be processed.

Among the machines which allow true variable-length byte operations, the CDC-3600 is notable.[4] It has three byte-oriented instructions which give it great power for part word and character manipulation. The first two of these are "load byte" and "store byte."

A load byte instruction (LBYT) is a 48-bit instruction and occupies a whole word. It is written in assembly code as follows:

$$\text{LBYT}, R_n, E, D, C \qquad m,b,v$$

where

$R_n$–specifies the position in the $A$ or $Q$* register of the right-most bit of the byte (after it gets loaded). Bits are numbered right to left in the 3600.

$E$–specifies the size of the byte.

$D$–specifies left indexing or right indexing or no indexing.

$C$–if equal to ONE, specifies that the other parts of the destination register ($A$ or $Q$) should be cleared to zero.

$m,b$–specify the effective address of the cell in memory from which the byte should be taken $M = m + (B^b)$.

$v$–specifies the index register which holds the position in the word $M$ from which the byte should be taken.

---

*The $Q$ register is a 48 bit register and in certain instructions it is treated as an extension of the $A$ register. At other times it holds the quotient of a division, hence the name.

If no indexing is specified, the byte designated by the combination of $m,b$ and the contents of $v$ is loaded into the $A$ or $Q$ register at the position indicated by $R_n$ with or without clearing the remainder of the register, and a full exit (to the next instruction pair) is taken. If right indexing is specified ($D=$ "$RI$"), then after loading the byte as described above the number specified by $E$ (the size of the byte) is subtracted from the contents of index register $v$

$$(B^v) - E \rightarrow B^v$$

so that $v$ now points to the next rightward byte of $M$. If *after* modification the contents of $v$ is still greater than or equal to zero, a skip exit is taken (one is added to the contents of the program counter), skipping over the next instruction pair and going on with the rest of the program. If, however, the contents of $v$ are negative, a normal exit is taken to execute the next instruction pair. This exit will be taken after all the bytes in the word $M$ have been loaded. Thus, this immediately following instruction pair can be used to set-up for the next word and reset $v$ to its initial left-most value.

```
ENI        initial, v
INI        1,b
```

Now with right indexing specified and, if the byte size is a sub-multiple of 48 (1,2,3,4,6,8,12,16,24), successive executions of the following short program:

```
LBYT, AO, 8, RI, CL        ARRAY 1,2
ENI        42,2
INI        1,1
```

will get successive (left to right) eight-bit bytes from a vector called ARRAY, which may if desired extend across many words and contain many, many bytes. A store byte (SBYT) works the same way, except that the information is stored rather than loaded.

---

*Question 8.1:* Suppose left indexing is specified (the next byte will be taken from the left of the present one), indicate what changes must take place in the LBYT instruction and what the following instruction pair should look like.

*Question 8.2:* Discuss how you might add such an instruction to our 24 bit word INDIGO. Hint: consider the possibility of "dedicating" some index registers, i.e., make their names implicit in the instruction.

---

The third byte oriented instruction in the 3600 is called SCAN and is written, in assembly language, as:

$$\text{SCAN, } Q_n, E, K \qquad m, b, v$$

where

    $n$–is the rightmost bit of the byte in $Q$ being searched for.

    $E$–is the size of the byte.

    $K$–is the condition to be satisfied.

  $m, b$–specify the effective address $M$.

    $v$–specifies the position in $M$ of the byte now being compared.

Right indexing (scan from left to right) is implied. The number of bytes to be compared is loaded into the $A$ register before executing the scan. $E$ must be a sub-multiple of 48 and the initial contents of $v$ must be $48 - e$. The condition to be met: "$K$," may be equal, greater than, less than, not equal, not less than, or not greater than. Execution proceeds as shown in Fig. 8.1.

## SEARCH INSTRUCTIONS

The character scanning instruction on the 3600 has just been discussed. It is a search for a byte bearing a certain relation to a given byte. A general search of arrays of whole words is required many times in the course of computation—searching symbol tables is but one example, albeit ubiquitous. We turn again to the 3600 for examples of powerful, well thought out instructions. There are four simple searches and one complicated one.

The simple searches are called "equality," "masked equality," "threshold," and "masked threshold." In an equality search (EQS), the search is successful (the searching condition met) if an item is found that matches the comparand exactly in all 48 bit positions. A masked equality search (MEQ) compares the items with the comparand only where the mask has ones. A threshold search looks for an item greater than the comparand, and a masked threshold search can best be explained as follows:
An item $I$ is "masked greater" than the comparand if there exists a bit $j$ such that

$$I_j = 1 \text{ and } c_j = 0 \text{ and } m_j = 1$$

and there is no bit $K$ to the left of $j$ such that

$$I_k = 1 \text{ and } c_k = 0 \text{ and } m_k = 1.$$

---

*Question 8.3:* Design a circuit to perform a bit parallel masked threshold comparison.

---

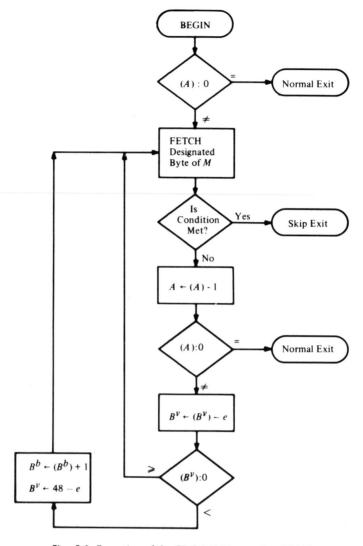

Fig. 8.1 Execution of the CDC-3600 instruction SCAN.

The item being searched for is placed in the $A$ register and the mask, if any, in the $Q$. The number of items to be examined is entered into an index register. The instruction itself is placed in a left half word. (The 3600 has many 24-bit instructions which can be, and are, packed two to a word—the left half being executed first and then the right half.) The search begins at the top end of the array and continues back down toward the starting address until either the condition is met or else the entire array has been scanned and no element meeting the condition has been found. In the latter case, the right half instruction is executed, which is usually a jump to a failure routine. This is called a "half-exit." If, on the other hand, the condition is met, a "full exit" is taken, skipping over the right half of this instruction pair. When a full exit is taken, the index register used (see below) will point to the element in the array that met the condition. Suppose, for example, we wish to search a table for an occurrence of the number 1234 and there are 100 elements in the table. The following short program accomplishes this handily:

| | | |
|---|---|---|
| ENA | 1234 | Enter the comparand. |
| ENI | 100, 5 | Set the number of elements in index |
| +EQS TABLE, 5 | | plus forces instruction to left half— EQS is an equality search. The candidate must match the contents of $A$ exactly. |
| JMP FAIL | | Half exit, we didn't find any. |
| FOUND | | We have found such an element. Go on with main program. |

The fifth search instruction uses three dedicated index registers. $B_1$ contains the word count, the number of items to be examined. $B_2$ holds the operand address modifier (the amount to be added to the address field), and $B_3$ contains the increment (the quantity that will be added to $B_2$ before examining the next element). Thus by putting $n$ in $B_3$, we examine every $n$th element and, if the number $n$ is positive, we scan upwards in core—if it is negative, we scan downwards. Searches may be made for equal the contents of $A$, masked equality, within limits (less than or equal to $A$ and greater than $Q$, and search magnitude within limits.

## PUSHDOWN STACKS

As was indicated previously, the English Electric KDF9[2] and the Burroughs B-5500[5] are machines organized around pushdown accumulators. Let us examine the KDF-9 in some detail, since descriptions of the Burrough's machines are more readily available, at least in this country.

The KDF-9 has a maximum of 32,768 words of 48 bits each in its main store. It has 16 $Q$-stores that were discussed in Chapter 6. It has a pushdown accumulator capable of holding 16 words and a 16-cell pushdown program counter. Since most arithmetic and logical instructions are zero addressed, a variable-length instruction format is employed where an instruction is composed of one or more "syllables" of 8 bits each. The instruction fetch is arranged to make sure that there are always at least three syllables available for decoding. Word boundaries are ignored within an instruction.

FETCH and STORE are three syllable instructions that perform "preserve the accumulator and copy from main store" and "write to main store and pop up the accumulator." Either may be indexed with one $Q$ store or doubly indexed using two.

Certain instructions refer to operations on the accumulator. ERASE is a pop up of the accumulator. ZERO causes a pushdown and the entry of a word of all zeros. DUP causes a pushdown, leaving a copy of the old head in the new head. DUPD causes the accumulator to be pushed down twice and the old contents of the top *two* cells to be reproduced in cells 3 and 4. REV interchanges the contents of the top two cells. REVD exchanges cells 1 and 3 and cells 2 and 4. PERM performs a cyclic shift of the top three cells (1)→3, (2)→1, and (3)→2. CAB is like PERM, but in the opposite direction.

Logical and arithmetic operations use the contents of cells 1 and 2 of the accumulator for operands and put the result in 1, popping up the rest of the accumulator one space to fill the now empty cell 2. For an example see Fig. 8.2. A set of conditional jumps on $A$ are available. Jump if contents of cell 1 are zero, not zero, greater than zero, not less than zero, less than zero, and not greater than zero. Two comparison jumps can also be used. Jump if (1)≠(2) (the first two cells differ), and jump if (1)=(2) (the first two cells are the same).

The pushdown program counter is used to facilitate subroutine jumps. "*JS r*" causes the program counter to be pushed down one and the address $r$ to be placed in the top cell,

$$PC \curvearrowleft —r$$

Since the next instruction is found at the address pointed at by the program counter's top cell, this effectively transfers control to the subroutine stored at $r$. The address of the instruction following the *JS* is preserved in the pushdown stack so that the subroutine can return to the calling program merely by popping up the program counter.

| *Before* | *After an* ADD |
|---|---|
| 1. 17 | 1. 53 |
| 2. 36 | 2. 12 |
| 3. 12 | 3. 18 |
| 4. 18 | 4. * |
| 5. * | 5. |

Fig. 8.2  An ADD instruction in the KDF.9.

This pushdown program counter together with the pushdown accumulator makes the use of recursive functions most attractive.  The only problem with them is that the pushdown stacks are 16 levels deep and it is easy to fill them up, thus preventing further recursion.  As a consequence, most compilers for the KDF-9 do not permit user programs to make use of these facilities for recursion, but force them to use standard ALGOL like methods.  The B-5500, on the other hand, has only two hardware registers in its accumulator, the rest of the stack being stored in reserved areas in main memory.  Here the user is permitted, even encouraged, to recurse with all the advantages that are obtained therefrom.

## MICROPROGRAMMING

Let us suppose that we own a computer (machine $A$) but wish instead that we had a different computer (machine $B$).  One thing to do would be to write a program for machine $A$ that would take as its input machine language instructions for machine $B$ and which would behave just as machine $B$ would except perhaps that it would be a little slower.  Such a program would be called an interpreter, and machine $A$ would be said to be "emulating" machine $B$.  If we further suppose that $A$ is especially well adapted to picking apart the machine language instructions of other machines, and if it is a fast machine and has a fast private store to hold the interpreter, we say that machine $A$ is an "inner computer" and that it is "microprogrammed" to behave like $B$.  The interpreter program is now called "*firmware*" to indicate that it is somewhere between *soft-* and *hard*ware.

Three separate meanings are attached to the word microprogramming.[6-12] None of them refer to the art of writing code for very small (one-chip) computers, sometimes called microcomputers or microprocessors.  The word "microprogramming" was coined by Maurice Wilkes[10] in the early fifties, and denotes an organized (as opposed to haphazard) method of designing the logic of a central processor.  His basic idea, if not the specific implementation, has become so much a part of the design process that the word is no longer used in this sense.

The second sense of the word is usually indicated with the adjective "vertical" preceding it.  Vertical microprogramming is much as we described above: a very fast, relatively simple, but more or less conventional inner computer (host machine) is programmed to behave like a slower, more complex, more desirable machine (the target machine).  The instruction set of the host is chosen to make decoding of target macroinstructions easy.  For example, a "branch on register field" is often included that lets the host pick off the macro op-code, the macro modifier field, and the macro address field conveniently.  Features of the macro machine such as registers are usually "faked" by using read/write locations of the micro store.

Horizontal microprogramming is the third use of the word. Here each microinstruction is typically very wide, up to 100 or more bits. Each bit controls the opening of one gate or one set of gates in the macro machine. These gates actually exist and are not faked as in vertical microprogramming. As an example of a horizontally microprogrammed machine, let us go to the ridiculous extreme of microprogramming BLUE on a hypothetical host of our own design. To continue with our Rainbow series, we will name it GREEN.

### Microprogrammed Version of BLUE

The version of BLUE that we presented previously was designed in a piece-meal fashion, one part at a time. It is possible to take a more organized approach to hardware design called "microprogramming." So that the reader may gain some insight into this process, we will now design a micropro-grammed machine and then program it to "simulate" (behave the same as) BLUE.

Our design will consist of an inner machine or micro machine called GREEN that draws one word at a time from a read only memory (ROM). Each such word is a microinstruction. Surrounding the inner machine there is a set of registers, an arithmetic logic unit (ALU), a bus connecting these registers, a core memory, and some input/output equipment. (See Fig. 8.3.)

The microinstructions control these surrounding units. The inner machine has a very fast cycle time—perhaps 50 nanoseconds—to read up a new micro-instruction. Then it waits 50 nanoseconds while the microinstruction is "executed" by being broadcast to the outer machine. After this a new micro-instruction is fetched up, and the process is repeated ad infinitum. As long as the computer is turned on, the inner machine buzzes along running through 10 million microinstructions per second.

Let us look first at the way in which the next microinstruction is selected. There are three ways that this may happen. The hardware required is shown in Fig. 8.4.

*Master Reset*  If the console button labeled master reset is pressed, the inner computer takes its next instruction from ROM location zero. This allows the operator to get the inner machine into a known state.

*Branch on Op Code*  The op-code field of the macro computer's instruc-tion register is used to select the location from which the next microinstruc-tion will be drawn. If the macro computer has $N$ different instructions numbered 0 through $N - 1$, then locations 0 through $N - 1$ of the inner com-puter's ROM are reserved for jumps to the $N$ micro-routines which will carry out the macroinstructions.

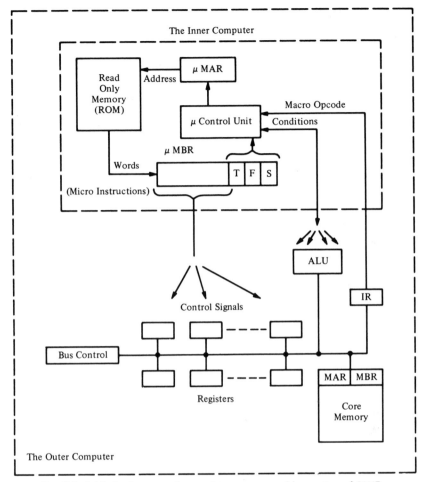

Fig. 8.3 A block diagram of our microprogrammable version of BLUE.

*Test Condition*  One of the fields of each microinstruction specifies a condition to be tested. If the condition is *false*, the next microinstruction is taken from the location specified in the "fail" field of the microinstruction. If the condition is *true*, the "success" field is used to indicate the next microinstruction location. These three fields are part of every microinstruction so that each microinstruction can serve as a conditional jump. Since both paths from the condition are specified by the success and fail fields, there is no need for a micro program counter.

Details of the decoding of the remaining fields of a microinstruction are

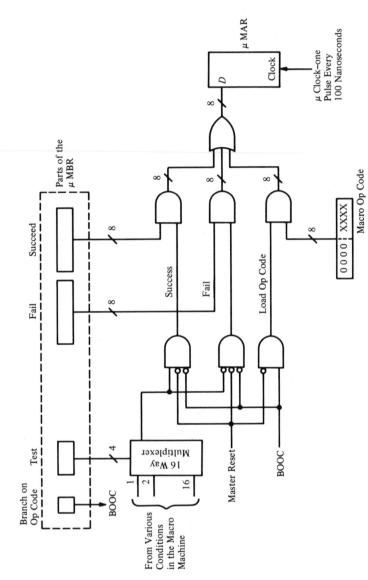

Fig. 8.4 Circuits for controlling the loading of the micromemory address register (μMAR).

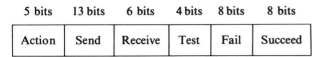

| 5 bits | 13 bits | 6 bits | 4 bits | 8 bits | 8 bits |
|--------|---------|---------|--------|--------|---------|
| Action | Send | Receive | Test | Fail | Succeed |

*Actions* perform some of the following actions:
       Initiate read cycle of core
       Initiate write cycle of core
       Set TRA flip-flop
       Clear TRA flip-flop
       Copy op-code (of BLUE instruction) to $\mu$ MAR

*Send* (gate some of the following registers onto BLUE's bus):
       Accumulator ACC
       Memory Buffer Register MBR
       Program Counter PC
       Switch Register SR
       Plus one +1
       Instruction Register Address-field AD
       Data Input Lines DIL
       sum ⎤
       or   ⎥
       xor ⎬ *ALU outputs*
       and ⎥
       $2*Z$ ⎥
       $\bar{Z}$ ⎦

*Receive* (gate some of the following off BLUE's bus):
       Accumulator ACC
       Memory Buffer Register MBR
       Program Counter PC
       $Z$ Register
       Macro instruction register
       $Y$ Register
       Memory Address Register MAR

*Test* (If the condition specified is met, take the next microinstruction from the location specified by "*succeed*." Else from "*fail*."):

| | |
|---|---|
| 0. no test | 6. Load PC button pressed |
| 1. $A_{15} = 1$ (accumulator is negative) | 7. Examine button pressed |
| 2. $R = 1$ (I/O device is ready) | 8. Deposit button pressed |
| 3. Memory is Free | 9. Overflow |
| 4. Stop button pressed | 10–15. Undefined |
| 5. Start button pressed | |

Fig. 8.5 Decoding of the microinstruction register.

shown in Fig. 8.5. The *action* field starts a read or restore core memory cycle, sets or clears the TRA flip-flop, or specifies a branch on macro op-code. The *send* field tells what register to gate onto the bus, and the *receive* field tells what register (or registers) to load from the bus. Note that we have one bit for each possible source and destination. If we wanted to send only one register at a time, we could have encoded these 13 bits onto 4 bits and used an external decoder to select which register should be sent. For simplicity, but not necessarily economy, we have made each possible sender independent.  For the receivers there are a couple of times when it is convenient to load two registers with the same data.  That requires either a separate bit for each register (in the general case) or if we know in advance what these cases are (and there are not too many of them), we encode "double loads" as further possible destinations in addition to the full set of single loads.

### Simulation of BLUE

The simulation of BLUE begins with a read next instruction (RNI) sequence which takes the place of the fetch cycle.  This is shown in Fig. 8.6. Its actions are as follows:

RNI:    copy the contents of the program counter into the memory address register and into $Z$.  If the stop button has been pressed, go to HALT.  Otherwise go to RNI1.

RNI1: initiate the core read cycle and send plus one to the $Y$ register.

RNI2: do nothing while the accumulator is forming the sum of (PC) + 1.

RNI3: send the incremented value for the PC back to the PC.

RNI4: when the core memory finishes the read cycle and loads the next macroinstruction into the MBR, go to RNI5.  We will assume that the MBR is automatically loaded from memory without our having to strobe it at the correct time.

RNI5: begin the write cycle to restore the core memory, and load the IR from the MBR.

RNI6: send the macro op-code (cccc) to the $\mu$MAR so the next microinstruction will be taken from ROM location cccc.

| $\mu$ location name | action | send | receive | test | fail | succeed |
|:---:|:---:|:---:|:---:|:---:|:---:|:---:|
| RNI: | — | PC | MAR,$Z$ | Stop | RNI 1 | HALT |
| RNI 1: | Read | +1 | $Y$ | — | RNI 2 | — |
| RNI 2: | — | — | — | — | RNI 3 | — |
| RNI 3: | — | sum | PC | Free | RNI 4 | RNI 5 |
| RNI 4: | — | — | — | Free | RNI 4 | RNI 5 |
| RNI 5: | Write | MBR | IR | — | RNI 6 | — |
| RNI 6: | branch on op-code | — | — | — | — | — |
| HALT: | Clear TRA | — | — | Start | H 1 | RNI |
| H 1: | — | — | — | Examine | H 2 | EXAM |
| H 2: | — | — | — | Deposit | H 3 | DEPOS |
| H 3: | — | — | — | load Pc | HALT | LPC |

Fig. 8.6 The read next instruction sequence for micro BLUE.

| $\mu$ location name | action | send | receive | test | fail | succeed |
|---|---|---|---|---|---|---|
| EXA: | Read | Pc | MAR,$Z$ | — | E 1 | — |
| E 1: | — | +1 | $Y$ | — | E 2 | — |
| E 2: | — | — | — | — | E 3 | — |
| E 3: | — | sum | PC | Free | E 4 | E 5 |
| E 4: | — | — | — | Free | E 4 | E 5 |
| E 5: | Write | MBR | IR | — | E 6 | — |
| E 6: | — | — | — | Examine | H 2 | E 6 |
| DEP: | Read | PC | MAR,$Z$ | — | D 1 | — |
| D 1: | — | +1 | $Y$ | — | D 2 | — |
| D 2: | — | — | — | — | D 3 | — |
| D 3: | — | sum | PC | Free | D 4 | D 5 |
| D 4: | — | — | — | Free | D 4 | D 5 |
| D 5: | Write | SR | MBR | — | D 6 | — |
| D 6: | — | — | — | Deposit | H 3 | D 6 |
| LPC: | — | SR | PC | — | L 1 | — |
| L 1: | — | — | — | load PC | HALT | L 1 |

Fig. 8.7 The console test sequences for micro BLUE.

At this point we branch off to start executing the macroinstruction. If the stop button was pushed in step RNI, we go to the halt routine where we test for a start button, a load PC, an examine, or a deposit button. These routines are shown in Fig. 8.7. When we finally detect a start signal, we go back to RNI (in case the PC was changed) and proceed to read up the next macroinstruction.

In the halt sequence (Fig. 8.6) we have a routine that is entered when the examine button is pressed. We fetch up from core the contents of the cell pointed at by the PC and display it in the instruction register. Then we idle (in microinstruction E6) until the examine button is released, at which point we go to test the deposit button. The deposit and load PC routines are similar.

Figure 8.8 shows the first 16 locations of $\mu$ store (ROM). In this figure we have shown nothing but jumps to the various routines for simulating BLUE's instructions. This is so the routines will appear as logical units. In actual practice one would store the first instruction of each routine in this transfer vector in order to save time and space.

Figure 8.9 shows nine non-memory referencing instruction sequences. (The HALT instruction was described in Fig. 8.6.) First of all we have NOP where the micro computer loops until the macro memory becomes not busy. This allows us to put on slow or fast core memory, as our economics may dictate, without reprogramming. In a real sense this makes the macro computer become asynchronous. This NOP loop is used by all the other instruc-

| $\mu$ location name | action | send | receive | test | fail | succeed |
|---|---|---|---|---|---|---|
| 0 | — | — | — | — | HALT | — |
| 1 | — | — | — | — | ADD | — |
| 2 | — | — | — | — | XOR | — |
| 3 | — | — | — | — | AND | — |
| 4 | — | — | — | — | IOR | — |
| 5 | — | — | — | — | NOT | — |
| 6 | — | — | — | — | LDA | — |
| 7 | — | — | — | — | STA | — |
| 8 | — | — | — | — | SRJ | — |
| 9 | — | — | — | — | JMA | — |
| 10 | — | — | — | — | JMP | — |
| 11 | — | — | — | — | INP | — |
| 12 | — | — | — | — | OUT | — |
| 13 | — | — | — | — | RAL | — |
| 14 | — | — | — | — | CSA | — |
| 15 | — | — | — | — | NOP | — |

Fig. 8.8 The first 16 cells of the ROM contain simple jumps to the beginning of the routines that simulate the 16 instructions of BLUE.

| $\mu$ location | action | send | receive | test | fail | succeed |
|---|---|---|---|---|---|---|
| NOP: | — | — | — | Free | NOP | RNI |
| CSA: | — | SR | $A$ | Free | NOP | RNI |
| RAL: | — | $A$ | $Z$ | — | RAL 1 | — |
| RAL I: | — | two $Z$ | $A$ | Free | NOP | RNI |
| JMP: | — | IR | PC | Free | NOP | RNI |
| JMA: | — | — | — | $A_{15}$ | NOP | JMP |
| SRJ: | — | PC | $A$ | — | JMP | — |
| NOT: | — | $A$ | $Z$ | — | NOT 1 | |
| NOT 1: | — | Zbar | $A$ | Free | NOP | RNI |
| INP: | Set TRA | — | — | Ready | INP | INP 1 |
| INP 1: | | data input | $A$ | — | INP 2 | — |
| INP 2: | Clear TRA | — | — | Free | NOP | RNI |
| OUT: | Set TRA | — | — | Ready | OUT | OUT 1 |
| OUT 1: | Clear TRA | | | Free | NOP | RNI |

Fig. 8.9 Nine instruction sequences that do not reference memory.

tion sequences to ensure that the memory is ready to do another cycle before we go to the RNI sequence.

Copy Switches to $A$ (CSA) does the transfer from the switch register to $A$ and then if the memory is free goes directly to RNI. Otherwise it goes to the NOP loop. Rotate $A$ Left, Jump, Jump on Minus $A$, Subroutine Return Jump and NOP are all similar enough to CSA to require no further discussion.

Input (INP) sets TRA and loops here in INP until the I/O device sends back a ready signal ($R = 1$). Then it transfers the contents of the data input lines to the accumulator, clears TRA and loops until core memory is free. Output is quite the same except that since the data output lines are always energized from the accumulator, no transfer of data is necessary.

Figure 8.10 shows some of the memory referencing instructions. Load Accumulator idles in LDA until the core memory becomes free. This could

| $\mu$ location | action | send | receive | test | fail | succeed |
|---|---|---|---|---|---|---|
| LDA: | — | — | — | Free | LDA | LDA 1 |
| LDA 1: | — | IR | MAR | — | LDA 2 | — |
| LDA 2: | Read | — | — | — | LDA 3 | — |
| LDA 3: | — | — | — | Free | LDA 3 | LDA 4 |
| LDA 4: | Write | MBR | $A$ | Free | NOP | RNI |
| STA: | — | — | — | Free | STA | STA 1 |
| STA 1: | — | IR | MAR | — | STA 2 | — |
| STA 2: | Read | — | — | — | STA 3 | — |
| STA 3: | — | — | — | Free | STA 3 | STA 4 |
| STA 4: | — | $A$ | MBR | — | STA 5 | — |
| STA 5: | Write | — | — | Free | NOP | RNI |
| ADD: | — | — | — | Free | ADD | ADD 1 |
| ADD 1: | — | IR | MAR | — | ADD 2 | — |
| ADD 2: | Read | $A$ | Z | — | ADD 3 | — |
| ADD 3: | — | — | — | Free | ADD 3 | ADD 4 |
| ADD 4: | Write | MBR | Y | — | ADD 5 | — |
| ADD 5: | — | — | — | — | ADD 6 | — |
| ADD 6: | — | sum | $A$ | Free | NOP | RNI |
| IOR: | — | — | — | Free | IOR | IOR 1 |
| IOR 1: | — | IR | MAR | — | IOR 2 | — |
| IOR 2: | Read | $A$ | Z | — | IOR 3 | — |
| IOR 3: | — | — | — | Free | IOR 3 | IOR 4 |
| IOR 4: | Write | MBR | Y | — | IOR 5 | — |
| IOR 5: | — | OR | $A$ | Free | NOP | RNI |

Fig. 8.10 Four memory referencing instructions of micro BLUE.

have been done conveniently in location 6, but was put here for ease of study. It then begins a read cycle and when that is complete starts the write cycle, loads the accumulator from the MBR and loops (at NOP) until the rewrite is over. Store Accumulator (STA) is comparable except that the data transfer is from the $A$ register to the MBR instead of the other way around.

ADD includes the usual one cycle "do nothing" microinstruction (ADD 5) to allow the sum to develop in the ALU. IOR is straightforward and is a prototype for the XOR and the AND instructions which are identical except for the last step in which they send the "xor" and the "and" outputs of the ALU instead of the "or" output.

### Extensions to Micro BLUE

Now that we have a nice inner computer hidden inside BLUE, there are a number of other ways we could use it. For openers we could give BLUE a completely different op code set. Perhaps we might want to add a subtract operation to the ALU, but even without that we could have controlled left or right shifts, or end off left shifts, or a twos complement of the accumulator or a replace add one instruction $((xxxx) + 1 \rightarrow xxxx$ and the Acc.) or even a fixed point multiply or divide.

---

*Question 8.4:* Assuming that op-code numbers are available for these instructions, write $\mu$-programs for them.

---

Again we might take all the non-memory referencing instructions and code them onto one op-code number with the low-order bits of the address field serving to distinguish them from each other.

---

*Question 8.5:* Try it. Hint: the contents of the IR could be shifted if you found it useful.

---

Still further we could add a macroinstruction that would jump on zero accumulator.

Many other variations could be dreamed up. But the inner computer we have described here is not as versatile as we might like if we wanted to simulate a machine that was completely different from BLUE. Too many short cuts have been taken in the design because we knew it was intended to simulate BLUE. For example, we could have to make fundamental changes if we wanted to add more macro registers or to have, say, a five bit op-code field. It seems that this is always true of microprogrammed machines.

But nonetheless, microprogramming is more organized than random logic, and it is surely more flexible than random logic (we change the contents of the ROM) even if it is not infinitely flexible.

### Firmware versus Hardware

Given that you have decided to develop a microprogrammed machine, you must make choices about whether to implement a particular facet of the machine in hardware or in firmware. I believe that the best practice is to try to fit each new facet you consider into firmware first. This may require minor changes to the inner machine if that is not yet committed to production. Only after you have tried to do it via firmware and you find out that a large amount of ROM is required or that the resulting operation is much too slow for the intended environment, should you consider adding extra peripheral hardware. Even at this point add external hardware like salt—a little bit at a time. The initial tendency is to say, "Ah yes, very nice," and then turn one's back on the micro machine and smother it with external gates, levers, wheels, and flashing lights.

These same remarks apply to the design of a system incorporating a microprocessor (see the next chapter). Remember, it's only CPU time you are spending (plus program storage space of course) and it's complexity, rigidity, cost, and unreliability that you are avoiding.

## SUMMARY

In this chapter we have looked at byte manipulating instructions, search instructions, the instruction set of a zero address machine, and that of a microprogrammed machine. Several hundred different machines have been designed to date. To be complete, this chapter should look at all of them. Instead we have selected only a few that seem to demonstrate interesting variations from the mainstream of computer design.

## REFERENCES

1. Turing, A. M. "On Computable numbers, with an Application to the Entscheidungs Problem." *Proc. London Math. Soc. Ser 2,* **42,** 230–265 (1936–1937).
2. *KDF-9 Programming Manual.* Kidsgrove, England, English Electric-Leo Computers Ltd., 1963.
3. *IBM Reference Manual 1620 Data Processing System.* White Plains, N.Y., IBM Corp., 1960.
4. *CDC-3600 Computer System Reference Manual.* St. Paul, Minn., Control Data Corp., 1966.
5. *Burroughs B-5500 Information Processing Systems Reference Manual.* Detroit, Michigan, Burroughs Corp., 1964.

6. Chu, Y. *Computer Organization and Microprogramming*. Englewood Cliffs, N.J., Prentice-Hall, 1972.
7. Davies, P. M. "Readings in Microprogramming." *IBM Systems Journal* **11**, 1, 16–41 (1972).
8. Fuller, S. H., Lesser, V. R., Bell, C. G., and Kaman, C. "Microprogramming and Its Relationship to Emulation and Technology." *Proc. 7th Workshop on Microprogramming*, 151–159 (Oct. 1974).
9. Husson, S. S. *Microprogramming: Principles and Practices*. Englewood Cliffs, N.J., Prentice-Hall, 1970.
10. Rosin, R. F. "The Significance of Microprogramming." *SIGMICRO Newsletter* **4**, 4, 24–39 (Jan. 1974).
11. IEEE Computer Society. *IEEE Transactions on Computers* **C-23**, 7 (July 1974). Special issue on Microprogramming.
12. Wilkes, M. V., and Stringer, J. B. "Microprogramming and the Design of Control Circuits in an Electronic Computer." *Proc. of Cambridge Philosophical Society* Pt. 2, **49,** 230–238 (April 1953).

# 9 | THE MICRO COMPUTER

*"When Gulliver awoke . . ."*
*—Jonathan Swift*

Probably the most exciting architectural event of the seventies has been the introduction of the micro computer.[1-7] The long awaited Large Scale Integration (LSI) has finally borne fruit, and one can now buy a CPU capable of executing 40 or 50 instructions, a 256 bit Random Access Memory (RAM), a 6048 bit Read Only Memory (ROM), 22 output lines, and 8 input lines all on a single 40 pin chip for $9.98 (in quantities of 10,000 or more).

It is called an S9209 and is made by American Microsystems Incorporated. It is not unique, although it has the lowest quoted price for a complete computer as of 1976. Starting in 1971 or 1972 Intel began delivery of the MCS-4004, a four bit micro computer requiring three chips for a minimum system. This was rapidly followed by the 8008, an eight bit system and the 8080, a faster eight bit system. Motorola introduced the M-6800, RCA the COSMAC, Western Digital the LSI-11 version of the PDP-11, and so on and on. Today there are several dozen micro computer systems available ranging in price from $10 to a couple of hundred dollars and in power and performance from virtually nil to thoroughly respectable, with price and performance not highly correlated.

This is exciting for a number of reasons. First of all, we can now consider putting a computer in a wristwatch or a hand-held calculator without its (a) weighing 200 pounds or (b) costing all outdoors. We can put a computer in a washing machine to control and select and time the various operations; in an alarm clock to wake us up at a different time each day of the week; in a calendar to keep track of leap year, the phase of the moon, movable feast days and birthdays and engagements; in a TV set to aid in band-width compression by keeping track of the changes from frame-to-frame rather than retransmitting the background 30 times per second; and in home entertainment games of ever increasing complexity and subtlety. How about a fourth for bridge? The limits are in our imaginations, no longer in the technology.

Second, this new device means we must reexamine our traditional (for the last 25 years) approach to computers as items of awe and (almost) worship. When a CPU costs less than a good meal, who gets concerned about CPU utilization? So it does sit there idle three quarters of the time. Who could care? Present-day time-sharing computers may cost a couple of million dollars and support perhaps 100 terminals. Two million divided by 100 is twenty thousand dollars per port. Let's see: $10 for a CPU, $500 for a teletype, . . .

Third, the advent of cheap processors means that really powerful systems with distributed logic such as STARAN or Illiac IV become practical. The Cray 1 computer can execute a new instruction every 12½ nanoseconds or 80 MIPS (million instructions per second). It costs on the order of $8 million, or 10 instructions per second per dollar. An S9209 can execute an instruction every 10 to 20 microseconds or .05 MIPS. That is 5000 instructions per second per dollar. Certainly there are unsolved problems in getting an assemblage of 800,000 microcomputers working intelligently on the same program. But after all, that is what computer architects are for, isn't it?

Finally, introduction of these devices means that universities can get back into the architecture business. For the last 20 years, with one or two federally funded exceptions, little realized computer architecture has been done at universities. Computer science departments have wandered off into theory, and industry has learned to ignore their writings and their graduates. Now, when we can give a graduate student, or even an undergraduate, a $100-handful of chips and say "go design your own computer," we may begin to turn out useful papers and, would you believe it, useful graduates.

This chapter will therefore concern itself with what has been called the "Little League" of computing. We will discuss three systems, AMI-S-9209, Intel-8080, and the Signetics 2650. In one book, let alone one chapter, we cannot present a great deal of detail about three different machines. But we will try to hit the highlights if not all the available options.

## AMI-9209

American Microsystems Incorporated is offering the 9209 for $9.98 apiece in quantities of 10,000. This machine gives every appearance of having been designed either by amateurs or by people who have never written a pro-

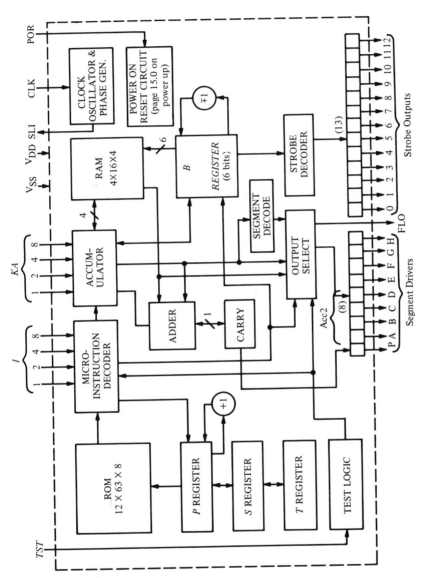

Fig. 9.1 9209 MPC general block diagram.

gram. It has two accumulators, a 4-bit ALU and its general architecture is shown in Fig. 9.1. The system's on-board clock produces seven minor cycles each of approximately 2 microseconds in length. Minor cycles 1 and 2 are used to fetch and decode the next instruction; minor cycle 3 is used to "pre-charge" the bus (this effectively gets the memory ready to do a read). In minor cycles 4 and 5 data are fetched from the RAM, and overlapping this fetch in cycles 5 and 6 we execute the instruction. During cycle 6 we pre-charge the bus to do the next instruction read, and minor cycle 7 is a wait cycle. Cycle 7 is used only to "provide a gap between cycles one and six." No indication is given of why minor cycle 7 exists at all.

Programs reside in the ROM, which is divided into 12 pages of 63 eight bit words. (It is not clear which address is nonexistent or what happens if an errant programmer invokes it.) Page name is contained in the 4 high-order bits of the $P$ (program counter) register and line number in the low order 6 bits. Pages 0 and 1 are used to hold commonly called subroutines called from the other ten pages. The remaining pages are numbered 2, 3, 4, 8, 9, 10, 11, 12, 14, 15 for reasons known only to the designers. What their prejudice is against the numbers 5, 6, and 7 escapes me completely. The program counter is 10 bits long [4 in $P$-upper ($PU$) and 6 in $P$-lower ($PL$)]. Associated with the PC are two other 10 bit registers called $S$ and $T$ (also divided into two parts each— $SU$, $SL$ and $TU$ and $TL$). These registers interact in a complicated fashion when the "transfer," "return," and "set $S$ register" instructions are executed.

Basically, $P$, $S$, and $T$ form a three-deep pushdown stack. The SSR $X$ instruction inserts the number $X$ into $SU$. This sets up the page number for a jump instruction. The RET instruction pops the stack [$(S) \rightarrow P$, $(T) \rightarrow S$]. This is the return from subroutine instruction and does just what might be expected of it. RET has two options: NS—no skip which behaves as above and S—skip which increments $P$ by one *after* the return in order to skip the first instruction following the return jump.

The transfer instruction has two versions which are called TRA0 and TRA1. First of all, we must remember that we are dealing with a machine with an 8 bit (2 four bit words) instruction and a 10 bit program counter. This makes for complications, because it is rather hard to change half the program counter at a time and still be around to change the other half. So an ordinary jump must consist of two instructions, the first to set up a new page address in $SU$ and the second to give a line number and cause the contents of $SU$ to go to $PU$. Their sequence, not necessarily one right after the other, is:

SSR    $X$
TRA1    $Y$

which causes a jump to line $y$ of page $X$. Since many jumps may be return jumps, the designers thoughtfully cause the old contents of $P$ (the address of the TRA1 instruction plus one) to be saved in $S$ when you execute the TRA1. Thus, at any time the address following the most recently executed TRA1 is available in $S$ and may be recalled using a RET instruction. The reader is cautioned that before using two TRA1 instructions in a row without an intervening SSR, he should read the instruction manual because things are a bit more complicated than I have pretended here.

The other transfer instruction TRA0 $X$ causes a jump to a subroutine beginning in page 0 and perhaps continuing into page 1. TRA0 pushes down the program counter stack so that the return address is available plus the address following the most recent main program TRA1. While in a subroutine a TRA0 $X$ causes a jump to $0X$ and a TRA1 a jump to $1X$.

---

*Question 9.1:* These unconditional jump instructions are pretty clumsy. Design better ones.

---

Conditional tests are all of the "skip next instruction" variety. One can skip if carry is zero, skip if bit $p$ ($p = 1, 2, 4, 8$) of RAM location $M$ is zero, skip if the $(A) = (M)$, skip if input line $Ip = 0$ (ground), or skip if one or more of the four $KA$ input lines is at ground.

The $B$ register is used to control access to the RAM. $BU$ is 2 bits and $BL$ is 4 bits. As a mask selectable option the purchaser may specify any six four-bit digits that he wishes to have the "$y$" parameter to translate to. For example, he may map $y_1 - y_6$ onto the BDC numbers 0, 11, 12, 13, 14, and 15. Then executing a load $B$ register instruction:

$$\text{LB, } X, Y$$

will put the 2-bit $X$ field in BU and the 4-bit translation of $y$ into $BL$. This allows one to treat the RAM as 4 sixteen-decimal-digit registers with the ability to conveniently select up to six of the sixteen digits. After executing an LB instruction at least one other instruction must be executed before any succeeding LB instructions have any effect. Thus, with the instruction pair

$$X: \text{ LB } v, w$$
$$P: \text{ LB } x, y$$

if we enter at $X$ we get $v$ in $BU$ and $T(w)$ in $BL$ because the second LB is skipped; but if we enter at $P$ we get $X$ in $BU$ and $T(y)$ in $BL$. There are also instructions for copying $A$ to $BL$ and vice versa.

Data transmitting instructions include setting and clearing the carry flip-flop $C$, setting or clearing bit $P$ of memory location $M$, load accumulator immediate and "load accumulator from RAM and then exclusive or a two bit parameter $X$ with $BU$ and put the result in $BU$."

*Question 9.2:* Why would one want this operation? Drop me a line if you get a good answer.

There is an "exchange RAM location with accumulator" which also provides $\text{XOR}(y, BU) \rightarrow BU$ and also allows you to add 0, +1, or −1 to $BL$.

There are five arithmetic operations: complement accumulator, add memory to accumulator, add memory to accumulator with carry in and carry out, add with carry and skip next instruction if carry out is zero, and add immediate 4 bits to the accumulator and skip if carry out is zero.

It is pretty obvious that this chip was designed to function as a decimal calculator and as such the arithmetic and data manipulation instructions are reasonable if not inspired.

*Question 9.3:* Using the instructions described so far write the programs for adding (and subtracting) two 10-digit numbers. Use $15_d$ to represent a decimal point.

Let us now discuss I/O for this chip. A seven segment digit display is shown in Fig. 9.2. The 9209 has a special ROM which translates 4 bit inputs into 7 segment outputs.

*Question 9.4:* Lay out the conditions under which each segment should be energized to display the digits 0–9 (binary codes 0000 through 1001).

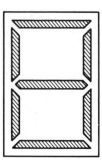

Fig. 9.2 A seven segment digit display unit.

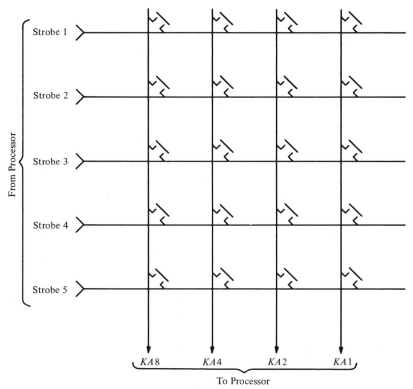

To Processor

Fig. 9.3 A 20-key keyboard for a micro computer.

The first I/O instruction (ATD) translates the contents of the accumulator to a 7 bit segment code, loads these seven bits into output flip-flops SEG $A-H$ and copies the carry flip-flop onto SEG $P$. Presumably the eighth bit is used to drive the decimal point of the display.

In order to select which digit of a display is to be loaded and to poll the keys of a keyboard there are 13 "strobe" output flip-flops: STB 0–12. The KSS instruction first clears all segment and strobe output flip-flops and then, two major cycles later, turns on the strobe output specified by $BL$. For an 8-digit calculator, 8 of these strobes would be connected to the display-enable inputs of the 8 characters of display. The remaining 5 strobes could be connected to a 20-key input keyboard as shown in Fig. 9.3. To detect a key operation we emit strobe 1 and examine the $KA$ input lines. Then we emit strobe 2 and examine the lines again. By scanning through the strobe lines one at a time and looking at the $KA$ input, we can rapidly discover any single key depressions.

*Question 9.5:* What happens if two or more keys are depressed simultaneously?

There is a circuit which detects "power up," and when the power comes on the processor is forced to page 15 line 0 to get its first instruction.

This completes our discussion of the S-9209. We have been somewhat harsh on the designers because of some apparently bad decisions they have made. In a book devoted to computer architecture, it would not do to let the reader come away with the impression that these decisions were good practice. Perhaps there are reasons dictated by the technology of the device which I don't understand, but I cannot imagine a technological (or any logical) reason for designing the PC with no carry out of *PL* to *PU* or for ROM pages with 63 words. If they exist, the writers of the handbook might have been wise to point them out.

## THE 8080

The next micro machine we will look at is the 8080. Pioneered by Intel as a development from its 8008 system, it is now being made by several of the large semiconductor houses. The 8080 has a .5-microsecond minor cycle time. Instructions consist of 4 to 18 minor cycles, and there are 72 distinct instructions. Figure 9.4 shows the general architecture of the 8080. There is an 8-bit wide ALU which can perform all the obvious instructions such as add, subtract, compare, and, or, exclusive or. It has five flags called zero, carry, sign, parity, and auxiliary carry. This last plus the contents of the accumulator can be tested for decimal correction and adjustment by a DAA instruction. The ALU is fed from a temporary register (TEMP), the accumulator latch (ACT) and the carry flag and places its results (other than the flags) directly on the 8 bit internal bus for delivery to the accumulator or another internal register. There are six 16-bit registers: the program counter (PC), the stack pointer (SP), a pair of 8-bit temporary registers not under programmer control (*WZ*) and three pairs of 8-bit registers called *BC*, *DE*, and *HL*. The stack pointer can be initialized to point at any of the 64K memory locations, and when data are "pushed" into the stack, the SP is automatically decremented. When data is pulled from the stack it is automatically incremented. There is an incrementer/decrementer circuit which can be used on any interregister transfer if desired.

There is a 16 bit address buffer output from the chip and an 8 bit bidirectional three-state data bus input/output buffer and latch.

Let us trace through the actions of an ADD *M* instruction which adds the contents of the memory cell to the contents of the accumulator and puts

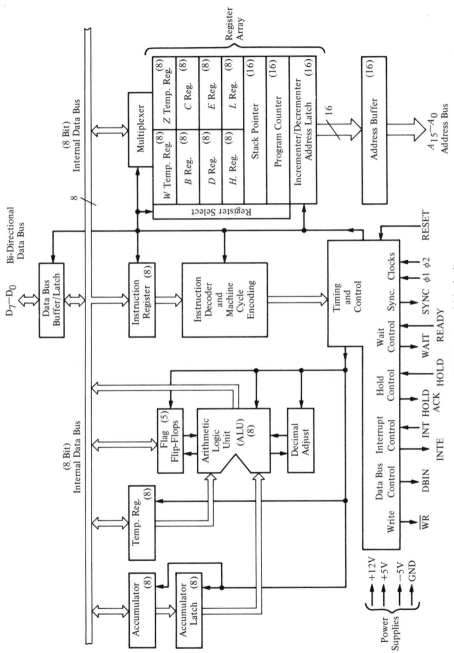

**Fig. 9.4** 8080 CPU functional block diagram.

the result in the accumulator. First, the contents of the program counter are sent out on the address lines and an 8 bit status word describing what is taking place is transmitted on the data output lines. This status word is saved external to the processor chip in status latches to direct subsequent actions and will be discussed a bit later. With the address sent out the PC is incremented; the next instruction is read in and copied to the IR and decoded. It takes 3 minor cycles to fetch an instruction. Next the contents of the $HL$ register pair are broadcast on the address line together with a new status word on the data lines and in 3 more cycles the contents of $M = ((HL))$ are in a temporary register within the chip. In the seventh minor cycle, the contents of the temporary register and the ACC are added together and stored in the ACC.

To take another example, the SHLD $X$ (store contents of $HL$ register in location $X$ and $X + 1$) takes 16 minor cycles. Four cycles fetch the opcode and then decode it, three more the high-order byte of the storage address ($x$), and three more for the low-order byte of the address. This address is stored in $WZ$. Now a write of three cycles stores the contents of $L$ at the address in $WZ$ and increments the contents of $WZ$. A final three cycles stores the contents of $H$, and the instruction is over.

Each time a new suboperation (called an "instruction cycle") is begun, the micro processor automatically broadcasts a SYNC signal and that indicates to the external status latches that a status word is on the data bus. The status word is placed on the data bus automatically without need for programmer action. There are 10 kinds of instruction cycles:

1. Fetch op-code
2. Memory Read
3. Memory Write
4. Stack Read
5. Stack Write
6. Input Read
7. Output Write
8. Interrupt acknowledge
9. Halt acknowledge
10. Interrupt acknowledge while halted

Each complete instruction execution consists of at least a Fetch of the Opcode plus some of the other nine. Each instruction cycle has a different pattern of status bits high. The 8 data bits (D0–D7) have the following meanings when interpreted as status bits:

D0 = INTA    —acknowledge signal for an interrupt request. When received externally, it should gate a restart instruction (subroutine jump) onto the data bus so that a transfer to the desired interrupt routine will take place.

D1 = $\overline{\text{WO}}$    —if $\overline{\text{WO}}$ = 0 this cycle will be a write or output function. If $\overline{\text{WO}}$ = 1, it will be a read or input cycle.

D2—STACK    —if = 1, the address bus holds an address from the stack pointer. (It is not clear to me why the external devices need to know this.)

D3—HLTA    —acknowledges a halt instruction.

D4—OUT    —indicates that the address bus contains the address of an output device and that the data bus is going to contain (when $\overline{\text{WR}}$ is active) some data to be sent to that device.

D5—$M_1$    —the CPU is in the fetch cycle and will be fetching the first byte of an instruction.

D6—INP    —indicates that the address of an input device is on the address bus and that the device should place data on the bus when DBIN goes active.

D7—MEMR    —data bus will be used for a memory read.

Figure 9.5 shows the connection of the status latch chip (8212), and Fig. 9.6 shows the use of the status bits in the 10 different kinds of instruction cycles. Other control signals are shown in Fig. 9.4. $\phi_1$ and $\phi_2$ are inputs from a two-phase external clock that control the minor cycle of the computer. The SYNC signal comes high during the first minor cycle of each instruction cycle and tells the status latches to capture the signals on the data bus as described above. If a memory device is referenced and it wishes to request a processor wait, it does so by pulling the processor READY line to ground. This will cause the processor to wait until the first $\phi_1$ pulse after READY goes back to ONE. While waiting the processor holds the WAIT line high. When it is desirous of absorbing data, the processor holds DBIN high. When it desires to output data, the processor forces the $\overline{\text{WR}}$ line low. When the interrupt enable line (NTE) is high, the processor is willing to accept interrupts on the INT line. When an interrupt is accepted, the processor enters a FETCH cycle sending a status word with $M_1$ and INTA both high. The contents of the PC are placed on the CPU's address lines, and it is up to the peripheral device to take over and cause any further interrupt actions. Typically, an 8 bit interrupt instruction (RESTART) is sent to the CPU in response to the instruction FETCH outstanding. RESTART $n$ causes a transfer to one of 8 locations in low store (0, 8, 16, 24, 32, 40, 48, or 56). Since this instruction is a subroutine call, it finishes up by storing the old contents of the PC on the STACK.

An external device can request use of the memory and the data bus for doing direct memory access (DMA) by raising the HOLD line. As soon as the memory is free (READY = 1) and there is a $\phi_2$ clock pulse, the CPU floats its address and data lines and raises HOLDACK. The peripheral

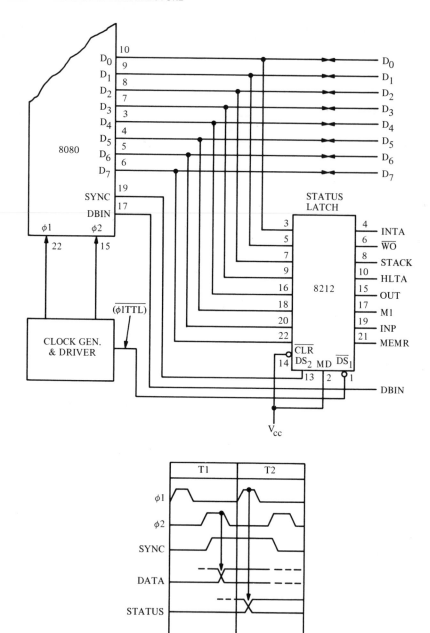

Fig. 9.5 The 8080 status latch.

Type of Machine Cycle

| Data Bus Bit | Status Information | Instruction Fetch | Memory Read | Memory Write | Stack Read | Stack Write | Input Read | Output Write | Interrupt Acknowledge | Halt Acknowledge | Interrupt Acknowledge While Halt |
|---|---|---|---|---|---|---|---|---|---|---|---|
| $D_0$ | INTA | 0 | 0 | 0 | 0 | 0 | 0 | 0 | 1 | 0 | 1 |
| $D_1$ | $\overline{WO}$ | 1 | 1 | 0 | 1 | 0 | 1 | 0 | 1 | 1 | 1 |
| $D_2$ | STACK | 0 | 0 | 0 | 1 | 1 | 0 | 0 | 0 | 0 | 0 |
| $D_3$ | HLTA | 0 | 0 | 0 | 0 | 0 | 0 | 0 | 0 | 1 | 1 |
| $D_4$ | OUT | 0 | 0 | 0 | 0 | 0 | 0 | 1 | 0 | 0 | 0 |
| $D_5$ | $M_1$ | 1 | 0 | 0 | 0 | 0 | 0 | 0 | 1 | 0 | 1 |
| $D_6$ | INP | 0 | 0 | 0 | 0 | 0 | 1 | 0 | 0 | 0 | 0 |
| $D_7$ | MEMR | 1 | 1 | 0 | 1 | 0 | 0 | 0 | 0 | 1 | 0 |

Fig. 9.6 Use of the 8080 status bits.

may then use the memory for as long as it wants before dropping HOLD. The RESET line, when energized externally as during a power up sequence, will clear the CPU's PC.

As will be obvious from reading the above, the 8080 is considerably more flexible than the 9209; but because of this flexibility it is also more complicated to program and to interface, and a number of outboard chips are required to make up a complete micro-computer system.

## SIGNETICS 2650

The Signetics 2650 is one of the nicer micro processors around, although it does have a few features that make it less than ideal. In the first place, unlike the 8080, data lines and control lines are separated, thus eliminating any need for outboard status latches or the like.

Let us begin our description with a block diagram of the major components of the CPU. (See Fig. 9.7.) There are an instruction register (8 bits), an instruction address register (IAR or more conventionally a PC) (15 bits), a return address stack RAS (15 bits by 8 words deep), an ALU, a program status word (PSU and PSL of 8 bits each), a separate address adder, a main accumulator RO (8 bits), and two banks of three general purpose registers

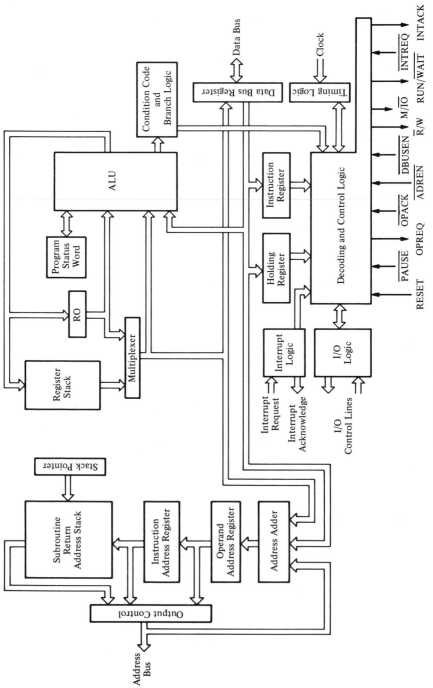

Fig. 9.7 Signetics 2650 block diagram.

(8 bits each). There are 15 address lines going off-chip and 8 bidirectional data lines, as well as a number of control lines that we will discuss below. The 2650 requires a single five-volt power supply at 100 ma, and a single phase clock running at 1.25 MHz. Each basic machine cycle takes three clock pulses or 2.4 $\mu$sec and instructions require 2–5 machine cycles for execution.

Memory may consist of up to 32,768 bytes and is arranged in 4 banks of 8,192 bytes each. The high-order address bits (ADR-14 and ADR-13) select the bank and also function as I/O control bits in certain instructions. Remember that this is a micro processor and not a super computer; it is unlikely that more than one bank of memory would be required for a given application, and so this particular complication will not usually be a bother. Which bank is being referenced is stored in a two bit bank register and may be changed either temporarily (for one instruction) or permanently under program control.

*Program Status Word*

The PSW consists of 16 bits divided into an upper and lower byte. Beginning at the left end of the PSU bit 7 is a sense line directly connected to a pin on the chip so that external events (one bit worth) can be sampled directly at any time. Bit 6 is a flag bit set or cleared by program and is also connected directly to the outside world. The designers suggest that these two bits can be used, among other things, to implement directly a teletype interface with bit 7 being the input bit, bit 6 being the output bit, and all timing and start and stop bits being taken care of by program control. Since micro processors exist in order to exchange logic circuits for program, this is a very reasonable suggestion.

Bit 5 of PSU is the interrupt inhibit bit, and when high prevents the processor from recognizing interrupts—this bit is set automatically when an interrupt occurs and is cleared by a "Return and Enable" instruction. It may also be set or cleared by the programmer at any time. Bits 4 and 3 are not used, while bits 2, 1, and 0 hold the pointer to the return address stack.

In PSL bits 7 and 6 form the condition code which is set any time a byte is put into a register. The pattern 01 indicates positive, 00 indicates zero, and 10 indicates negative. Bit 5 is the interdigit carry and is used for detecting carry out of bit 3 in an arithmetic operation. This allows one to easily perform decimal arithmetic on two digits per byte. Bit 4 of PSL is the register bank select and determines whether registers 0, 01, 02, 03 are addressed or registers 0, 11, 12, and 13. Note that register 0 is common to both banks. Bit 2 conditions the ALU to perform arithmetic with or without carry (borrow) added (subtracted) in. Bit 2 is the overflow bit and is set when an unwarranted change of sign occurs. Bit 1 tells whether to do a comparison operation on 8 bit unsigned integers or on 8 bit two's complement integers.  Finally, bit 0 of PSL is the carry/borrow bit.

### Interface

The interface between the CPU and the outside world is quite well thought out.  We have already mentioned the flag and sense lines that allow direct communication between a program and the real world.  In addition, there are a number of other lines mostly taken care of automatically. The RESET line comes into the chip and when raised clears the interrupt inhibit bit and also clears the IAR to ZERO.  Then when RESET drops, the next instruction is taken from location ZERO of page ZERO.  The RESET line may be raised at any time by user intervention or automatically during a power up sequence.  The $\overline{\text{PAUSE}}$ line causes the CPU to finish its present instruction and then enter a wait state until the $\overline{\text{PAUSE}}$ line goes low again. This is useful for DMA.

The most important line out of the chip is the OPREQ or operation request line.  It basically tells the world that the CPU wants an operation performed and that the information on other control, address, and data lines is valid.  For example, in a read-operand-cycle OPREQ goes high, indicating that the address lines are valid and that an 8 bit datum is requested. The memory unit raises $\overline{\text{OPACK}}$ (operation acknowledge), fetches up the datum, and then drops $\overline{\text{OPACK}}$.  The CPU waits as long as $\overline{\text{OPACK}}$ is high, thus allowing completely asynchronous memory operations. If the datum will be available within 1 $\mu$sec after OPREQ is sent, $\overline{\text{OPACK}}$ may be left down, and data will be captured by the CPU properly and without any delay to the program.

Address enable ($\overline{\text{ADREN}}$) and data bus enable ($\overline{\text{DBUSEN}}$) are used by an external DMA device and force the CPU to float the address and data lines.

The $\overline{\text{R}}$/W read-write line, if high, indicates a write operation and if low indicates a read into the CPU is desired.  The M/$\overline{\text{IO}}$ line indicates that a memory operation is in progress (if high) or an input output operation is being executed by one of the 6 I/O instructions.  When memory operations are indicated, ADR-14 and ADR-13 are the bank address lines.  When an I/O instruction is in progress, ADR-14 is interpreted as a data-control (D/$\overline{\text{C}}$) line.  Write control (WRTC) and read control (REDC) instructions make D/$\overline{\text{C}}$ low to tell external devices that information on the data bus is control information.  Read instructions (read data REDD and read control REDC) cause one byte of data to be transferred from the data bus to a central register.  Their only difference is that REDD makes D/$\overline{\text{C}}$ high and REDC makes it low.  This might be used to select one of two I/$\overline{\text{O}}$ devices or to read status information as opposed to data.  Write data and write control are similar except for direction of the information transfer. These four I/O instructions are each one byte long and they all cause ADR-13 (which is called E/$\overline{\text{NE}}$ when M/$\overline{\text{IO}}$ is indicating input output) to go low—meaning "nonextended." The other two I/$\overline{\text{O}}$ instructions REDE and WRTE are two byte or extended operations. When these are executed, the 8 low-order address bits contain the value of the second byte of the instruction. They can thus be used to read or write one of 256 input or output devices if the addresses are fully decoded or one of eight if each address line enables one device.

RUN/$\overline{\text{WAIT}}$ goes low whenever the CPU executes a HALT instruction or the PAUSE line requests a temporary stop and stays low until the processor starts again either by releasing $\overline{\text{PAUSE}}$ or by a RESET or an interrupt.

Vectored interrupts are available on the 2650. Action is as follows:

1. A device pulls $\overline{\text{INTREQ}}$ to ground, indicating that it wishes to interrupt the CPU.
2. The CPU finishes its current instruction.
3. The CPU sets the interrupt inhibit bit in PSU.
4. The CPU loads a Zero Branch-to-Subroutine Relative (ZBSR) instruction into the IR.
5. The CPU generates an interrupt acknowledge signal on the INTACK line.
6. The device sees the high INTACK line and places a vector address from $-64_d$ to $63_d$ on the data lines (negative addresses wrap around to the high end of the current page); this forms the second byte of the jump instruction—the offset from page 0, location 0.
7. The CPU executes the ZBSR instruction, saving the old value of the PC on the return address stack.
8. Device releases $\overline{\text{INTREQ}}$ and the CPU drops INTACK.
9. The interrupt routine specified by the vector address supplied by the device is executed (this address may be all ZERO's for a simple I/O system) and is ended by a return instruction which pops the stack back into the PC and clears the interrupt inhibit bit.

Without going into the details of timing it would seem worthwhile to tie some of the above together by running through a memory read operation.

1. The CPU sets OPREQ to ONE, $\overline{\text{R}}$/W to read, M/$\overline{\text{IO}}$ to memory, and places the memory address on the address lines.
2. The memory device puts the desired byte on the data bus and then pulls $\overline{\text{OPACK}}$ to ZERO, indicating that the data are available.
3. The CPU sees $\overline{\text{OPACK}}$, strobes in the data, and drops OPREQ.

*Addressing Modes*

The 2650 has four basic addressing modes. Instructions are 1, 2, or 3 bytes in length depending on the addressing mode being used. Most instructions are 6 bits in length, leaving two bits to specify which register in the current bank is being referenced. Sometimes these bits have other uses, in which case the default register is always register 0. Let us look at the variations in loading a register that are possible.

1. LODZ, *r*—load register zero (1 byte, 2 cycles—4.8 $\mu$sec). Transfer the contents of register *r* to register 0. (Called register addressing.)
2. LODI, *r v*—load immediate (2 bytes, 2 cycles). The second byte of the instruction—*v*—is loaded into register *r*. (Called immediate addressing).
3. LODR, *r* (*) *a*—load relative (2 bytes, 3 cycles). The low-order 7 bits of the second byte—*a*—form an offset from the beginning of the next instruction (present location plus two). The contents of the cell so designated are loaded into register *r*. If the optional star (*) is present, the assembler sets the high-order bit of *a* to ONE, indicating indirect addressing. If indirect addressing is specified, two bytes from EA and EA + 1 are fetched, and the low 15 bits are used as the address of the operand. (Called relative addressing.)
4. LODA, *r* (*) *a*—load absolute (3 bytes, 4 cycles). The low-order 13 bits of bytes 2 and 3 specify an address within the current page. The 8 bits stored at *a* are loaded into register *r* if direct addressing is specified. If indirect addressing is specified, *a* and *a* + 1 contain a 15-bit address at which the data are found.
5. LODA (*) *a*, *x*—load absolute indexed (3 bytes, 4 cycles). The contents of register *x* are added to the address *a*, and the contents of that byte are loaded into register zero. If indirect addressing is specified, the index is added to the indirect address (postindexing).

## DESIGN OF A SMALL SYSTEM USING A MICRO PROCESSOR

Perhaps one of the most instructive ways of learning about micro processors would be to pick a problem and try to solve it using a micro processor. As an example, we will consider the design of a teaching aid called "Electric Ed" developed by Mary Lou Foster. It consists of a box with a red and a green light on it, a battery inside, a socket, and a probe about 2 feet long. Into the socket one plugs a "book" which consists of several pages of questions, each question with a metal contact next to it. When the probe is touched to one of the contacts, a circuit is completed and either the green or the red light goes on. To drill students on the difference between the long A and short A sounds, a page might exist with the following information on it:

Select the words from the following list which have a short A sound as in the word "hat":

- CAT
- CANE
- BARE
- RAM

.
.

.
.

Contacts 1 and 4 would light the green light, while 2 and 3 would light the red light. Simple, straightforward, and of high interest for the third grade. Original plans called for construction using a printed circuit board for each page with colorful overlays glued onto the PC board with the printing and some pictures on them. The point of having each page as a separate PC board was that the positions of right and wrong answers could vary from page to page and the children could not learn the location of the right answers. That was before we discovered that PC boards cost about 5¢ per square inch. An 8½ × 11 inch board would cost just under $5, and a book covering the short-long A sound of 10 pages would cost around $50 to produce. Covering the five vowels and selling at three times cost would mean a sale price of $750–$1,000.

So the question of interest is: can we redesign using a micro processor at a lower cost and possibly provide some additional functions such as keeping a score of right and wrong responses?

To begin with, let us settle on one PC board with removable cardboard or heavy paper overlays with the printing on them. This will immediately reduce the price substantially, but it generates two new problems. First, we have lost the flexibility to place the contact studs anywhere we wish on the page and thus give some variety to the visual impact of the different pages. That, we are going to have to live with, since we plan to substitute stored program information in the micro processor for the "random logic" embodied in different PC boards. The second problem is: how do we keep the program informed of what overlay the student is presently using?

Probably the simplest and most foolproof way would be to flush-mount a set of 8 photo transistors in such a position that they would normally be covered by the overlays. Then we could punch holes in each overlay where we wanted light to hit the photo transistors and turn them on. Since we can assume that there will be light in the room by which the student may read the information on the overlays, we will rely on room lighting to trigger the exposed photo transistors. With 8 holes or no-holes we could distinguish 128 different pages and include a parity bit to allow for dog-earing, grease and grime, probing fingers, and other aspects of the hostile third grade environment. We will let "all ONE's" when an overlay is removed put the device into a "no page" state, and as soon as the photo transistor input is stable for say 5 seconds, we will read the overlay number and then ignore any shadows or covering fingers until we go through the no-page state again.

Multi-position rotary switches might be more reliable, but they present the problem that students might forget to change them when they changed overlays. It is better to build that function in than to rely on a human.

On the original Electric Ed, the student could find one right answer and keep touching it with the probe, getting a green light each time until the battery ran down. Now with a complete computer built into the machine, we can be as structured as we like, counting each question only once, subtracting errors from corrects, ceasing operation after all questions on a page have been answered correctly, or whatever other procedures seem good. We will not choose here, because that question certainly lies outside the realm of computer architecture. Suffice it to note that the capability is present to be as organized as we and third grade teachers might like.

How many response contacts should there be on a page? Surely a multiple of 8, since that is the common data path width of most micros. If we have just 8 and the question involves selecting the members of a set, the students will have to change cards after every 3–5 responses. If we have too many, we will get cluttered overlays and perhaps induce boredom. I propose 24 contacts arranged along the right-hand edge of an $8\frac{1}{2} \times 11$ page (long way up). If these are equally spaced, they can each be individual questions (member/nonmember) or can be paired with printed brackets and the words YES and NO, or indeed be divided into any convenient subsets for multiple-choice responses.

Immediate feedback to the student can be in the form of two light-emitting diodes (LED's), indicating right or wrong. Allowing 10 "right" answers per page and 10 pages per "book," the total number right can be displayed using two LED decimal characters. Wrong would take another two characters, and since individual characters cost about $1 each, it seems worthwhile to display both right and wrong simultaneously.

Finally, we need a reset button to clear the response counters and initialize the system.

Now with all those decisions out of the way—subject to change if we find any startling inefficiencies—we are ready to begin discussing the micro processor part of the design.

First, let us estimate the amount of RAM and ROM we are going to need. We need RAM to hold the current page number (8 bits) and the current count of right and wrong responses (8 bits each) plus a 24 bit word to indicate if the questions on the current page have been answered or not. That's about 6 bytes of RAM. With luck we could use central registers to hold this information. Let us assume, however, that a small RAM (64 words of

4 bits each) is necessary. For permanent storage we will need space to hold our program and the correct/incorrent value of each possible response for each overlay page. There are 128 overlays maximum with 3 bytes per overlay to hold ZERO's (wrong) and ONE's (right) or 384 bytes of fixed data. How much space for program storage? Well, we certainly can't estimate that very accurately before we have selected the processor, but let us guess at 256 bytes (it's going to be pretty simple) but allow for the possibility of up to 512 bytes. Adding 512 bytes for program plus 384 for data storage (right/wrong), we get 896 bytes of ROM. The nearest convenient-size ROM is 1024 bytes, so we will specify that.

Figure 9.8 shows the outline of our system so far. There are 1024 words of ROM. Let us assign them addresses $0-1023_d$ and put the RAM in address space $1024_d-1083_d$.

There are 4 input devices (phototransistors plus 3 contact banks of 8 contacts each) and 4 output devices (4 characters plus the red/green lights; these red/green lights are the 8th bits of the low-order digits of the wrong counter and the right counter).

Now we must choose a micro computer with which to drive the system. But before we can answer that question we need to know how many of these devices we can expect to sell. There are somewhere around 20,000 schools in the U.S.—give or take a factor of 2. If our teaching aid sold to 10% of them

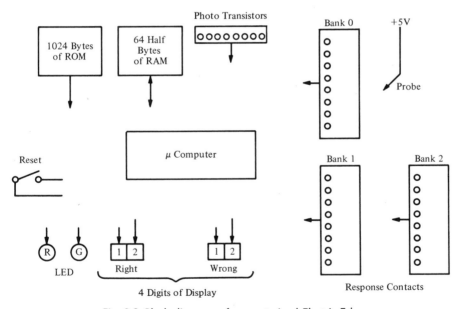

**Fig. 9.8 Block diagram of computerized Electric Ed.**

and each school bought a couple, we might expect to sell 4,000–5,000—about the right range for a specialized textbook. But the 9209 comes in minimum lots of 10,000. Still, at under $10 apiece, we might buy the 10,000, store the surplus, price the device a little higher, and hope that sales would exceed our estimate. On the other hand, should we go with the 2650, the price might be somewhat higher, but we wouldn't be committed to any fixed number, and should the device be unsuccessful, we wouldn't be stuck with an inventory of $90,000 worth of unmarketable chips. If that isn't complicated enough, you might consider the possibility of marketing the device as a home entertainment game if the price is low enough.

---

*Question 9.6:* Which micro processor of the three described here would you choose? Justify your choice.

---

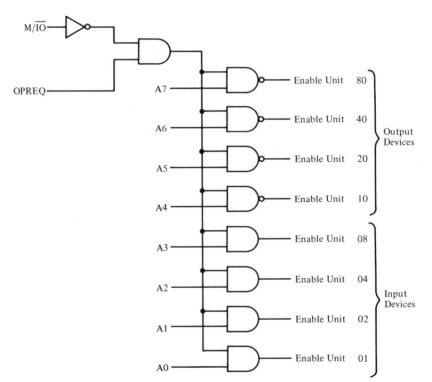

Fig. 9.9 Circuits to enable the input and output devices of Electric Ed. Output devices will be loaded when their enable line goes low. Input devices will put a byte on the data bus when their enable line goes high.

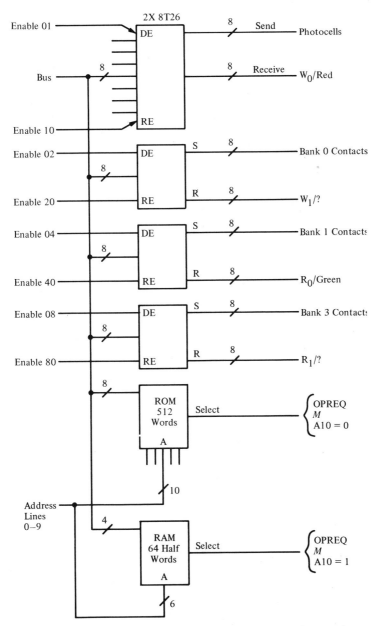

Fig. 9.10 Organization of the peripheral devices for Electric Ed.

I think that if I were actually going to launch such a venture I would go with the 9209—preferably using somebody else's money. But for the purposes of this book, we are going to choose the Signetics 2650, because we want to learn something about interfacing and because I personally prefer that one to the others we have discussed.

We have 8 I/O units, so we will use the extended I/O instructions and select which I/O unit we want to talk with by taking the AND of OPREQ, IO command (the not of $M/\overline{IO}$) and one of the 8 low-order address lines. Thus I/O unit names will be 01, 02, 04, 08, 10, 20, 40, and 80 in hexadecimal. See Figure 9.9. If one were to specify a device name with two ONE's in it, he would get two units responding—which might, or might not, be interesting. We will not buffer the character displays, but will hit them in turn as often as we can and rely on the integration of the human eye to eliminate flicker.

We will use a pair of the Signetics 8T26 tristate quad bus driver/receiver to interface the bus to the I/O units. The 8T26 enables the bus drivers (for a read operation) when the DE input pin goes high (disabled bus drivers have high impedance), and it enables the receivers when the RE pin goes low. The receiver gate will sink 16 ma, and that is enough to drive the segmented display directly and to drive LED (light-emitting diodes) to indicate right or wrong responses by the students. Since the displays need only 7 bits, we will put the right/wrong lights on the high-order bits of two of the display characters. This leaves us room for two more response lights if we can think of a use for them. The program will have to translate each BCD character into a segment pattern, but this is a simple table-look-up operation. Since the send and receive lines of the 8T26 are independent, we can group an input and an output device together on each pair of 8T26's—as in Fig. 9.10.

There is no guarantee implied that the device described here will actually work. There are loading and timing problems that we have not fully considered, but the point we want to make is that it is possible to design a simple system, using a microprocessor and a few outboard chips. Estimating the 2650 plus ROM and RAM at $75 in unit quantity, and general logic chips at $1 each (that is high) we have a system that will cost around $100 in parts and should sell at around $300.

## REFERENCES

1. *AMI 59209 Microprogrammable 4-bit controller.* Santa Clara, Calif., American Microsystems Inc., July 1, 1975.
2. *Intel 8080 Micro Computer Systems User Manual.* Santa Clara, Calif., Intel Corp., September 1975.
3. *Signetics 2650 Micro processor.* Sunnyvale, Calif., Signetics Corp., no date.
4. Foster, C. C. "A View of Computer Architecture." *CACM* **15**, 7, 557–565 (July 1972).

5. *Computer*, July 1974. Microprocessor Architecture.
6. *Computer*, August 1974. Microprocessor Applications.
7. Holt, R., and Lemas, M. "Current Microcomputer Architecture." *Computer Design* **13**, 2, 65–73 (Feb. 1974).

# 10 | VERY LARGE COMPUTERS

*"Oh, it is excellent to have a giant's strength;*
*but it is tyrannous to use it like a giant."*
*Measure for Measure*

The so-called super computer is perhaps a typically American phenomenon in which we demonstrate again our love for the largest, the flashiest, and the most chromium-plated. Be that as it may, the world of computers is divided quite cleanly today into the very small and the very large. In this chapter we are going to investigate the large. We have a choice as to whether this chapter should be organized around specific machines or around concepts. Last time I wrote it I chose machines. Now seven years later I am going to try the other approach.

## INCREASING MEMORY SPEEDS

It has long been recognized that memory speeds are one of the major bottlenecks of computing. When one attempts to build a very fast machine, one spends considerable effort on the problem of getting memory speeds as high as the proposed price of the machine will permit.

### Multiple Blocks

One of the oldest approaches to speeding up the apparent cycle time of memory is to buy many independent blocks of storage.[1] Then perhaps we can be fetching from several blocks at once and thus increase the number of words fetched per second and hence the apparent cycle speed of the store. This is called "memory interleaving" or "banking," depending upon how it is organized. In the CDC-3600 the high-order bits of the address select which "bank" one is conversing with. The idea behind this was that one could put his program in one bank and his data in a second, and the drum could be simultaneously loading or emptying yet a third unit, without access to one unit of memory interfering with access to another. In many other machines the selection of which physical unit one is addressing is done by the low-order bits of the address. This is called memory interlace or "interleaving." The argument here is that one is seldom organized enough to have program parts so neatly separated as above, nor fortunate enough to allow one user to have several blocks. It is far better to rely on statistics. Suppose interlace is on the 3 low-order bits. Words 0, 8, 16, etc., come from one block, words 1, 9, 17, etc., from a second, and so forth. (See Fig. 10.1.) Then there is only one chance in eight (on the average) that any two memory references will "collide" or contend with each other for access to a word from a given bank.

Still other machines like the Univac 1108[2] and the CDC-3800 rely on a mixed strategy using one or more low-order bits and the rest from the high-order end of the address. Nobody seems to have done a study of which mode is better or worse under what conditions.

| Block 0 | Block 1 | | Block 2 |
|---------|---------|---|---------|
| 0 | 1 | | 7 |
| 8 | 9 | | 15 |
| 16 | 17 | •••• | 23 |
| 24 | 25 | | 31 |
| ⋮ | ⋮ | | ⋮ |

Fig. 10.1  Word assignments to memory block with interlace on the three low-order bits of the address.

### Wide Words

Another way to get apparent memory speeds up is to make the words very wide. For instance if the CPU uses words of 32 bits each, then fetch 64 or 128 bits at a time from the memory block. On the assumption that the next instruction will come from the location following the present one, this is certainly good for instruction fetches.[3]  (See Fig. 10.2.)

For data the benefit is less obvious except for array (vector) operations, but certainly there is no harm done by fetching up some extra bits that don't happen to be used. So on the average wide words will help. The higher-numbered members of the IBM 360 used variously double word and quadruple word fetches as do many others of the giant computers.

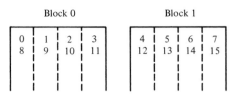

Fig. 10.2 Two blocks of wide words. Block selection is done on the third bit of the address and the two low-order bits determine which portion of the wide word is referenced.

### Caches and Buffers

Another way at least to appear to speed up memory is to reduce the load on it by not going there so often; that is to put high speed buffers in or around the CPU so that we can park data and instructions temporarily without going back to the slow main storage.[4-8]

Some of these buffering schemes are under programmer control; some are carried out automatically by the hardware. On the one hand, it is said, "Who wants to be bothered with managing data in and out of buffers? Hard wire it!" And on the other hand, "That's all very well but I know better what to save and what to discard than any bucket of bolts ever will." Shades of the compiler/assembly language controversy! The solution is obvious: let the management be automatic, but let the user override the default conditions when he desires—the same solution as was found by making compilers accept assembly language statements for the "sticky parts." But nobody seems to have applied that approach to hardware buffer and cache management.

The first type of buffer is the general purpose register. Back in the days of the IBM 650, which was a drum machine with a single accumulator, the clever programmer used the "distributor" (MBR) as a temporary register and sometimes could save a memory fetch of up to 17 milliseconds. Nowadays many machines have a set of general purpose registers. The PDP-11 has 8, the Sigma 7 and the IBM 360 have 16, the CDC-6600 has 24, and the Cray 1 has 144 general purpose plus 256 special purpose high speed (12.5 nanosecond) registers. In some senses 8 or 16 is probably the most difficult number to manage. With exactly one general purpose register, every reference flows through that. With a thousand or so registers, you just go ahead and spend them—it will be hard to use that many up. But with a dozen or so . . . . Naturally, compilers exist that will handle the registers assignment for the lazy user.

An alternative to cutting down data fetches is the cutting down on instruction fetches or at least on the contention caused by them. The first such scheme to took at is the instruction pre-fetch used by the CDC-3800.

It has a few words of buffers for holding instructions, and if the memory block in which the next unfetched instruction lies is not doing anything else useful, and if the instruction buffer isn't full, then another instruction will be fetched and placed in the buffer. No big deal, no attempt to pre-decode instructions to see if there are any jumps coming up—just a "if you happen to be free, old chap . . ." sort of design. So we come up to execute an instruction and find that it is an unconditional jump and all the "instructions" in the buffer are really just garbage—well, at least we tried. Nothing got lost because the memory bank was going to be idle anyway, and maybe we did some good and had instructions there ready to execute.

---

*Question 10.1:* What happens in the 3800 if the buffer runs out of instructions?

---

Next more formal in its operation is a pre-fetch stack that is automatically kept full but which it is possible to "freeze" for holding a tight loop. Suppose I have an innermost loop that is known to be short enough to fit into the instruction stack. Just before the code for the loop I issue a "freeze" to the stack which says "don't throw anything more away." The stack will keep on pre-fetching until it is full; but it will not overwrite anything after the freeze instruction.

Now when the user's program executes a "test and branch back" instruction, execution continues from the stack without ever going to memory for another instruction until a transfer is made out of the loop. Then normal pre-fetch resumes.

---

*Question 10.2:* Rough out the design for a stack with a freeze instruction. What criterion do you have for unfreezing?

---

In order to decrease memory references caused by indirect addresses, we find the 360/67 with a small associative store that is used to short-circuit the three stages of address translation in a segmented machine (segment table to page table to datum). This is not a buffer for instructions or for data but rather a place to hold the most recent translations of virtual addresses to physical addresses.

The IBM 360/85[5,8] employs a full-fledged "cache" memory whose action is entirely automatic and not modifiable by the programmer. This cache or slave storage is used to very nearly match an 80-nsec CPU with a 1-$\mu$sec core store. The idea in modified form has also been proposed by Wilkes.[4]

When a main memory reference is made in the 85, sixteen 8-bit bytes (4 words of 32 bits each) are fetched in parallel from a bank of core. We define a *block* of storage to be 64 contiguous bytes (16 words) of storage and a *sector* to be 1024 bytes (256 words or 16 blocks). Since main storage is four words wide and interlaced four ways, one reference to each storage unit is all that is necessary to fetch a block of 64 bytes into the slave store. These references may be executed more or less in parallel, since they are independent.

The slave store consists of 16*K* bytes of fast storage divided into 16 sectors. Associated with each sector of the slave store, there is a 14 bit *tag* register and 16 *validity* bits.

Consider now a main storage address which is 24 bits in length. This is broken into three parts. The left-most 14 bits specify the sector, the next 4 the block within the sector, and the right-most 6 the byte within the block. When a word is referenced in storage, the upper 14 bits of its address are compared (associatively) with the contents of the 16 tag registers of the slave. If a correspondence is found, then at least a portion of the sector of which that word is a part is in the slave store. But not all of the sector may have been fetched up from main store yet. So the next four bits of the word's address (the block number) are used as an index to determine which validity bit should be examined. If the indicated validity bit is ONE, that particular block of words has been copied into the slave store and the desired word is there to read. If the validity bit is zero, that block has not yet been copied up from main store, so a FETCH of the required block is initiated. The quarter of the block (4 words) that contains the one desired word is fetched first (followed by the other 3 quarters) and is sent simultaneously to the CPU and to the slave store. Then the validity bit of the block in the sector is set to one.

If a search of the tag registers reveals no comparison, a sector of slave store is selected (see below), its validity bits are all cleared to zero, its tag register is set to correspond to the high-order 14 bits of the address, and the block within the sector containing the desired word is fetched as described above.

Whenever a sector in slave store is referenced, it is promoted to the head of a "usage" list and it is the sector at the bottom of the list that is replaced when a new sector is brought in.

Writing is different from reading. When a WRITE occurs, the word is written into main store and, *if* its sector and block is in the slave, it is updated there as well. If it is not in the slave, a WRITE does not change the contents of the slave in any way. Since words are always rewritten into main store, when a sector of slave is reassigned, it is not necessary to take any action to preserve its contents.

This is not as expensive of time as one might at first suspect. Writes are much less frequent than reads. Furthermore, the memory units are buffered to the extent that once a write operation has been initiated the CPU can be released to go about other business while the memory unit takes care of completing the write. Only in the reasonably rare case in which two writes to the same memory unit overlap in time does the CPU have to wait until the first one is finished before it can initiate the second. The KDF .9 took this one step further by double buffering. It had the normal MBR and MAR to buffer (hold) the first write plus another set of registers to hold the data and address for a second write, so that only if three overlapping writes were issued would the CPU be held up. In an unpublished study of instructions executed on a CDC-3600, Dr. Edward Riseman and I found that there were on the average 9.5 fetches for instructions and data for each store. Of the several million instructions executed, approximately 61% were non-memory referencing (jumps, register operations, etc.), 13.5% were data fetching, and 17.6% were data storage.

Fairly extensive studies by the design group at IBM[5] indicate that the performance of an 80 nsec slave store with 1 $\mu$sec main store is approximately equivalent to 80% of that obtainable with a conventional main store of 80 nsec cycle time. This means that the system is functioning about the same as if all its store had a 100 nsec cycle time. This is an impressive gain in performance at a cost much less than what would be necessary to actually buy 100 nsec storage.

---

*Question 10.3:* Design a circuit that will compare an effective address with the tag registers and validity bits of the slave store described above. Since speed of operation will be critical, minimize (as much as possible) the number of gates through which a signal must pass.

---

The MU-5 designed at Manchester University[9] has an interesting variation on a cache. Operands are divided into "literals" (integer or real variables, data descriptors, names of functions and subroutines) and secondary operands, which include array or vector elements and strings of elements. The first class of these operands, called primary operands, are kept, when they occur, in a 32 word associative memory. Each word has an access time of 40 nsec and can store the "name" of the operand together with a 64 bit value. Replacement is via a cyclic (longest in residence?) algorithm, and the designers predict an almost incredible 99% hit rate. Secondary operands have their own unit called the secondary operand pipeline (SEOP), which does effective address calculation for elements of arrays that are located by indexing.

As an example of how concepts first introduced in top-of-the-line machines gradually make their way downward toward the less expensive end, we have the Data General Corporation's new Eclipse computer, which might be classed as a large mini-computer and which has a cache memory. Main memory is 700 nanosecond semiconductor interleaved four ways, and between that and the CPU there is a 64 word, 200 nanosecond cache. These 64 words are divided into blocks of four words each. When a reference is made to main store, the addressed word and the next three sequential words are all fetched and loaded into a block of cache. Blocks are managed with a least recently used (LRU) algorithm. Stores to memory are done on a write through basis.

Finally, let us look back at demand paging for a minute. Is it not the case that by trivial renaming "main storage" becomes a large cache and "backing store" becomes main memory? Then a page fault causes a failure of the cache and a reference to main memory for the datum. Let us leave the subject there with the perhaps gloomy thought that thrashing is just as likely to occur in a cache as in a paged virtual store.

---

*Question 10.4:* That gloomy thought is probably wrong. Why?

---

## INSTRUCTION DECODE OVERLAP

Let us return to the simple case of an instruction stack that is kept full by a pre-fetch unit. Since we have the instructions sitting there in a hardware stack waiting their turn at execution, it is extremely tempting to sneak a look at these instructions to see what is coming up. This temptation was irresistible to the designers of the IBM 360/91 (370/195),[10,11] the CDC-STAR,[12] the Texas Instruments ASC,[13] the MU-5,[9] the CDC-6600,[1,14] the IBM Stretch, and a number of other super computers.

Consider the phases of preparing an instruction for execution:

1. Fetch the instruction from memory.
2. Examine the op-code to see what kind of instruction we have.
3. If it is memory referencing, develop the effective address.
4. Send the effective address to the MAR to cause a read of the specified operand.
5. Present the operand plus the op-code to an execution unit to carry out the instruction.

One should note that parts outlined above are reasonable independent of each other. That is, for example, the hardware used in developing the effective address is not used in any of the other steps. Let us divide the in-

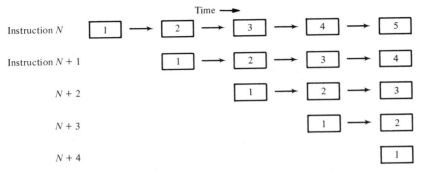

Fig. 10.3 An example of an instruction decode overlap.

struction decoding unit into five parts corresponding to the five steps listed above. Consider the first line of Fig. 10.3. An instruction moves from box 1 to box 2, etc. Time increases to the right. Now as soon as instruction $N$ has left box 1 for box 2, box 1 falls idle with nothing more to do for instruction $N$. Since eventually we will have to perform operation step 1 for instruction $N + 1$, why not begin now as soon as unit 1 goes idle? In the fullness of time instruction $N$ moves on to unit 3, leaving unit 2 to accept instruction $N + 1$, which leaves unit 1 free to accept instruction $N + 2$. When instruction $N$ finally leaves unit 5, we have unit 4 working on $N + 1$, 3 working on $N + 2$, 2 working on $N + 3$ and unit 1 working on instruction $N + 4$.

Everything goes along swimmingly, with non-memory referencing instructions skipping step 4 and perhaps load accumulator and store accumulator taking slightly different paths.

---

*Question 10.5:* The paths differ from step 3 on. Display them.

---

Until we detect a jump instruction in the sequence. Let it be an unconditional jump that was stored at memory location $M$. We decide what type of op-code we have in step 2; so by the time the jump gets to unit 2 to make the decision, we will already have started to fetch the instruction from location $M + 1$ using unit 1. Now $M + 1$ is the very last place a reasonable jump in location on $M$ will be going to jump to, so we compute the effective address in step 3, and then when unit 1 finishes the fetch from $M + 1$ (which we throw away), we have unit 1 start fetching from the effective target address of the jump instruction.

---

*Question 10.6:* If that sounds simple, go ahead and rough out the circuits to accomplish it.

---

So an unconditional jump causes a momentary hiccup in the instruction decode overlap but no major problems.

Now consider a conditional jump instruction arriving at unit 2. The instruction that just preceded the conditional jump is probably the one that will generate the condition the jump is testing. And it is only now in unit 3 of the decoding operation. So nobody in the world knows which way the "cat is going to jump." At this point, machine designers part ways. One group brings their pre-fetch and decode machinery to a dead halt until the condition is "resolved" and it is known which path to take. Others make an assumption about which path is most likely (fall-through or take-the jump) (and there are naturally two schools of thought here) and proceed to pre-fetch down the "likely" path. If they have guessed right, all is well and they continue without a hitch. If they are wrong, they are no worse off than the dead-stop group (except for some wasted fetches); and since pre-decoding *does not change any part of the machine or the context of the running program*, they simply abandon the wrong path and start over on the right path. The MU-5 keeps a record of which path was taken on the most recent execution of each jump instruction and pre-fetches from that path until proved wrong.

Finally, the most ambitious group of designers does it both ways. They alternately pre-fetch instructions from first one path and then the other either until the condition is resolved (in which case the untrodden pathway is abandoned) or until another jump instruction is decoded. Trying to go beyond this point would be too bloody-minded for the most sanguine contemporary designer, so they bring the pre-fetch to a halt until the old conditional jump is resolved, and they can discard one path and then pursue the other with full vigor.

## MERRY-GO-ROUND DESIGNS

As indicated in the previous section, conditional jumps cause difficulties in instruction pre-fetching because we don't know what to pre-fetch. Some studies of this problem have been made,[15-17] with quite startling results. There are two forms of dependencies that prevent a program from running infinitely fast. One of these is called "data dependency." Assume each instruction takes some reasonable time to complete. An instruction can be begun when all of its inputs (sources) are available and when there is a unit free to execute it. Assume for a moment that there are always enough units to execute an instruction and that the path through the program is known. Then the only barrier to infinite speed is the fact that one instruction must wait until another finishes before it can use the data the first is supposed to generate. Under these assumptions, Foster and Riseman found that an average program would run 51 times faster than on a normal computer.

But now we must consider control dependencies. We don't know which path to execute until the data needed to select the path become available. If we are going to jump on negative accumulator, we have to have a number in the accumulator. Given this restriction, the average program ran approximately 1.7 times as fast with unlimited resources, pre-fetch, etc., as it would have run on a standard computer—a loss of a factor of 30 in potential speed.

One way to attempt to regain this factor of 30 is to make successive instructions presented to the CPU be independent of each other. One good way to ensure that this is the case is to draw successive instructions from different programs. Several machines designed around this approach will now be described.

### The PPU's of the 6600

The Control Data Corp. 6600 has a set of 10 peripheral processing units (PPU's) which handle input and output. The most interesting feature of the PPU design is what is called the "barrel." (See Fig. 10.4.) Instead of each PPU having its own control and arithmetic unit, all ten of them share one fast unit on a time-division multiplex scheme.

This common unit operates at a 100 nsec rate. As the barrel rotates, one PPU after another comes into the "slot," at which point it is connected to the processor. A private memory reference is perhaps initiated and exactly one $\mu$sec later, the memory cycle is finished and the PPU is back in the "slot" again ready to proceed. This barrel is actually 51 circular-shift registers (each 10 bits long) which are used to store the registers of the 10 PPU's (18 bit $A$, 12 bit PC, effectively a 21-bit instruction register). Note that using this technique relies on the synchronism between the barrel's rotational velocity and the length of the private storage memory cycles. If a particular PPU doesn't need a memory reference for some instruction, it still has to take a trip around the barrel before beginning

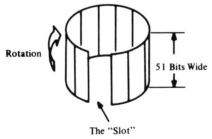

Fig. 10.4 The organization of the peripheral processors of the CDC-6600.

its next FETCH cycle. Some instructions require several trips around. None the less, this is an exciting idea that results in a considerable saving in hardware and still keeps a good balance between memory cycle time and the "apparent" control unit speed.

### The Honeywell 8200

This machine has a number of interesting features, but what concerns us here is the way in which successive instructions are taken from different programs.

The 8200 processor[18] is somewhat similar to the PPU's of the 6600—it has 9 pseudo machines, each with 32 registers. These registers are stored in a scratch pad and the 8200 differs from the 6600 in that only if a register group is active will it be fetched for a turn in the slot. Once fetched, the register group is allowed to execute one complete instruction. Since these are 3-address instructions, this implies four memory references, including the next fetch. Then the registers are put away in the scratch pad and the next active register group is given a turn. Any inactive group is skipped over so that there may be from 1 to 9 pseudo computers running at one time. If only one is running, it gets every turn. If two, they each execute at half speed and, if all 9 are active, each gets 1/9th the computation speed it would get if it were alone. Eight of these register groups are assigned to user programs while the 9th group has all the privileged instructions and is used by the monitor.

The advantage of this scheme is that up to 8 user programs can be running "simultaneously" with no interference and no overhead. Each one runs 8 times as slowly as if it were alone, but that is the best you could expect on the average in any case. If one group is put to sleep to wait for an I/O, the other 7 pick up the slack and run that much faster. The 9th group (called "Master Group") becomes active only when an I/O request is to be handled or some conflict or error is detected. Notice that unlike the 6600, the 8200 waits until the execution of an instruction is complete and the next instruction fetched before moving on to the next register group. Thus, it does not gain the possible increase in speed that could be attained this way. But as we will see below, that increase in speed is to be bought only with a fair amount of complexity.

### The Edinburgh Design

The Edinburgh design exists only on paper at this time.[19] Nonetheless, some of the ideas in it are worth examination, since they seem to offer considerable improvement in cost effectiveness over conventional designs. It was developed by the author while he was at the University of Edinburgh. Professor Sidney Michaelson, Chairman of the Computer Science

Department there, made many helpful suggestions during the development phase.

Consider if you will a vastly expanded H-8200 or CDC-6600 PPU system with, say, 255 register groups. Let there also be many independent storage units with relatively long cycle times and one very fast central processor. Operation will be as follows:

Memory unit $M$ finishes fetching an operand for register group $R$ and obtains the attention of the CPU. Register group $R$ is fetched and, together with the operand, is given to the CPU, which proceeds to execute one instruction for $R$ (say it was an ADD). Now $R$ needs a new instruction from some memory unit, say $M'$. The FETCH request is sent to unit $M'$ and register group $R$ is rewritten into the scratch pad. That is all for $R$ until $M'$ finishes its FETCH cycle. Meanwhile, memory unit $Y$ has completed a cycle on behalf of register group $G$. Register Group $G$ together with the information (if any) from $Y$ goes to the CPU and has a crack at execution.

Note that in this scheme, it is *not* the case that register groups take successive turns in a slot like in the 6600; nor is it the case that the register groups are scanned for "activity" as in the H-8200. Rather it is the storage devices that are scanned for cycle completion and it is the order of their completion that determines which group gets the next execution cycle. Thus, we can mix all kinds and speeds of storage together and, except for the relative speed of execution, they will be identical from a programmers point of view. This is obtained without incurring any system overhead for "hierarchy management." We can install one or two high-speed units for use by number crunching programs, several medium speed units for use by average type programs, and lots of low-speed units for use by I/O bound programs. Certainly there will have to be some level adjustment when a program passes from compute bound to I/O bound status, or vice versa, but this will be reasonably rare and easily handled.

Since successive instructions arriving at the CPU will come from different and independent programs, we can have what amounts to pipelining of instructions through the CPU, without worrying about interlocks. Further, we can take complete advantage of the overlapping of fetches from different storage banks, since again there will be many independent programs in execution. Finally, we can buy slow and hence inexpensive storage and still keep a high speed CPU busy.

### Stacking Memory References

In a machine like this with many programs running more or less asynchronously, there will of course come times when program $A$ references a block of storage now serving program $B$. Indeed, this will be quite common if, as we propose, the addresses of the storage units are interlaced on the low-order bits.* There must, therefore, be a mechanism for queueing up these requests. The method we propose is a direct adaptation of the method used in the Bull Γ-60 Computer (see below, Chapter 12).

Let each storage unit have two registers associated with it called the USER and the END registers. Let there be a scratch pad called the NEXT PAD containing one slot for each register group. Register groups will be numbered from 1 through 255. Figure 10.5 shows the situation when register groups 12, 100, 205, 71, and 36 have requested service from storage unit $M$ in that order and register group 12's request is presently being processed.

$$\left.\begin{array}{l} \text{USER } (M) = 12 \\ \text{END } (M) = 36 \end{array}\right\} \text{ associated with storage unit } M$$

$$\left.\begin{array}{l} \text{NEXT } (12) = 100 \\ \text{NEXT } (100) = 205 \\ \text{NEXT } (205) = 71 \\ \text{NEXT } (71) = 36 \\ \text{NEXT } (36) = \text{all zeros} \end{array}\right\} \text{stored in the NEXT PAD}$$

Fig. 10.5 The queue for memory unit M. (See text.)

Now suppose that register group 65 finds it needs to write a word $\beta$ into location $\alpha$ of unit $M$. It examines the user register of $M$ and finds that the unit is busy. Looking in the END register, it finds that RG 36 is the last one on the queue, so it writes its own name (65) in NEXT of 36 and then into END $(M)$. (See Fig. 10.6.) In order to free up the CPU for other activity, we must record somewhere the fact that 65 wishes to write word $\beta$ into location $\alpha$. Since we must make a reference to NEXT of 36 anyway (to record the fact that 65 follows 36 on the queue) let us expand the NEXT register to contain not just one but four fields as:

NEXT:    1. name of successor on the queue.
           2. type field (read, write, instruction fetch, indirect).
           3. word the successor wishes to write if it is a write.
           4. the address within $M$ at which read or write is to occur.

Therefore, in the situation just described, we would deposit

$$\text{"65,W,}\beta,\alpha\text{"}$$

in NEXT (36).

*Even if we interlace on high-order bits, two programs may wish to use a single copy of a common subroutine.

USER $(M) = 12$
END $(M) = 65$

NEXT $(12) = 100$
NEXT $(100) = 205$
NEXT $(205) = 71$
NEXT $(71) = 36$
NEXT $(36) = 65$
NEXT $(65) =$ all zeros

Fig. 10.6 Register group 65 is added to the queue of memory unit M.

Now let us suppose that unit $M$ finishes working for RG 12, gets its chance at the CPU, and then looks around for something else to do.  In the slot in NEXT PAD belonging to RG 12 is the name of an RG desiring service and also the three fields describing what service is desired.  In our example, it is register group 100 and we may imagine that 100 wants an instruction FETCH from location $\gamma$.  Then the NEXT (12) will contain

$$\text{``100, Inst,----,}\gamma\text{''}$$

We read from NEXT PAD the NEXT (USER($M$)), that is NEXT (12). The first two fields are sent to the USER register so that when this reference is finished, $M$ can tell the CPU for whom the reference was made and what kind it was.  The third field is sent to the memory buffer register (in this case no information) and the fourth to the memory address register.  A read cycle is begun to fetch the desired instruction.  If, after the read from the NEXT pad, the user number is now zero (not a legal register group number), we have cleaned up the queue waiting for $M$ and so set the END register to ZERO.  When a request for service is made to an idle memory unit, the appropriate information is written into the USER, MBR, and MAR registers and the name of the user is copied into the END register. We note that the NEXT PAD should be read destructively, leaving zeros behind, since the information stored there is needed only once and the zeros can be used as an indicator of the fact that the end of the queue has been reached.

The management of information transmission is in the hands of two devices called LOADER and SAVER.  Let us divide one CPU cycle into four parts called the 0, 1, 2, 3 subcycles.  We will consider all the registers of all the various I/O devices to be collected into an IOD scratch pad.

### Loader

Using a look-ahead scan, the LOADER will have identified a memory unit $M$ which has completed a reference by the beginning of a CPU cycle. Thus in subcycle 0, we read from the IOD scratch pad the contents of

USER ($M$) and MBR ($M$). The register group number stored in USER ($M$), say 12, is used as an index into the register group scratch pad. In subcycles 2 and 3, the contents of RG 12's registers are read up (destructively) and, at the beginning of the next CPU cycle, the register contents, the reference type (read, write, etc.), and the retrieved data (if any) are ready to present to the CPU. Meanwhile, in subcycle 1, the present user of $M$ (that is 12) is used to retrieve (destructively) the contents of NEXT (USER ($M$)) from NEXT PAD. In subcycle 3, this information (about the next task for $M$) is written into $M$'s slot in the IOD scratch pad. The LOADER device is now free to work for the next memory unit found by the scanner. (See Fig. 10.7.)

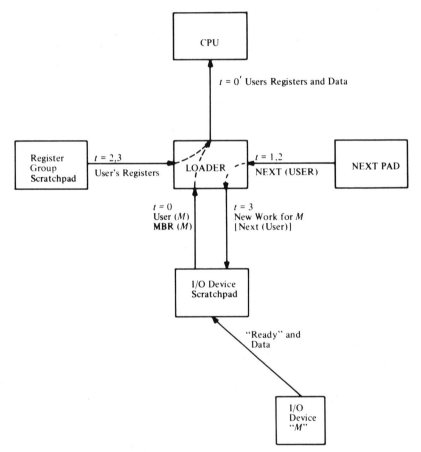

Fig. 10.7 The operations of the LOADER.

*Saver*

While the CPU is working on the "present" instruction and the LOADER is setting up the "future," the SAVER is busy preserving the "past." In subcycle 0 and 1, SAVER puts away the registers of the old register group from the CPU in the register group scratch pad. In subcycle 1, it interrogates the I/O device referenced by that register group and, if the device is idle, writes the information about this reference into the I/O device in subcycle 2. If the device is busy, it merely updates the END register. If the I/O device was idle, SAVER is through with its tasks, but if the device was busy, SAVER must preserve the information about the just generated reference in the NEXT PAD in the slot pointed at by the old contents of the END register. It does this in subcycle 3. (See Fig. 10.8.)

A consideration of the timing cycles above will show that the register group scratch pad and the NEXT PAD must be able to perform one read (destructive) and one write (without clearing) in one CPU cycle, while the IOD scratch pad must perform two of each in the same period. If the CPU has a cycle time of 100 nsec, the speed requirement on these scratch pads is not too demanding.

### Further Details of the Design Process

We should observe the two following rules in "designing" an installation:

1. The expected number of I/O transfer completions per second should be roughly equal to the expected number of CPU operations per second.
2. There should be enough register groups so that, considering the ones that are waiting for teletype input and the ones that are being "interferred" with (by access to a block already busy), they will generate the number of I/O requests per second needed to conform with Rule 1.

Let us consider a simple situation in which there are $A$ active register groups and $B$ blocks of storage that run $S$ times slower than the CPU (on the average). We will assume a worst case situation in which each effective address requires access to one of the blocks chosen at random with probability $1/B$. In order to keep the CPU busy (and attain a maximum throughput), we must have $B \geq S$.

Consider an instant of time at which there are $A$ requests outstanding (not yet honored). Then the average number of requests per block will be

$$\lambda = A/B \qquad (1)$$

and the probability that a block will have *no* requests for its services will be (assuming a Poisson distribution).

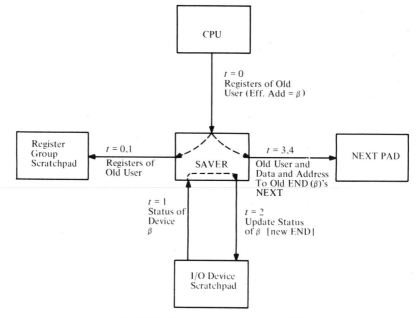

Fig. 10.8 The operations of the SAVER.

$$P(0) = e^{-\lambda} \cdot \frac{\lambda^0}{0!} = e^{-\lambda} \tag{2}$$

The number of "idle" blocks will then be

$$B \cdot P(0) = Be^{-\lambda} \tag{3}$$

and the number of "busy" blocks will be

$$B(1 - e^{-\lambda}) \tag{4}$$

which should be greater than or equal to $S$.

Thus,

$$S \le B(1 - e^{-\lambda}). \tag{5}$$

Table 10.1 shows a few representative values of $\lambda$ versus $B/S$. If we assume that a block of storage costs $K$ times as much as a register group, we can minimize the cost of the storage and register groups for a given CPU. Two values of $K$, 2 and 10, are included in Table 10.1.

From this table we can conclude that if a block of storage is twice as expensive as a register group, we should choose a $\lambda$ of 1.5 and a $B/S$ ration of 1.29. If a block costs 10 times as much as a register group, we

TABLE 10.1    CALCULATION OF THE RELATIVE COST OF A MACHINE FOR VARIOUS
AVERAGE NUMBERS OF REQUESTS PER BLOCK OF STORAGE ($\lambda$). $K$ IS
THE RATIO OF THE COSTS OF A BLOCK OF STORAGE TO THE COST OF A
REGISTER GROUP

| $\lambda$ Average No. of requests | $B/S$ No. of blocks/ Relative speed | $K=2$ Relative cost | $K=10$ Relative cost |
|---|---|---|---|
| .5 | 2.54 | 3.15 | 2.65 |
| 1 | 1.57 | 2.36 | 1.73 |
| 1.5 | 1.29 | 2.25 | 1.48 |
| 2 | 1.16 | 2.32 | 1.39 |
| 3 | 1.05 | 2.63 | 1.365 |
| 5 | 1.10 | 3.53 | 1.515 |

should pick a $\lambda$ around 3 and a $B/S$ ratio of 1.05. In both cases, taking
a $\lambda$ of 2.0 and a $B/S$ ratio of 1.16 results in a change of cost of less than
3%. We, therefore, recommend that choice.

Now given a value of $S$ we can specify the rest of the machine. For a
speed ratio of 10:1 ($S = 10$), we need 12 storage blocks and 24 active register groups. For $S = 100$, we should have 116 blocks of storage and 232
register groups. Since we are all partial to powers of two, I suggest 128
blocks and 256 active register groups.

*Dedicated I/O Devices*    Certain of the input/output devices can serve many
programs at once (storage blocks for instance or disks). Others should be
dedicated to a single program while that program requires them at all.
One thinks in particular of teletypes, card readers, and line printers which
do not lend themselves well to "interlacing."

There are at least two ways of dealing with such devices and the choice
between these ways will depend in part on the cost of a register group.

*Case 1: Cheap Register Groups*    If the cost of a register group is, say, under
$1,000, then the obvious solution is to leave the group assigned to the pro-
gram which references one of these slow dedicated devices. In this case,
the device does not need any queueing mechanism, but merely the user number (register group number) and a buffer capable of holding either one
character or one word, depending on the device.

For example, to have 256 *active* register groups we probably need 4
times that number of teletype terminals. This implies (under the present
scheme) about 1024 register groups and the same number of ports on the
I/O multiplexor. But these ports need have only an 8-bit information
buffer (one character) and can have their "user number" wired in.

*Case II: Expensive Register Groups*    If the register groups are relatively expensive, we don't want to buy 100 of them if we can help it. This indicates that we should "dump" the program referencing a slow device and use the register group for something else.

What we must store with the I/O device now is not the Register Group number, but the address at which the registers have been stored in main storage. Perhaps this also could be wired in if an area of low core were reserved for each I/O device. The register group should be automatically dumped when it references a slow device and, when the dump is complete, the register group is marked "idle."

When a slow device completes a transfer the Highway Control Unit "looks around" for an idle Register Group. When it finds one, it initiates a "load register" from the address supplied by the I/O device. If there are *no* idle groups, the I/O device flag should be left up and an attempt should be made again after the next scan.

This latter method doesn't sound terribly attractive and it requires some specialized operations by the Highway Control Unit. One would much prefer to see Case I implemented. It leads to a cleaner design.

### Backing Store

At the present time there does not appear to be a reasonable substitute for moving head disks. They have large capacity, low cost per bit, and are erasable.

Unfortunately, they can transfer at best around 10 pages per second when the pages are selected at random. They have the further undesireable property that a receiver must be ready to gulp down each word when it is presented, unless a very severe degradation in performance is to ensue.

Coupling such an "impatient" device on to our asynchronous machine is something of a problem, since we cannot in the normal course of events guarantee a time within which a storage cycle will be completed. Once again we suggest two possible approaches.

*Method I Fast Buffer Store*    The simplest method is to provide a storage unit for absorbing the information from the disk as fast as necessary and then moving it out to main storage at a rate compatible with the rest of the machine.

Assume all backing store transfers are in units of one page of 1024 words each. For the read operation, we need 4 instructions:
1. Request assignment of a buffer (respond with buffer number).
2. Load buffer $b$ from disk address $d$.
3. Copy buffer $b$ to main store page $p$.
4. Release buffer $b$.

These could all be part of one (or perhaps 2) instructions with the assignment and release of the buffers being automatic.

The question to ask now is how many buffers of what speed do we need per disk. Loading a buffer will take about 100 msec for seek and transfer. Copying the buffer to main store will take no more than an average of 50 $\mu$sec per word in our 256-register-group machine. 1000 words can then be moved in 50 msec. With two buffers per disk, one of them can be filling (or draining) from the disk while the other is being transferred to main storage and then loaded from main storage for a subsequent write to the disk.

With 4 big disks, we then need 8 one page buffers. Each disk can produce one word, say every 8 $\mu$sec, and four of them produce 4 words in that period. Allowing for the fact that all of the four buffers being transferred to or from main storage may request a word in any one 8 $\mu$sec time interval, we see that $8K$ of 1 $\mu$sec core will do nicely as a buffering device for 4 disks. This configuration can exchange about 40 pages per second between main store and backing store.

*Method II Preemptive Demand*    Suppose that the blocks of storage are interlaced to a depth of $2^b$ on the $b$ low-order bits of the address. Loading a page into such a memory will require access to a given block only every $2^b$th word. Suppose further that there exists a "preemptive demand" which places a register group at the head of the queue of groups waiting for service from a given block. Let the storage cycle time be $\tau_s$ and the time between words coming off the disk be $\tau_d$.

Then if there are $n$ disks which can issue preemptive demands, we see at once that

$$2^b \cdot \tau_d \geq (n+1)\tau_s.$$

The factor of $n$ plus one arises because the block may be busy when initially requested. The other $n-1$ disks can preempt this preemption. For $\tau_d = 8\,\mu$sec, $\tau_s = 10\,\mu$sec and $b = 3$ we may have up to 5 disks. For $b = 4$ we may have up to 11.

This unfortunately is not quite all that is required. The register group which is handling the transfer must have certain unusual characteristics. Since it may be on up to 8 queues ($b = 3$) at one time, it must have 8 NEXT registers. Perhaps the best solution would be to provide a special register group for each disk and handle the problem that way. Method I is more straightforward, but method II is probably less expensive.

## MULTIPLE FUNCTIONAL UNITS

A second method of speeding up the CPU is to provide many units for executing instructions that can operate in parallel. Perhaps the foremost examples of this approach are the IBM 370/195[10] and the CDC-6600.[1] The 195 is too complicated to explain here but the reader is urged to consult the January 1967 issue of the *IBM Journal of Research and Development*, which is devoted to a description of the 360/91. The 91 and the 195 have identical CPU's. We will however look quickly at the CDC-6600.

The main CPU can communicate only with memory. (All I/O is handled by the PPU's.) It has eight 18-bit address ($A$) registers, eight 18-bit increment ($B$) registers, and eight 60-bit operand ($X$) registers. The increment registers function primarily as index registers and the operand registers as accumulators. When an 18-bit address is inserted into one of the address registers, a transfer of the correspondingly numbered operand register to or from core is initiated. $A1$–$A5$ cause loads of $X1$–$X5$, respectively, and $A6, A7$ cause storage of the contents of $X6$ and $X7$. $A0$ and $X0$ are used to refer to what is called "extended core," i.e., a collection of a million or more cells of slow (2 $\mu$ sec) core that can be attached to the 6600. $A0$ holds a central memory address while $X0$ holds an extended core address. Instructions exist which will transmit blocks of data in either direction, using these addresses as source and destination.

Instructions are either 15- or 30-bits long and are packed several to a 60-bit word with the restriction that a 30-bit instruction may not cross over a word boundary. There is an 8-word × 60-bit instruction stack which is kept filled automatically and may contain between 16 and 32 instructions, depending on their length. Tight inner loops can be contained therein and can execute without any references to storage at a consequent increase in speed. Most instructions consist of an op-code and three register designators (two sources and a results destination).

The CPU has 10 functional units which can operate independently. There are two multipliers and two incrementing units and one each Boolean, Brancher, Shifter, Floating point adder, fixed point adder, and a divider. Since these units operate asynchronously, three rules are necessary to keep order.[20] These rules are enforced by a reservation control unit.

1. An instruction is *issued* to a functional unit when
   a. The unit is free (if there are two identical units the first free one is used),
   b. the specified result register is not reserved.
2. A unit *starts* executing an instruction when both operands become available.
3. After completing an operation, the result is *stored* in the destination register only when all previously issued instructions which specify the register as an operand have begun.

---

*Question 10.7:* Show that elimination of any one of these rules could lead to false results.

---

## PIPELINING

In an earlier section we discussed instruction pre-fetch and postulated a five-stage unit for speeding up the process by having each stage perform one independent task and then pass the instruction to the next stage for further processing. The same idea can be applied to the execution process. Consider a floating multiply operation for example. We must multiply the two mantissas (signicands), normalize the result, add the two exponents (exrads), correct the resulting exrad for normalization, and finally put the word back together. This is just a superficial analysis. Clever designers have discovered as many as 20 or 30 independent steps in the performance of a floating multiply. If we had a string of floating multiplies to perform and if the multiplier were designed in successive independent stages as described above, we could stream these instructions through the unit at a high rate of speed. Such a situation is likely to occur when we are manipulating vectors or matrices. Hence a machine designed with a pipelined execution unit is sometimes called a "vector processor." The Texas Instruments Advanced Scientific Computer (ASC), the CDC string array processor (STAR) and the Cray Research Inc. Cray 1 are all such machines.

Let us examine the vector operations on the Cray 1.[21] To begin with, there are 8 vector registers ($V$ registers), each containing 64 elements or words. Access time to a word of a vector (and also the basic machine cycle time) is 12.5 nanoseconds. Main memory of up to one million words of semiconductor storage has a much slower access time of 50 nanoseconds. Note that there is no cache involved here. This is the genuine main memory speed. There are six independent functional units that can use the $V$ registers. These are: integer add, shift, logical, floating add, floating multiply, and reciprocator (there is no divider, so division is accomplished by taking the reciprocal of the divisor and multiplying). Each of these functional units can be called into play by a three address instruction which specifies three of the $V$ registers or two $V$ registers and main memory. Suppose the instruction is:

$$\text{ADD } V1, V2, V3.$$

The first element $V1$ and the first element of $V2$ are added; then the second elements of each vector are added and so forth. The contents of a vector length register ($VL$) determine how many elements are to be processed.

After a certain number of clock periods (6 for the floating point adder), the first sum appears and is stored in the first element of $V3$. On each successive clock period thereafter, another sum is spit out and stored in $V3$. Since a clock pulse is 12.5 nanoseconds, one is clearly pipelining at a high rate. But this is not the limit. As soon as the first sum has been stored in $V3$, it is available for another vector operation. For example, we may wish to multiply the result by the corresponding element of $V4$ and put the product in $V5$ to form:

$$V5_i = V4_i \times (V1_i + V2_i) \qquad \text{for } i = 1 \text{ to } 64.$$

This is called "chaining" of vector operations. The multiply functional unit has 7 internal stages. The first sum is available in clock period 6 and is fetched in CP 7, and the first product appears in CP 14. Another product appears in CP 15 and so on until all products are produced. Since main memory is interleaved 16 ways, it has a fast enough effective access time to serve as a source or as an ultimate destination. Chaining can be compounded with three or four or perhaps more vector operations involved, as long as there are separate functional units for each step of the chain and we don't run out of vector registers. Long vectors must be segmented into sub-vectors of lengths 64 or less, and then a program loop is required to process successive sub-vectors.

In STAR[12] and the ASC,[13] there are up to four pipelines but they are functionally interchangeable with each other rather than specialized as in the Cray 1 or the 6600. In the ASC each "pipe" can produce a result every 60 nanoseconds. Main memory consists of 8 independent blocks. Each block is 8 words wide, so data are fetched in 8 word units. Each pipe has 6 buffers, each capable of holding an 8 word unit. (See Fig. 10.9.)

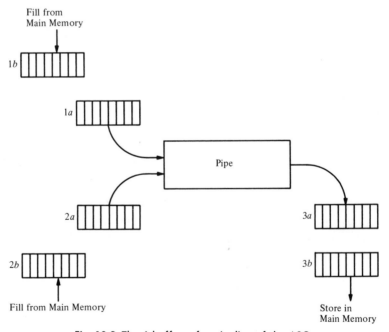

Fig. 10.9 The 6 buffers of a pipeline of the ASC.

While operands are being read from buffers 1*a* and 2*a* and results are being stored in buffer 3*a*, we have buffers 1*b* and 2*b* being filled from main memory and buffer 3*b* being copied into main memory. For vector operations the buffers are refilled and emptied automatically, so the pipeline can be kept supplied with data.

Up to 36 instructions in total can be in execution at any one time. Four are in the process of being decoded or executed in the Instruction Processing Unit and eight in each of the four pipes. Naturally a vector instruction will occupy a complete pipe (if it is longer than 8 elements), so the

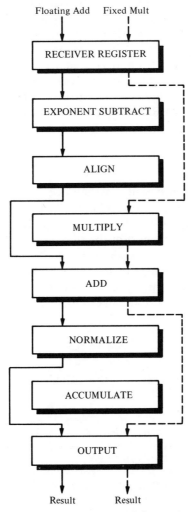

Fig. 10.10 Arithmetic unit pipeline concept.

count of *different* instructions may be less than 36 even if everything is completely busy. Scalar (nonvector) operations are reordered by the compilers to "achieve optimal overlap of instruction execution in the pipelined instruction and arithmetic processing units." Figure 10.10 shows the overlaps possible in a pipe. Each box may contain a partially executed instruction.

The STAR machine[12] has a 40 nanosecond clock period. It also utilizes 8-word-wide memory units called in this case "super-words" or "swords." The floating point arithmetic unit is divided into two pipes. Pipe 1 is used for register add, subtract, and multiply and all vector arithmetic except divide and square root. Pipe 2 is used for register divide and square root, and all vector instructions. In addition to the usual two sources and destinations, STAR provides a third input called the control vector. This is a string of ZERO's and ONE's and is used when sparse vectors are to be operated upon. A ONE indicates that that element of the source exists and a ZERO that it does not. Thus sparse vectors can be packed up close with only the string of ZERO's in the control vector remaining to indicate the squeezed-out spaces.

## SUMMARY

This chapter is concerned with methods of speeding up the computer. Certain sample machines were investigated: the CDC-6600, the IBM 360/85, the Texas Instruments ASC, the Cray 1, the Honeywell 8200, and the Edinburgh Design. A large part of the chapter is devoted to this last paper tiger. An attempt is made to make some design decisions on the basis of what statistics we can estimate in advance. Alternate approaches are presented and an attempt is made to lead the reader through a preliminary investigation of the proposed architecture.

## REFERENCES

1. Burnett, G. J., and Coffman, E. G. Jr. "A Study of Interleaved Memory System." *AFIPS Proc. SJCC* **36,** 467–474 (1970).
2. Stanga, D. C. "Univac 1108 Multiprocessor System." *AFIPS Proc. SJCC* **30,** 67–75 (1967).
3. Skinner, C. E., and Asher, J. R. "Effects of Storage Contention on System Performance." *IBM Systems Journal* **8,** 4, 319–333 (1969).
4. Wilkes, M. V. "Slave Memories and Dynamic Storage Allocation." *IEEE Trans. on Elect. Comp.*, 270–271 (April 1965).
5. Conti, C. M., Gibson, D. H., and Pitkowsky, S. H. "Structural Aspects of the System/360 Model 85, I General Discussion." *IBM Systems J.* **7,** No. 1, 2–14 (1968).
6. Bell, J. R., Casasent, D., and Bell, C. G. "An Investigation of Alternative Cache Organizations." *IEEE Trans. on Computers* **C-23,** 4, 346–351 (April 1974).

7. Kaplan, K. R., and Winder, R. O. "Cache Based Computer Systems." *Computer*, 30–37 (March 1973).
8. Liptay, J. S. "Structural Aspects of the System/360 Model 85, II—The Cache." *IBM Systems J.* **7,** No. 1, 15–21 (1968).
9. Ibbett, R. N. "The MU5 Instruction Pipeline." *The Computer Journal* **15**, 1, 45–50 (Feb. 1972).
10. *IBM System/360 Model 91, Functional Characteristics Form 22-6907-2.* Poughkeepsie, N.Y., International Business Machines Corp., 1966.
11. Anderson, D. W., Sparacio, F. J., and Tomasulo, R. M. "The IBM System/360 Model 91: Machine Philosophy and Instruction Handling." *IBM Journal of R&D* **11**, 1, 8–24 (Jan. 1967).
12. *Control Data STAR-100 Computer Systems Reference Manual*, Pub. No. 60256000. Control Data Corp., Arden Hills, Minn. (1971).
13. *A Description of the Advanced Scientific Computer*, Pub. #930034-1. Austin, Texas, Texas Instruments (April 1973).
14. Thornton, J. E. *Design of a Computer—The Control Data 6600.* Glenview, Ill., Scott Foresman (1970).
15. Riseman, E. M., and Foster, C. C. "The Inhibition of Potential Parallelism by Conditional Jumps." *IEEE Trans. on Computers* **C-21**, 12, 1404–1411 (Dec. 1972).
16. Foster, C. C., and Riseman, E. M. "Percolation of Code to Enhance Parallel Dispatching and Execution." *IEEE Trans. on Computers* **C-21**, 12, 1411–1415 (Dec. 1972).
17. Tjaden, G. S., and Flynn, M. J. "Detection and Parallel Execution of Independent Instructions." *IEEE Trans. on Computers* **C-19**, 10, 889–895 (Oct. 1970).
18. *Honeywell Series 200, Model 8200 General Systems Description.* Wellesley Hills, Mass., Honeywell Elect. Data Processing, 1965.
19. Foster, C. C. "Uncoupling Central Processor and Storage Device Speeds." *The Computer Journal* **14**, 1, 45–48 (Feb. 1971).
20. Tomasulo, R. M. "An Efficient Algorithm for Exploiting Multiple Arithmetic Units." *IBM Journal of R&D* **11**, 1, 25–33 (Jan. 1967).
21. *The Cray 1 Computer Preliminary Reference Manual.* Chippewa Falls, Wisc., Cray Research Inc. (1975).

# 11 | PARALLELISM AND DISTRIBUTED LOGIC

*"Many as the sand which is by the sea in multitude."*
*Kings IV, 20*

There are limits to the amount of speed one can squeeze out of a computer, whether by increasing the horsepower or by decreasing the wind resistance. One such limit is the propagation velocity of electrical signals. If the computer is a 1-ft cube, light takes 1 nsec to get from one side to the other and signals sent down shielded cable take about 10 nsec just to get across the machine. This does not include any delays inside gates.

One way of increasing a computer's speed is to provide many processing units which operate in parallel. If there are only a few such units, the machine is called a multiprocessor; If there are many units, it is often called a parallel machine or a "distributed logic device."

## EARLY DESIGNS

One of the earliest multiprocessing machines might be thought to be the Honeywell 800 described above but that was actually a multiplexed single processor and does not fall into this category. Probably the earliest multiprocessor ($\sim$ 1959) actually built was the Gamma-60[1] made by the French concern Compagnie de Machine Bull. This machine consisted of a central memory (32$K$ words of 24 bits), a central "control unit," and up to 128 "elements," each of which was capable of concurrent autonomous action once it was triggered off by the central control unit.

The elements normally included in a system were:

|       | Arithmetic unit | – | Decimal arithmetic. |
|-------|-----------------|---|---------------------|
|       | Logical unit | – | Binary arithmetic and AND and OR. |
|       | Comparison unit | – | Compares a number $X$ with numbers $A$ and $B$ and reports relative magnitude. |
| 1 each |                |   | Also used for transfers within core. |
|       | Transcoder unit | – | Automatic table look-up—128 characters for I/O translation. |
|       | Magnetic drum | – | 128 tracks, 200 words/track, 20 msec revolution. |
| 1–10 | Uniselectors | – | For driving 1–48 magnetic tape units. |
| any | Card readers | – | 300 cards/min. |
| any | Punched tape reader | – | 200 char./sec. |
| any | Line printer | – | 300 lines/min—120 characters. |
| any | Card punch | – | 300 cards/min. |
| any | Paper tape punch | – | 25 char./sec. |

To provide for autonomous operation, each element had sufficient storage to remember:

1. The location of its operands in memory.
2. The operation to be performed.
3. The number of times the operation should be repeated.
4. The location in memory of the next instruction of the program it is working for.
5. A "qualitative" register to store information about the outcome of the operation.
6. 2 registers to store the "head" and "tail" of the queue of programs waiting to use this element.

Instructions are picked up from memory and interpreted by the central control unit (when notified by an element that its current task is completed). Notice that this is almost the inverse of the Edinburgh design. Most instructions are executed by the elements, but BRANCH and CUT instructions are handled in the central control. Branches, of course, allow jumps on various conditions, but the CUTs require some explanation. Figure 11.1 shows the instruction layout and the meaning of the various bits.

The $tc$ field determines the type of CUT to be executed. The normal cut ($tc = 1$) releases the element being used and places the program containing this cut on the queue waiting for service from element $X$. The word following every CUT instruction is left blank by the assembler and acts as the NEXT slot for this cut. (See the description of the queueing mechanism of the Edinburgh design.)

| CUT *instruction* | T | K | tc | m | F | A | X |
|---|---|---|---|---|---|---|---|
| | 0 | 1 | | | | | |
| | 24 | 23 22 | 20 | 19 18 | 17 | 16 15 | 1 |

$m$ = number of times this instruction must have been called up previously if this call is to result in further action. If $m \neq 0$, $m-1$ replaces $m$ and the instruction is stored again without further action. If $m = 0$, the program continues from this point.

$X$ = the name of the real element transferred to ($0 \rightarrow 127$) or the address of the first cell of the virtual element transferred on.

$tc$ = 1, normal transfer to real element designated in $X$–pick up chain is utilized. Previous real element is released. (transfer)

= 2, as in 1, but previous element *not* released. (transfer and hold)

= 3, as is 1, but pick up chain not utilized. (preempt)

= 4, transfer on a virtual element, $X$ designates address of first image cell of virtual element. Pick up chain is utilized.

= 5, release virtual element designated in $X$.

= 6, SIMU–*first*–go to instruction sequence which begins at $X$ and initiate it. When control unit is released, go to instruction immediately following the SIMU and initiate that sequence. (AND branch)

= 7, STOP–release the previous real element and do not transfer.

**Fig. 11.1 The CUT instruction of the Γ-60.**

$tc$ fields equal 2 and 3 are seldom used, since they do not obey normal queueing discipline.

Just as in normal assembly language, the programmer wants the ability to construct MACRO's, so in the Gamma-60, he is given the ability to construct virtual elements or pseudoprocessors. The first two words of each virtual element (a string of instructions) are reserved to act as "image catenas" to hold the head and tail registers for its queue. One bit of these words is used to indicate whether the virtual element is busy or idle. A cut with $tc = 4$ tests this bit automatically and, if it is ZERO (idle), sets it to ONE (busy) and proceeds to execute the subsequent code. If the bit is already ONE, the present cut to that virtual element is put on the queue. A CUT with $tc = 5$ examines the queue of virtual element $X$ and, if it is *not* empty, starts off the next process on the queue. If the queue is empty, it sets the status bit to ZERO, indicating an idle virtual element.

A $tc$ field of 6 is called a SIMU cut. Control first goes to location $X$ and starts up the string of code located there. Once that has set an element into activity or been placed on a queue, the SIMU cut returns to the original line of code and continues with that. This might be called an "AND branch" and is used to set two elements into parallel activity. Successive SIMU cuts can set many elements going. A SIMU cut is used by the monitor to initiate a new program. Thus there may be many programs running at one time and each of them may have several activities going on.

The $m$ field is called the regrouping field and is used in conjunction with the SIMU cut. Suppose I have three tasks to perform, $A$, $B$, and $C$. I don't care which order $A$ and $B$ are performed in and indeed they use different elements, but task $C$ requires the results of both $A$ and $B$ and must not start until both are done. In such a case, we will start task $C$ with a CUT with an $m$ field of one. $A$ or $B$, whichever finished first, CUTs to the beginning of $C$. It picks up the CUT there, sees that $m \neq 0$, subtracts ONE from $m$, and lays the CUT back down. Nothing else happens. Now the other task CUT's to the beginning of $C$, finds an $m = 0$ and executes the remainder of the CUT instruction. Up to four tasks can be "regrouped" with one CUT and cascading several allows as many as may be desired.

At the time the Gamma-60 was designed, core speeds were slow (11 $\mu$sec cycle times) and the many elements soon swamped the single bank of core available. Redesigned with today's technology, a new Gamma-60 might make quite a splash in the computing world.

Another early ($\sim$1960) attempt at multiprocessing was the Thompson-Ramo-Wooldridge TRW-400.[2] This was to consist of 16 processors, 64 peripheral devices (including banks of core storage), and an electronic cross-bar switch which permitted the peripherals to be divided into 16 subsets (any device in any desired subset), one connected to each processor. One processor, although physically the same as the others, was to be designated as the master unit. This unit was to assign jobs and the required peripherals for the other 15. This was called a Polymorphic computer and was supposed to have the ability to "fail-soft" or have "graceful degradation." That is, if one processor or peripheral failed, the system could be reconfigured and go on with its function, albeit at perhaps a somewhat slower pace. This ability to keep on working after a failure is very important in some applications.

Although a lot of work was done on the design of the TRW-400 and construction actually begun, the total machine was never completed.

---

*Question 11.1:* Design a 4 × 4 crossbar for a small version of the TRW-400. Assume 48 bit words are to be transferred in parallel.

---

## DISTRIBUTED LOGIC

As one progresses beyond the Gamma-60 or the TRW-400, one reaches a stage at which a certain amount of logic is associated with each memory cell. The associative memory we discussed in Chapter 4 is an example of this type of computer—each cell contains enough logic to recognize whether or not its contents are the same as the comparand.

The purpose of distributing logic to each memory cell is to permit certain operations to be carried out in parallel instead of having to bring the operands one by one to the CPU for processing. When this purpose is realized, a group of operations that would be programmed as an iterative loop in a conventional machine can be executed in parallel and in a time independent of the number of elements to be processed. Associative memories are a form of distributed logic and we have already seen how searches can be carried out in parallel in them. A little later we will present an algorithm for parallel addition in an AM.

In all, five functions have been "distributed." Three of them are clearly local in nature and the last two might be called "global." They are:

Comparison — the ability to compare the contents of a cell with the contents of a master comparand register.

Communication— the ability to influence the state of selected neighboring cells.

Control — the ability to determine, on the basis of its own contents or state, what operation is to be performed.

Feedback — the ability of the total array of cells to tell the central control unit information about the state of the array.

Priority — the ability of a cell in the array to determine whether or not it is the "first" cell of the array in a given state.

In Chapter 4 we discussed an associative memory with the abilities to compare, to feed back "some or none" information about the state, and to select the first responder. Let us now design a machine around that memory.

### CACS-I (Content Addressable Computing System—first version.)

We postulate a $32K$ cell array of 48 bits per cell with two independent sets of sense lines and tag flip-flops called the $I$ and the $J$ response stores. The $I$ response store is used to retrieve instructions while the $J$ store is used to hold the information that the cell is or is not a "responder."

The $I$ response store is connected like a shift register and can be caused to "advance" (shift down) one step at a time on signal from the CPU.

---

*Question 11.2:* Indicate how this might be accomplished using cryotrons as storage and logic elements.

---

The CPU contains an instruction register ($IR$) a comparand register ($C$), a mask register ($M$) and 64 scratch pad registers ($S_{00}-S_{77}$). $S_{00}$ is wired to contain all zeros and $S_{77}$ is wired to contain all ones. The other 62 may be used to hold words retrieved from the AM and serve as the operating registers for various instructions. Instructions consist of 1, 2, 3, or 4 fields of 6 bits each and are stored one instruction per cell left justified. This is done both for simplicity and for programmer convenience. The basic machine cycle is as follows:

Read the responder on $I$ into the instruction register.
Begin decoding instruction.
Advance activity on $I$ one position.
Execute instruction.

Let us now look at what instructions should be included in the machine.
There are the usual interregister operations of which

$$\text{ADD } p, q, r$$

is a typical example. It adds the contents of $S_p$ to the contents of $S_q$ and puts the result in $S_r$. This class includes add, subtract, multiply, divide, and, or, and exclusive or. Then we have a group of "immediate" instructions:

BIT $r, b, k$—which affects the $b$-th bit of register $r$ according to the value of $k$. If:

$k = 0$—no operation.
$\phantom{k} = 1$—set the bit to ONE.
$\phantom{k} = 2$—clear the bit to ZERO.
$\phantom{k} = 3$—complement the bit.
$\phantom{k} = 4$—add the bit.
$\phantom{k} = 5$—subtract the bit.
$\phantom{k} = 6$—clear register and then set bit.

BYS $r, y, c$—byte substitute. Replaces the 6 bit byte of register $r$ whose right most bit is indicated by $c$ with the contents of the $y$ field.

ENR *r*    —Enter word in register. Takes the contents of the cell following the one containing this instruction and enters it into register *r*. Activity on *I* is advanced an extra step, skipping the cell that is loaded into *r*.

Next we have control operations which include skips on zero, non-zero, positive and negative registers, skips on particular bits of a register being zero or one (ZBS *r*, *b* and NBS *r*, *b*) and,

SSR        —skip if some responders on *J*.
SNR        —skip if NO responders on *J*.
DSZ *r*, *n*—decrement register *r* by *n* and skip if zero.
HLT        —halt.

There is a group of four instructions used for subroutine cells. These are:

USK  *α*—unconditionally skip the next instruction.  *α* is a seven byte field ignored in this instruction.
NOP  *α*—a do nothing instruction.  *α* is seven bytes.
JMP  *α* —search, using the *I* response store for an instruction of the form "NOP *α*" and jump to that location.
RJP  *r* —jump to the location which contains the same bit pattern as is contained in register *r*. Search using *I*.

The use of these four instructions is best explained by reference to **Fig. 11.2.  We have a main program on the left which wishes to use a sub-**routine named JONES located beginning in cell *γ*. The call will take place from cell *α* of the main program. When the ENR 35 is placed in the instruction register, the effect will be to put the contents of *α* + 1 into register 35. This is the instruction "USK SMITH" where the field SMITH is any desired bit pattern that is unique to this call and appears nowhere else in memory after an USK.  After loading register 35, activity on *I* is advanced one extra step so that the *I* bit of cell *α*+2 will be ON and all the rest will be OFF.  When this instruction (JMP JONES) is loaded, it will cause all the *I* bits of memory to be set to ONE and a search

|  | *Main Program* | *Subroutine* |
|---|---|---|
| *α* | ENR 35 | *γ* NOP JONES |
| *α*+1 | USK SMITH | : |
| *α*+2 | JMP JONES | : |
| *α*+3 |  | : |
|  |  | RJP 35 |

Fig. 11.2 Subroutine calling procedure.

will be performed for a cell containing the bit pattern corresponding to:

### "NOP JONES"

The only cell in memory containing this pattern had better be the first instruction of the subroutine and, as this is the case in our example, we end with $I_\gamma$ set to ONE and all other $I$ bits set to zero. Consequently, the next instruction is selected from $\gamma$. $I$ is advanced one position and the subroutines activities begin. Parameters may be passed through various scratch pad registers or by having their $J$-response bits set.

When the subroutine has completed its activities, it executes an RJP 35 which causes a search (using $I$) for the pattern "USK SMITH" stored in $S_{35}$. This is found in $\alpha+1$ and, when executed, causes an unconditional skip to $\alpha+3$ where the main program resumes. Although this method appears to be somewhat clumsy, the author knows of no other method that will work even this easily.

---

*Question 11.3:* Can you think of another method of calling subroutines? Remember that the cells of an AM don't have any "names." We have used the labels above purely for convenience in referring to them

---

We have a set of operations involving the associative properties of the memory:

SET —turn ON all the $J$ response bits.

LDR $r$ —load register $r$ with the logical AND of all responders.

SVF —save the first responder. Reset all others.

MUW $m, c$—load the mask register from $S_m$ and the comparand register from $S_c$. *Multiwrite* in all responders. Write the contents of the comparand register in memory for those bit positions in which the mask contains ONES.

WIN $m, c$ —load the mask register from $S_m$ and the comparand register from $S_c$. *Winnow* the responders, keeping only those that match the comparand where the mask contains ONES.

Finally we should include a set of register shifting instructions: left, right, end off, cyclic, sign extended, and single or double length. For example,

DRL $q, r, n$—double right logical will shift the concatenated contents of $S_q$ and $S_r$ to the right $n$ places end off with no sign extension.

---

*Question 11.4:* Sketch out a design for the CACS-I CPU laying out timing charts for the instructions including the AM.

---

*Parallel Addition*    Falkoff[3] presents several algorithms for searches for maximum and minimum contents of an array. Here we will present an algorithm for CACS-I that will add field *a* to field *b*, placing the result in field *b* for all responders in parallel.[4] In order to keep the example simple, we will assume TWO's complement notation for negative numbers and that there will be no overflow to bother about. Further, we will specify that the *b* field runs from bit 0 (the right-most bit) through bit 9, that the *a* field goes from bit 20 through bit 29, and that bits 47 and 46 are used, respectively, as MARKER and CARRY bits in each word. Since we will have to use the *J* response store during the addition process, we will begin by identifying the cells we wish to work on with a ONE in their marker bits. We assume that upon entry to the algorithm all marker bits are ZERO and that the set of responders corresponds to the set upon which addition is to be performed. Now consider the addition process for the *i*th bit. Figure 11.3 shows on the left the eight possible initial conditions and on the right the 8 possible final conditions. $A_i$ and $B_i$ are the bits of the respective fields and $C_{i-1}$ is the carry (if any) from the next less significant position.

Note that in the first, second, seventh, and eighth rows the final configuration is the same as the initial, so that no action needs be performed. Note also that the final state of the third row labelled I is the same as the initial state of row II so that the action to carry out II must precede that carrying out I. Similarly, III must precede IV, but no other dependencies are present. Therefore, we will carry these out in the order II, I, III, and IV.

|      | Initial $C_{i-1}A_iB_i$ | Final $C_iA_iB_i$ |
|------|-------------------------|-------------------|
|      | 000                     | 000               |
|      | 001                     | 001               |
| I    | 010                     | 011               |
| II   | 011                     | 110               |
| III  | 100                     | 001               |
| IV   | 101                     | 100               |
|      | 110                     | 110               |
|      | 111                     | 111               |

Fig. 11.3 The possible initial and final bit configurations for the bit-serial addition of field A to field B (*i*th-step).

Let us assume that scratch pad registers 1–4 are used as follows:

$S_1$—holds a 1 in bit 47, otherwise zero—marker bit.
$S_2$—holds a 1 in bit 46, otherwise zero—carry bit.
$S_3$—holds a 1 in the $i$th bit, otherwise zero, to mark the place in the $B$ field.
$S_4$—holds a 1 in bit $(20+i)$, otherwise zero, to mark the place in the $A$ field.

Registers $S_3$ and $S_4$ initially have a ONE at zero and a ONE at 20, respectively, pointing to the right-most bits of their fields. Let us follow case II, the fourth row of Fig. 11.3.

SET        —turn on all response bits.
WIN  1, 77  —using $S_1$ as a mask (1 @ 47) and all ones as a comparand keep only those cells whose marker bits are ONE.
WIN  2, 0   —using $S_2$ as a mask (1 @ 46) and all zeros as a comparand keep only those cells whose carry bits are zero.
WIN  3, 77  —keep those with $B_i$ equal to ONE.
WIN  4, 77  —keep those with $A_i$ equal to ONE. This leaves set only those cells we wish to work on that correspond to case II. $(C=0, A=B=1.)$
MUW  2, 77—write the carry bit to ONE.
MUW  3, 0  —write $B_i$, the sum bit, to ZERO.

Next we do case I followed by III and IV. We shift registers 3 and 4 left one position in one instruction:

DLL  3, 4, 1—shift 3*4 left logical (end off) one position,

test to see if we are done, and otherwise loop back. The entire algorithm is shown in Fig. 11.4. Note that, upon termination, it will restore all marker bits to ZERO.

---

*Question 11.5:* Assume that bits 47 and 46 are always used for marker and carry bits. Design the hardware to execute the following instruction:

PAD $p, q, r$—parallel add in all responders. The field beginning with bit $p$ to the field beginning with bit $q$, both extending $r$ bits.

What is the minimum number of special registers you will require in the "PADDER" to carry this out efficiently? How much faster (per bit added) will it be than the algorithm shown in Fig. 11.4?

---

| *Instruction* | *Comment* |
|---|---|
| MUW 1, 77 | Write marker bits to ONE. |
| MUW 2, 0 | Clear carry bits to ZERO. |
| ENR 5 | Enters the octal number "12" ($10_d$) into register 5 for |
| 12 | looping-purposes. |
| BIT 3, 0, 6 | Clear $S_3$ and set bit 0 to ONE. |
| BIT 4, 24, 6 | Clear $S_4$ and set bit $20_d$ to ONE. |
| NOP LOOP | Serves as a "finder" for jump instruction. |

SET
WIN 1, 77
WIN 2, 0
WIN 3, 77          Case II.
WIN 4, 77
MUW 2, 77
MUW 3, 0

SET
WIN 1, 77
WIN 2, 0
WIN 3, 0          Case I. Note that we don't need to change the carry bit.
WIN 4, 77
MUW 3, 77

SET
WIN 1, 77
WIN 2, 77
WIN 3, 0          Case III.
WIN 4, 0
MUW 2, 0
MUW 3, 77

SET
WIN 1, 77
WIN 2, 77          Case IV. Note: Again no change in carry bit.
WIN 3, 77
WIN 4, 0
MUW 3, 0

DSK 5, 1          Decrease ($S_5$) by 1 and skip if result is ZERO. Not
JMP LOOP              done. Go back to "NOP LOOP."
SET              Clear all marker bits.
MUW 1, 0

Continue.

Fig. 11.4 An algorithm for CACS-I to add two fields of every word together. (See text.)

## CACS-II

The machine described above is reasonably elementary, as far as distributed logic machines go. In this section we will add some more features that will simplify the operation and increase the power of the design.

*Multiple Tags*  One thing that would make a content-addressable computer system easier to use would be to provide several response stores. CACS-I had two such stores: one for keeping responders to normal searches and one for keeping the identity of the next instruction. We indicated in the preceding section that each would have its own sense lines and set of flip-flops. If we wish to expand the number of program-usable response stores to four, this approach would require five separate sets of sense lines, which might conceivably get a little crowded.

Let us instead add five special bits to each word and to the mask and comparand register. These bits are "special" only in the fact that the programmer cannot use them in a normal fashion to store information. We will call these bits $I$, $J_1$, $J_2$, $J_3$ and $J_4$ and they will be used to hold the $I$ response store and four $J$ response stores. We will have only one sense line and only one response flip-flop (tag bit) per word.

Consider now the instruction FETCH cycle. This will be composed of several steps that will be executed by a wired-in program.

1. SET—turn on all tag bits.
2. Winnow for $I = 1$, using only the $I$ bits of mask and comparand registers. ($C_I = M_I = 1$.)
3. Read the responder and put it in the instruction register.
4. Begin decoding the instruction.
5. Write a ZERO in $I$ bit of responder. ($C_I = 0$, $M_I = 1$.)
6. Advance activity of the tag bits (shift down one position).
7. Write ONE in $I$ bit of the responder. ($C_I = M_I = 1$.)

This requires a one-bit search, a read, two writes, and a one bit shift. Depending on the way the associative memory is built, one might find it advantageous from a speed point of view to implement the $I$ and $J$ bits in flip-flops that are considerably faster than the rest of the bits of the AM. On the other hand, we might well decide to have this information stored in high-speed cores (5 words of $32K$ bits each). Should we adopt this latter approach, we would have destructive read out, thus eliminating step 5, and indeed the entire algorithm would change.

1. Read $I$ to response store. (The response store functions as the MBR.)
2. READ responder from AM to the instruction register.
3. Begin decoding instruction.
4. Advance activity of the response store.
5. Write contents of response store in $I$.

Exactly which method is chosen will depend on details of desired speed, economics, and the technology of the day. The point to be made is that it is possible to have only one real response store and several "virtual" ones.

Now that we have four tag bits per cell, all tag manipulating instructions will need another field to specify which tag bit is to be used. For example, WIN $m$, $c$ must become WIN $t$, $m$, $c$ (where $t$ specifies which tag bit, $m$ the location of the mask, and $c$ the location of the comparand).

Given four tag bits per word we can have some instructions that perform logical operations on the tag fields.

TND $t, u$—Tag AND. For each cell of memory form the logical product of $J_t$ and $J_u$ and store the result in $J_u$.

TOR $t, u$—Tag OR.

TXR $t, u$—Tag EXCLUSIVE OR.

This permits us to combine searches on different criteria, thus increasing the power and flexibility of the machine.

---

*Question 11.6:* Design a response store that will permit these three instructions. Why did we not allow the programmer to specify three tag bits (two source and one destination)?

---

*Shifts* Several more instructions can be added. Since the real response store must be capable of being shifted to advance activity on $I$, we can do the same for any of the tag bits:

MAF $t, n$—will move activity forward, $n$ cells on the $t$ tag bit.

If the $x$th tag bit of $t$ was ONE, then after execution the $(x+n)$th tag bit of $t$ will be ONE, otherwise it will be zero. This will allow us to do complex searches on records that extend over several cells.[5,6]

Given the ability to move forward, a programmer will want the inverse of that operation to move activity backward. This means making the real response store a two way shift register. Then we can have:

MAB $t, n$—will move activity on $t$ backward $n$ cells.

---

*Question 11.7:* Would you make these shifts "end off" or "end around?" Why?

---

Since we have gone this far, let us take one more step and imagine the cells of the AM arranged on a square grid instead of on a line.[7] Then each cell has four neighbors, except for the edge cells (see below). Let us choose $2^{16}$ or $65K$ cells as the memory size so that the array can be square.

This will give us a grid of $256 \times 256$ locations. Making the response store a four way shift register, we have the following possible instructions instead of MAF and MAB:

MAU $t, n$—move activity up (toward the top of the grid) on $t$ by
        $n$ places.

MAD $t, n$—move activity down.

MAL $t, n$ —move activity left.

MAR $t, n$—move activity right.

This provides us with a "spacially oriented computer" à la Unger that is well adapted for spacially oriented problems like picture processing and relaxation problems. Indeed it can be shown that this machine as so far stated is equivalent, in its ability to process in parallel, to SOLOMON[8] and to its descendent ILLIAC IV.[9]

---

*Question 11.8:* Design a response store that permits the four-way shift described above. Assume a shift greater than ONE will be accomplished by iteration.

---

What we have done here is to provide each cell with a "neighborhood" that it can influence. This is in distinction to a conventional coordinate addressed computer where the only relation between cells is that induced by the use of index registers. The computational powers this provides have been only partially explored, but when ILLIAC-IV comes on the air (even though it does not have quite the same structure as CACS-II), it will provide a testing ground for much fruitful exploration.

Now let us examine an example of what we might call "design fallout." Since we can shift activity of the response stores in four directions, we can obviously shift activity on $I$ in four directions. Let us add one more field, this time to *every* instruction, that tells the machine in which direction it should move the $I$ activity. This will make CACS-II a one address type of machine, since the instructions of CACS-I had *no* memory addresses. Now we can write iterative "loops" as genuine loops in memory: "go down halfway, step right one, come back up, and step left one." Moreover, all the skip instructions of CACS-I can become "branch" instructions. For example, skip on register zero, non-zero, positive, and minus can combine into one instruction:

> BCR  $r, a, b, c$—branch on contents of register $r$. Go in direction $a$
> if minus, $b$ if zero, and $c$ if greater than zero.

A good bit of the details of which directions to go in could be left to a reasonably simple assembler. Little work has been done in this area, but it appears to be quite interesting in its potentialities.

*Input/Output*  So far we have not presented any input or output commands for either CACS-I or CACS-II. There are three possibilities that should be examined.

The first and simplest would be input and output via one of the scratch pad registers. The two instructions would be:

> INP  $r, d$  —input a word from device $d$ to register $r$.
> OUT  $r, d$ —output a word from register $r$ to device $d$.

Even if the machine were designed to permit it to do other computation while a word was being transferred, this would be a relatively slow operation and many of the virtues of high-speed parallel processing would be lost, because data could not get in and out of the machine fast enough.

A second approach in CACS-II would be to use the edge cells as I/O points.[8] Consider the left edge of the array. The cells there have no left-hand neighbors, so a Move Activity Left dumps information into oblivion. Upon execution of a Move Activity Right, we are uncertain as to what we should enter into the left edge. It is tempting to think about attaching a 256-bit wide input highway to the left edge and a similar output highway to the right edge. These highways might be connected to a 256-track drum that could act as a buffer and format translator connecting the CACS-II to the outside world via more conventional I/O devices. With a drum bit rate of 1 megacycle, we would have an effective transfer rate of 256 megabits per second, or 32 megabytes per second, or about 5 megawords per second. With this device, assuming it was coupled to some kind of back up storage, we could load $65K$ words of 48 bits each in roughly 10 msec and then search for the presence or absence of a particular word or pattern of words in perhaps ten $\mu$sec. We are still badly I/O bound and need another factor of 100 or more in I/O speed. This brings us to our final suggestion. Let a memory load of $65K$ words be arranged as a set of 48 photographs, each picture containing one bit of every word.[10] Let there be a photodiode connected to each response flip-flop so that when light strikes the diode, the flip-flop is reset to zero. Upon the execution of the command "PROJECT," let successive pictures be projected onto the photodiodes. Then the following algorithm will load all of memory in 100 $\mu$sec or there abouts, assuming the memory was previously cleared to all zeros.

1. SET—set all response store flip-flops.
2. PROJECT—resetting those flip-flops receiving light.
3. Write ONE in bit $i$ of all words whose flip-flops are still set.
4. Increase $i$ by one and repeat 48 times.

This algorithm would have to be wired in and each memory load would have to contain a copy of the searching program. Conversely, one could follow step 1 by a winnow operation on some given bit of each word that would be ONE for data cells and ZERO for cells storing program material that was to be preserved. Optical projection via birefringent beam splitters or using cathode ray tubes would present no major problems. Such an input device would have a bit rate of $65K$ bits every 2 $\mu$sec or 4 gigabytes per second ($4 \times 10^9$).

Output could be made comparably fast, using light emitting semiconductors to expose film, but quite often a content addressable machine will be used to search large files and the amount of output is much less than the input. Therefore, in many circumstances, one could get by with output from a scratch pad register. Note that this parallel I/O just described could be used on either CACS-I or II.

*Response Counting* Sometimes we wish to know not just that there are some responders or none, but how many. Kaplan[11] has suggested a machine that provides an approximate count via an analog method in 24 $\mu$sec and an exact count in 410 $\mu$sec. His machine had $4K$ cells so he was obviously counting at a rate of 10 cells per $\mu$sec. Most other methods of obtaining the exact count of responders rely on serial counting techniques and are thus dependent on the number of items to be examined. While the present author was at Goodyear Aerospace Corp., he and Dr. K. E. Batcher designed an exact counter that has a delay proportional to the log of the number of cells to be counted and requires no more than one full adder per cell.[12,13]

We wish to add up a long column of ZERO's and ONE's and arrive at an answer we will call the COUNT. Our approach is based on the following reasoning: the least significant bit of the COUNT will be ZERO if there are an even number of ONE's in the input. The next least significant bit of the COUNT will be ZERO if there are an even number of *pairs* (disregarding any odd ONE discovered in the previous step), and so forth. Consider now a full adder. It has three inputs, which may between them contain 0, 1, 2, or 3 ONE's and it maps the state of the inputs onto the two binary digits called CARRY and SUM. Let us, therefore, take the original inputs three at a time and present them to full adders. (See Fig. 11.5.)

| Original Input | Full adder Output (CS) | Meaning |
|---|---|---|
| 0 0 1 | 01 | No pairs and an odd ONE. |
| 1 1 1 | 11 | One pair and an odd ONE. |
| 0 0 0 | 00 | No pairs and no odd ONE. |

Fig. 11.5 The first stage of an adder pyramid.

In the example shown, we have found 1 pair and 2 odd ONE's. But in general, we might have had 0, 1, 2, or 3 odd ONE's. The 2 odd ONE's we found should be combined to make another pair. Had we found 3, we should generate another pair and still produce 1 odd one. But a full adder does just this. So we take the sum outputs of the first stage described above and put them into another full adder. (See Fig. 11.6.)

The reader is urged to satisfy himself that any odd number of ONE's at the left side will generate a ONE on the right and any even number will generate a ZERO.

If the number of inputs at any level is not a power of three, so that an exact number of full adders can be used, half adders may be substituted to combine two signals or the extra signals can be passed unchanged up to the next level.

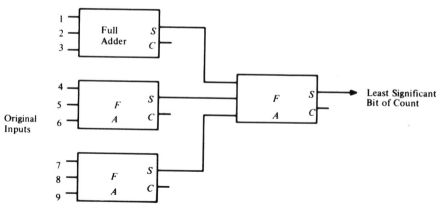

Fig. 11.6 The adder pyramid for the least significant bit of the count of 9 inputs.

We have taken care of the least significant bit of the count and now we are concerned with the next least significant bit. That involves the odd-ness or evenness of the number of pairs in the input. But the CARRY outputs of the pyramid we have just constructed represent the number of pairs in the input, and what worked before should work again. So let us take these CARRY outputs from the first pyramid and put them into a second pyramid whose final SUM output will be the second least signifi-cant bit of the COUNT. We can then take the CARRY outputs from this second pyramid, which represent the quadruples, and put them into a third pyramid, etc. Figure 11.7 shows the three pyramids required to generate a COUNT from 15 original inputs.

---

*Question 11.9:* Show that for $N = 2^n - 1$ cells, we require exactly $N - n$ adders.

---

*Question 11.10:* Derive an expression for the maximum number of adders a signal must pass through as a function of $N$. In Fig. 11.7, the number is 6 if we connect the successive pyramids together "any old which way." (As shown, the maximum is 5.)

---

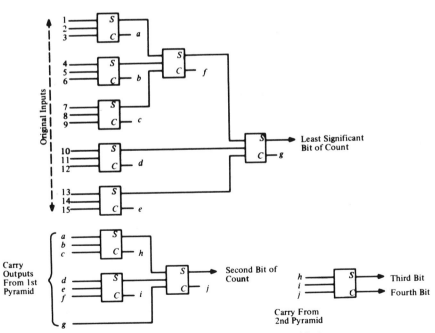

Fig. 11.7 Three pyramids to add up 15 possible inputs.

## STARAN

Staran[14] is a content addressable parallel processor designed and built by the Goodyear Aerospace Corporation of Akron, Ohio. It is a very complex machine and is capable of great speed in executing algorithms in parallel over a number of cells. We will gloss over most of the complexities in order to present a brief description of its major features.

Staran stores programs in a program memory and data in a Content Addressable Memory. As we saw in the discussion of CACS I and II, this is quite reasonable, given the problems of jumps in a completely content addressable machine. The data memory comes in blocks of 256 words and 256 bits wide. Up to 32 such blocks may be attached to the machine. Because the number of words per block and the number of bits per word are equal, Staran allows the user to address either a word or a bit slice with the same circuitry.

Instructions are 32 bits long, and of course data referencing instructions in general have no addresses, so there is lots of room for sub-op codes to specify all sorts of interesting variations and options. Many search operations across several bits can be expressed as one-word loops—and a "repeat instruction $N$ times" operation keeps the loop overhead way down. Addition of fields requires four instructions in the loop, and other parallel processing operations are comparable.

Because of its complications, its basic novelty, and its stiff price, Staran has not yet had a major impact on the field, but it is, I believe, the forerunner of a new generation of machines. Because of its ability to perform parallel processing, Staran can be looked on as a 256 element array processor. Provisions have been made via a "flip" netowrk to allow at least two-dimensional layouts of the words with immediate neighborhood communication.

REFERENCES

1. *Gamma-60, A New Concept.* Data Processing (Jan.-Mar. 1960).
2. Conway, M. E., "A Multiprocessor System Design." *Proc. AFIPS 1963 Fall Joint Comput. Conf.*, 139–146.
3. Falkoff, A. D., "Algorithms for Parallel Search Memories." *J. of ACM* **9**, No. 4, 488–511· (Oct. 1962).
4. Foster, C. C., "Parallel Execution of Iterative Algorithms." *Ph.D. Dissertation, Ann Arbor, Mich.,* U of Mich., 1965.
5. *Hybrid Associative Computer Study, RADC-TDR-65.* Griffiss AF Base, N.Y., Rome Air Devel. Center, 1965.
6. Lee, C. Y., "Inter Communicating Cells. Basis for a Distributed Logic Computer." *Proc. AFIPS 1962 Fall Joint Comp. Conf.*, 130–136.
7. Unger, S. H., "A Computer Oriented Toward Spacial Problems." *Proc. IRE* **46,** No. 10, 1744–1750 (Oct. 1958).
8. Slotnick, D. L., Borck, W. C. and McReynolds, R. C., "The Solomon Computer." *Proc. AFIPS 1962 Fall Joint Comp. Conf.*, 130–136.

9. Slotnick, D. L., "Unconventional Systems." *Proc. AFIPS 1967 Spring Joint Comp. Conf.*, 477–481.
10. Foster, C. C., "Parallel I/O for an Associative Memory."    GER-11772, Akron, Ohio, Goodyear Aerospace Corp., 1964.
11. Kaplan, A., "A Search Memory Subsystem for a General Purpose Computer." *Proc. AFIPS, 1963 Fall Joint Comp. Conf.*, 193–200.
12. Favor, J. N., "A Method of Obtaining the Exact Count of Responses Using Full- and Half-Adders."    AP-111770, Akron, Ohio, Goodyear Aerospace Corp., 1964.
13. Hill, C. A., "Fast Adding Technique to Obtain Exact Count of AM Responders." GER-12181, Akron, Ohio, Goodyear Aerospace Corp., 1965.
14. Rudolph, J. A., "A Production Implementation of an Associative Array Processor—STARAN." *AFIPS Proc. FJCC* **41,** 229–241 (1972).

# 12 | TESSELLATED COMPUTERS

> *"I ever loved to see everything on the square."*
> *Cervantes*

If we carry the idea of distributed logic one step beyond what was explored in the previous chapter, we have what Holland has named "tessellated" computers.  In this class of machines each cell is capable of "executing" its own instruction or program independent of what the rest are doing.  This type of computer is interesting in its own right, as being perhaps the most "distributed" of all, and is even more interesting in that it was for a "paper machine" of this kind that von Neumann developed his self-reproducing automata.

In this chapter, we will discuss von Neumann's design.  We will examine the Holland Machine, and Squire and Palais' modification thereof, and finally we will look at a device called the "Orthogonal Row Computer" (ORC) and show that, even without local control, an associative memory and some clever programming can simulate a Holland Machine and perhaps a little bit more.

## THE COMPUTER WITH 29 STATES

Between 1949 and 1953, von Neumann[1] devoted considerable thought to the theory of automata and developed among other things a self reproducing automaton.  Let us look at the machine he used for this.  We begin with a large array of identical cells, hence the name "tessellated" from the hexagonal tiles used in some floors.

Each of these cells is a small automaton or computer capable of independent action and of influencing and being influenced by its immediate neighbors. Both Holland and von Neumann worked with a square grid on a plane, although other configurations of space filling objects are clearly possible. These cells are relatively primitive compared even with BLUE.

There are three types of signals that exist within von Neumann's machine and, of course, the absence of all signals. These we will designate by:

$\emptyset$   an ordinary pulse
$\$$   a special pulse
$\mathcal{C}$   a confluent pulse
$\mathcal{N}$   no pulses at all

### Transient States

Generally speaking there are three classes of states that a cell may be in: *unexcited*, *transient*, and *stable*. As is usual in automata theory, when the machine is first turned on all but a finite number of cells are to be in the unexcited state. Left to itself, an unexcited cell will remain unexcited forever, but if it receives a special or ordinary pulse (they have the same effect here), an unexcited cell is converted into the first transient state, called $S_\theta$. Once in the first transient state, the eventual stable state that the cell will end in is determined by the history of "pulse" or "no pulse" over the next few time periods. For the purposes of this history, ordinary and special pulses count as "a pulse" and confluent or no pulses at all count as "no pulse." Figure 12.1 shows the possible transient states with a pulse represented by a 1 and no pulse by a 0.

At most, five time periods after leaving the unexcited state, the cell reaches one of nine stable states, which, again if left to themselves, will persist indefinitely. There are four ordinary transmission states, "right," "up," "left," and "down," and four similar special transition states and one confluent state.

### Transmission States

The eight transmission states serve as OR gates with a unit delay. Figure 12.2 shows four ordinary transmission states with their "directions" indicated by single arrows. Each ordinary transmission state has two conditions: active and passive. Suppose that at time period $t$, cell $b$ or $c$ or $d$ becomes active (emits an ordinary pulse). Then at time period $t + 1$, cell $a$ will emit an ordinary pulse in the direction shown (to the cell on its right). Thus, a chain of ordinary transmission cells, as shown in Fig. 12.3, can serve to propagate a signal from one point to another with one unit of delay at each stage. Note particularly that the emitted pulse (if any) is emitted only in the direction of the arrow.

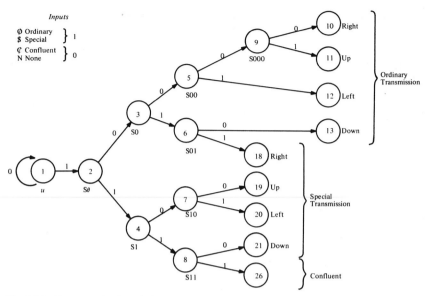

Fig. 12.1 The unexcited and the transient states of von Neumann's cellular computer.

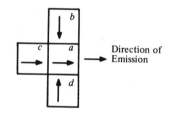

Fig. 12.2 Four ordinary transmission states.

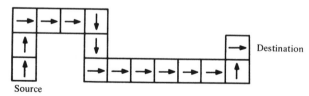

Fig. 12.3 A chain of ordinary transmission cells to send a pulse from "source" to "destination."

$t = t_0$        $t = t_0 + 1$

Fig. 12.4 An ordinary pulse (*) impinging on a special transmission state converts the cell to the unexcited state.

Special transmission states have these same properties, except that they emit special pulses, and can also be used to propagate signals. This time "special" signals. If an ordinary pulse impinges on a cell in a special transmission state that cell is "killed." It reverts to the unexcited state. (See Fig. 12.4.) Similarly special pulses hitting either ordinary or confluent states "kill" them.

### Confluent States

The confluent state is used to communicate between ordinary and special transmission states and, further, it serves as a two unit delay AND gate of all those ordinary states adjacent to it and directed toward it. Figure 12.5 shows a typical configuration. A confluent cell, when it becomes active, broadcasts a $\mathcal{C}$ pulse to those of its neighbors who are not "pointing" at it. This $\mathcal{C}$ pulse will activate both ordinary and special transmission cells.

Since the confluent cell has a dual delay, it has four possible internal conditions (active-active, active-passive, passive-active, and passive-passive). This leads to the total of 29 distinguishable states and/or conditions for each cell. Table 12.1 shows these 29 states and what state they will go to given: no input, some of the ordinary neighbors emitting $\mathcal{P}$'s, all of the ordinary neighbors emitting $\mathcal{P}$'s, some of the special neighbors emitting $\mathcal{S}$'s, or a confluent neighbor emitting a $\mathcal{C}$. It also shows the output (if any) of each state.

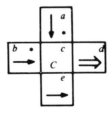

Fig. 12.5 Cells a and b are active at time t. At time t + 2, the confluent cell broadcasts a C pulse and at t + 3 both cells d and e become active.

*Question 12.1:* Design a von Neumann cell that will behave as indicated in Table 12.1. You may find it convenient to use more than the minimum

**TABLE 12.1    STATE TRANSITIONS FOR VON NEUMANN'S CELLULAR COMPUTER**

| Number | State | Input | | | | | Output |
|---|---|---|---|---|---|---|---|
| | | None | Some $\wp$ | All $\wp$ | Some $ | $\mathbb{C}$ | |
| 1 | Unexcited Transient | 1 | 2 | 2 | 2 | 1 | ... |
| 2 | $S_\theta$ | 3 | 4 | 4 | 4 | 3 | ... |
| 3 | $S_0$ | 5 | 6 | 6 | 6 | 5 | ... |
| 4 | $S_1$ | 7 | 8 | 8 | 8 | 7 | ... |
| 5 | $S_{00}$ | 9 | 12 | 12 | 12 | 9 | ... |
| 6 | $S_{01}$ | 13 | 18 | 18 | 18 | 13 | ... |
| 7 | $S_{10}$ | 19 | 20 | 20 | 20 | 19 | ... |
| 8 | $S_{11}$ | 21 | 26 | 26 | 26 | 21 | ... |
| 9 | $S_{000}$ | 10 | 11 | 11 | 11 | 10 | ... |
| | Ordinary transmission Passive | | | | | | |
| 10 | → | 10 | 14 | 14 | 1 | 14 | ... |
| 11 | ↑ | 11 | 15 | 15 | 1 | 15 | ... |
| 12 | ← | 12 | 16 | 16 | 1 | 16 | ... |
| 13 | ↓ | 13 | 17 | 17 | 1 | 17 | ... |
| | Active | | | | | | |
| 14 | →* | 10 | 14 | 14 | 1 | 14 | $\wp$ |
| 15 | ↑ * | 11 | 15 | 15 | 1 | 15 | $\wp$ |
| 16 | ←* | 12 | 16 | 16 | 1 | 16 | $\wp$ |
| 17 | ↓ * | 13 | 17 | 17 | 1 | 17 | $\wp$ |
| | Special transmission Passive | | | | | | |
| 18 | ⇒ | 18 | 1 | 1 | 22 | 22 | ... |
| 19 | ⇑ | 19 | 1 | 1 | 23 | 23 | ... |
| 20 | ⇐ | 20 | 1 | 1 | 24 | 24 | ... |
| 21 | ⇓ | 21 | 1 | 1 | 25 | 25 | ... |
| | Active | | | | | | |
| 22 | ⇒* | 18 | 1 | 1 | 22 | 22 | $ |
| 23 | ⇑* | 19 | 1 | 1 | 23 | 23 | $ |
| 24 | ⇐* | 20 | 1 | 1 | 24 | 24 | $ |
| 25 | ⇓* | 21 | 1 | 1 | 25 | 25 | $ |
| | Confluent | | | | | | |
| 26 | PP | 26 | 26 | 27 | 1 | 26 | ... |
| 27 | AP | 29 | 29 | 28 | 1 | 29 | ... |
| 28 | AA | 29 | 29 | 28 | 1 | 29 | $\mathbb{C}$ |
| 29 | PA | 26 | 26 | 27 | 1 | 26 | $\mathbb{C}$ |

number of flip-flops. *Remember* that a confluent cell must be able to detect not only that a neighbor is emitting an ordinary pulse toward it, but also that a neighbor is an ordinary transmission cell pointing toward it and *not* emitting a pulse.

---

### A very Brief Outline of the Self-Reproducing Automaton

The full development of von Neumann's automaton takes some 200 pages of closely reasoned argument, and any attempt to compress it into a few paragraphs is bound to do it insult if not injury. None the less, we will try to present an outline.

The principle idea is to have a machine (constructed of many cells) which is "programmed" by a long "tail" of cells, the state of each cell of the tail determining the next action to be taken by the machine. What this program directs the machine to do is first to make another machine identical to the original and then copy the tail and attach it to the new machine. When this is completed, the original machine sends the new machine a "start" signal and now there are two identical machines both ready to reproduce themselves.

A reader trained in mathematical logic will notice immediately that, although von Neumann has provided elementary AND's and OR's, he has failed to provide an elementary NOT. This omission must be remedied by destroying a cell in a pathway which serves to inhibit the transmission of a signal, and thus functions as a NOT.

Next von Neumann shows that one can construct "coders" and "decoders." The first generates an arbitrary, but determined, sequence of pulses upon receipt of a start pulse and the latter generates an output pulse if, and only if, it receives the "correct" sequence of input pulses. In addition to this, he shows how to construct a "reading head" to sense the state of a cell in the tail, how to build a "constructing arm" to make the new machine with, and how to allow two signal pathways to cross each other without interferences.

Using these functional organs, he designs a "constructing unit" and a "memory control" that together comprise a "universal constructor," which, together with a proper tail, comprise the self-reproducing automaton. Finally, to keep his device from being "trivial," he throws in a "universal computer" as part of the pattern to be reproduced.

What von Neumann has accomplished is to create a "pattern" that is capable of generating another "pattern" that in turn is capable of generating yet another copy of the same pattern, and so on and on. Why the excitement? The reason is that until he had done it, the ability to reproduce itself was the one thing that the "vitalists" could claim as irrefutably distinguishing animate from inanimate objects. Now their last refuge has been destroyed and the question of "what is living?" is up for grabs.

## HOLLAND'S ITERATIVE CIRCUIT COMPUTER

In two papers published in 1959 and 1960 John Holland[2,3] presented a design for a cellular computer that generated considerable interest in the computing world.

Holland proposes a square grid of cells all identical in structure. Each cell consists of a storage register and several auxiliary registers. As in von Neumann's machine, time is quantized and occurs in discrete steps, $t = 0, 1, 2, \ldots$. At each time period, a cell may be active or inactive. If it is active, it interprets the contents of its storage register as an instruction and executes it. Generally when the active time period comes to an end, an active cell goes inactive, but passes its activity to its "successor" (one of its four immediate neighbors specified as part of the instruction). The single most important aspect of the Holland Machine is that many cells may be active at any given time, each with its own independent instruction being executed. Time periods are divided into three phases called:

1. Input
2. Path building
3. Execution

During the input phase, any cell connected to an input device may have a word copied into its storage register. Holland does not consider this phase in any detail.

As part of each instruction, there are two bits which specify the "predecessor" of the cell. Since each predecessor must have a predecessor of its own, it is clear that, except for certain pathological cases, each cell has a chain of predecessors stretching through the machine. Note that the chain of predecessors and successors may be distinct. Of particular interest along this chain of predecessors are two cells which are in certain special "states." One of these is the first cell encountered along the chain that is in the $A$, or *accumulator*, state. The other, again the first such found, must be in the $P$, or *path*, state. The accumulator cell functions as might be imagined. The $P$ status module is the initial cell of yet a third chain of cells called the "path." From the $P$ cell, there is a set of path segments, each parallel to one of the axes of the grid, which constitute the path. The cell just beyond the end of the last segment is called the "termination cell." During the path building phase, some bits of the instruction specify how long a segment is to be constructed (the length may be zero) and in what direction it should go. Construction begins at the termination cell and proceeds as indicated. It is also possible to specify that the last segment of a path be erased. A cell may be part of at most four paths at one time.

During the execution phase, the termination cell at the end of the path serves as the "operand." Holland proposes that signals can pass along the chain of predecessors and along the path at infinite velocity, which is convenient from a theoretical point of view, but difficult to achieve in practice—particularly since the grid is unbounded and the length of a path may be indefinitely long.

Be this as it may, the following set constitutes the eight instructions that can be executed:

| | |
|---|---|
| ADD | add the contents of the termination cell to the contents of the accumulator. Put the result in the accumulator. |
| STORE | copy the contents of the accumulator into the termination cell. |
| TRANSFER ON MINUS | If the accumulator contains a negative number, "activate" the termination cell. Otherwise activate the normal successor. |
| ITERATE SEGMENT | this serves as a one-step loop for building long straight path segments. If the accumulator contains a positive number, one is subtracted from that number and activity is retained by the cell containing this instruction. When the accumulator contains a negative number, the instruction does nothing and passes activity onto the normal successor. |
| SET REGISTERS | *copies* 9 bits from the high-order end of the accumulator into the auxiliary registers of the termination cell. Note that this can cause the termination cell to become active, as well as the normal successor, thus starting a second program going. |
| RECORD REGISTERS | the inverse of the above. |
| NOP | a pass. |
| STOP | do not activate any successor. |

The auxiliary registers consist of:

| | |
|---|---|
| $E$ register | contains ONE if this cell is active. |
| $A$ register | contains a ONE if this cell is an accumulator. |
| $D$ register | contains a ONE if this cell is the initial cell of a path segment. |
| $D_1 D_2$ register | has two bits to indicate the direction of the path segment originating in this cell. |
| $(b_1 b_2)$* registers | are four one-bit registers which contain ONE's if the cell is part of a path in the indicated direction and ZERO's otherwise. |

Holland includes a number of rules for resolving race conditions and for taking care of pathological cases, as when for instance two lines of predecessors have a common accumulator or when there is no $P$ cell in a line of predecessors. For details, the reader is referred to the original papers.

Holland states that "by using complements and iteration all the arithmetic operations, such as subtraction and multiplication, can be accomplished...." It is not clear how one can, without using excessively clumsy artifices, take the difference between two positive numbers. The interested reader is urged to prove the present author wrong.

### Comments on the Holland Machine

As Holland points out, this machine is but one example of a large class of possible machines that could be built along these general lines. Two aspects of this type of machine should be emphasized.

First, the cells being identical, the machine is a "natural" for integrated circuit technology. Holland has estimated approximately 1000 basic elements (NOR gates?) would suffice for a 40 bit storage register cell. Single chips of this complexity are well within the technology and, since a single type of cell is required, could even become relatively inexpensive in large volume.

Second, as we have already mentioned, many programs can be active concurrently. That is, we can introduce as much parallelism into our computational process as the problem itself will permit. Moreover, by use of programmed interlocks, one can have several problems passing down one "instruction stream" at the same time (just as several railroad trains can use a common track), provided appropriate block signals are set up to prevent rear end collisions. What this means is that we can build computers with unlimited throughput capacity. Unlimited at least by the things that constrain conventional organizations—circuit rise times, speed of light, etc. One thinks of the possibly apochryphal story of the stellar dynamacist who programmed a model of stellar evolution for a 7094 and found that it ran in real time. With a large enough Holland organization, he could speed this up by as many orders of magnitude as he could afford.

### The N-Cube Holland Machine

There are two problems that arise in a machine of the Holland type if one considers the actual construction of one. The first we have alluded to by implication. Since a given cell may be a part of at most 4 paths at one time, it is possible to have a situation in which "you can't get there from here." That is, it may be impossible, because of interfering pathways, for a given instruction stream to reach a desired operand. The second difficulty involves the speed of signal propagation.

Squire and Palais[4] have suggested a modification to the square grid which helps to overcome both these problems. They propose to put the cells at the vertices of an $N$-cube, where $N$ may be quite large, say 30 or 40. They show how one could construct such a device by folding and refolding a planar structure.

On an $N$-cube, each cell would have $N$ neighbor cells and between two cells (a distance of $k$ apart) there would exist $k!$ possible pathways, which should help immensely to relieve the congestion problem. On an $N$-cube, the maximum distance between two cells would be $N$, that between opposite extremes of a diagonal. This means that for $N=40$, which provides $10^{12}$ cells, the longest path would be through 40 other cells, which is a lot less than would be the case for a planar array.

If one were to set out to construct a machine of the Holland type, one would want to give their suggestion serious consideration.

### Hypercube

In 1975, IMS Associates introduced a family of machines called Hyper cube II, III, and IV. Hyper cube III consists of 81 nodes arranged on a four-dimensional cube (logically speaking of course), three nodes on a side ($3 \times 3 \times 3 \times 3$). Each node has 8 immediate neighbors with which it can communicate. Each node consists of a pair of LSI-11s (small one-board minicomputers made by Digital Equipment Corp.), one to do the communicating and one to do the computing at that node. Every node has $8K$ words of storage (expandable to $32K$), executes one instruction per microsecond, and has a Direct Memory Access (DMA) capacity for I/O of 2 megabytes per second. Thus the Hypercube III can execute 81 MIPS (million instructions per second), has DMA capacity of 162 megabytes/second, and a total user program memory of .6 megawords (expandable to 2.5 megawords).

Suggested applications include on-line information storage and retrieval, time sharing network tasks, large-scale message switching, and array processing. So far as is known, this is the first commercially available multi mini array processor. Price for the H-III is $400,000, which is not high considering its performance. There may be considerable problems involved in keeping all 81 processors busy, but that is left as an exercise for the user. Hyper cube II has 16 nodes and H-IV has 256.

## THE REDEFINABLE NEIGHBORHOOD

In von Neumann's cellular computer, as in CACS-II, each cell has exactly four neighbors that it can influence. In Holland's machine, each cell has these four plus two more, the Accumulator and the Termination cell. These last two may be anywhere on the grid. We have called this a "redefinable neighborhood." Possession of this property permits programs in Holland's machine to be free from geometric considerations, at least as far as retrieving and storing operands is concerned.

## RESIDENCE OF CONTROL

In Holland's machines, each cell controls its own destiny. That is, it has logic built into it which can decode and execute an instruction. Consider CACS-II, the spacially arranged machine with content addressability. This clearly has no decoding circuitry, yet it can be made to simulate, except for the velocity of signal propagation, the Holland machine. Consider first instruction execution. Let three bits of each cell be used to hold an op-code.[5] Select all those cells holding an op-code of "000" and perform an ADD (we explain below how to reach remote accumulators and operands). Next select those cells holding an op-code of "001" and execute a STORE. Proceeding through the possible op-codes, we find it takes us eight steps or stages to get all active cells executed, regardless of how many there may be. In fact, with a certain amount of clever programming, we find that we can execute many of the subsidiary parts of the 8 steps at the same time. In one simulation of a Holland machine done by the author,[5] it was found that (averaged over the whole execution cycle) approximately half the active cells could be processed on each sub-step.

## ACCESSING REMOTE CELLS

All the activities involving path building operations and the line of predecessors of a given cell involve the transfer of information from one cell to another.

If we are to simulate a Holland machine in CACS-II, we must provide a way to get information transferred between two non-adjacent cells. Clearly this can't be done at infinite speed, but we have yet to show that it can be done at all. That we will do now.

Consider the following problem "Cell $(i, j)$ wishes to know the contents of cell $(i+x, j+y)$, that is, $x$ columns to the right and $y$ rows above it." The method is as follows: let the original cell send out a "messenger" that will move one row or column at a time until it gets to the destination. There it will pick up the desired information and bring it home again. In addition to various flags and a "carrier field" to bring the data back in, this messenger will have four fields called: $H_x$, $H_y$, $D_x$, $D_y$. Initially we set these fields to

$$H_x = -x$$
$$H_y = -y$$
$$D_x = x$$
$$D_y = y$$

The $D$ fields indicate the distance yet to go towards the destination and the $H$ fields hold "the way home." The "retrieval" algorithm first looks for any messenger wanting to go to the right $[(D_x) > 0]$.

All such messengers are copied (one bit at a time) into the "messenger" fields of the cells immediately to their right. In the process, the old copy of the messenger is erased and the contents of the $D_x$ field are diminished by one. Next we move *up* all messengers with positive $D_y$. Then those with negative $D_x$ are moved *left* and one is added to $(D_x)$. Finally we move down all messengers with negative $D_y$. A messenger is allowed to move only if the messenger field of the adjacent cell in the desired direction is empty. Collisions between messengers wishing to move right (up) and those wishing to move left (down) are taken care of by an "exchange messengers" subroutine.

After a set of moves (right, up, left, down, exchange-left-right, exchange up-down) is completed, we look for any messengers that have arrived at their destinations. These will be the messengers with ZERO in both $D_x$ and $D_y$. Now we do two things. First we copy the desired information into the carrier field and then copy $H_x$ into $D_x$ and $H_y$ into $D_y$, clearing out the $H$ fields at the same time. This will start the messenger moving towards home. When the messenger arrives there, its data can be unloaded and the originating cell can go on about its business.

One complete cycle of moves, exchanges, and reversals when at the destination, takes the place of Holland's path building phase. We have here exchanged Holland's rather complex hardware for a quite complex and, consequently, slow piece of software. But remember in a Holland type machine, we can get throughput as high as we desire.  Further, much of this communication algorithm could be wired into the CPU and, hence, be executed at high speed.

In any event, we have shown that it is possible to do without local control if we absolutely have to.

## THE ORC

Many other designs have been proposed for distributed logic or tessellated machines.  Some of them are most interesting in their intended functions. Lee has proposed a device for manipulating strings of characters.[9]  Comfort[6] has simplified and modified the Holland design.  Fuller[7] has examined several ways of constructing content addressable memories. Rosin[8] has proposed a complete cryogenic machine.  The list goes on. In this section, we are going to present a design[5] that has some abilities none of these other machines have: namely, the ability of *each* cell to carry out a content addressable search of the other cells, all at the same time.  This would be useful, for instance, if one wished to "tag" the common items of two separate lists.

Figure 12.6 shows the general design of an Orthogonal Row Computer (ORC).  There is a horizontal row of cells $(H_1, \ldots, H_n)$, a vertical row of cells $(V_1, \ldots, V_n)$, and an array of intersection points $(P_{11}, P_{12}, \ldots, P_{nn})$. The horizontal and vertical cells are identical and consist of $d$ binary

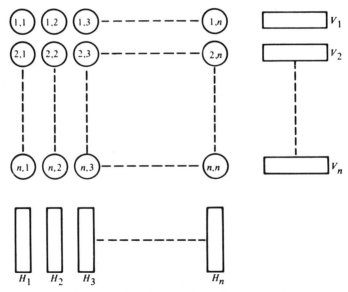

Fig. 12.6 The configuration of the main memory of ORC.

digits each.    The intersection points consist of an exclusive-or and a flip-flop. A horizontal cell $H_i$ is considered to be a "horizontal responder" if any of the flip-flops in column $i$ are SET.    A vertical $V_j$ is a "vertical responder" if any flip-flop in row $j$ is SET.

On a COMPARE command, the most significant bit from the horizontal and vertical cells are transmitted along columns and rows and, at each intersection point, the exclusive-or compares the horizontal bit with the vertical bit (providing a central MASK register has a ONE in this bit position).    If the two bits differ, the flip-flop at that point is RESET. We will include the same 64 word scratch pad as in CACS-I.

---

*Question 12.2:* Design an intersection point.

---

The commands available in the machine include:

SET                     turn on all intersection point flip-flops.

COMPARE $m$     reset any intersection point flip-flop for which the corresponding horizontal and vertical cells differ under the mask. $S_m$ is used as the mask.

SFV                     save first vertical responder (resets all succeeding rows).

SFH                     save first horizontal responder (resets all succeeding columns).

MWV $m, c$     multiwrite in vertical responders.

MWH $m, c$     multiwrite in horizontal responders using $S_m$ as a mask and $S_c$ as a comparand.

LRH $r$     load register $S_r$ with the logical AND of all horizontal responders.

LRV $r$     load register $S_r$ with the logical AND of all vertical responders.

SNR                     skip if no responders.

To begin with, we can make ORC act like CACS-I by storing a comparand in $V_1$ and using that for a search:

SET                     set all flip-flops.

SFV                     reset all but first row.

MWV 77, $C$     write contents of $S_c$ in $V_1$

COMPARE $m$     reset any flip-flop in first row (others already reset) for which ($H_i$) does not agree with the contents of $V_1$ under the mask in $S_m$.

We should note that we have only one instruction to test whether there are any responders or not. It is impossible to have a vertical responder without having a horizontal one at the same time.

It seems reasonable with a design like ORC to store commands in an auxiliary coordinate addressed memory. We will not explore details of this design, except to show that it is easy to program a redefinable neighborhood into the machine. We will do this for two neighbors called $A$ and $T$. Let each horizontal cell be assigned a unique name and let there be a vertical cell with the same name as each horizontal one. We wish to set flag $F_1$ in every horizontal cell if flag $F_2$ of its $A$ neighbor is set. If we can accomplish this we can generalize, bit serially, to a more complex arithmetic and logical interactions. Let the format for the corresponding vertical and horizontal cells be:

| $H_i$ | NAME | Data | | 1 | ? | 1 |
|---|---|---|---|---|---|---|

|  |  |  |  | $F_1$ | $F_2$ | $F_3$ |
|---|---|---|---|---|---|---|
| $V_i$ | NAME | $A$'s name | $T$'s name | ? | 1 | 1 |

First we write ONE's in $F_3$ of all cells, $F_2$ of all vertical cells, and $F_1$ of all horizontal cells. Let us consider the case for which cell $H_1$ has an $A$ neighbor of cell $H'_{11}$ and $H_2$ has an $A$ neighbor of $H_{12}$ as shown in Fig. 12.7. We will ignore what neighbors $H_{11}$ and $H_{12}$ may have.

1. Swap the contents of the name and $A$ fields of all vertical cells and SET and compare on the name field. This will leave $P_{1,11}$ and $P_{2,12}$ SET and all other $P$'s RESET.

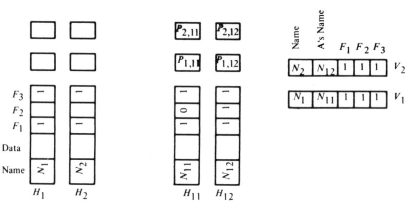

Fig. 12.7 $H_1$ has A-neighbor $H_{11}$ and $H_2$ has A-neighbor $H_{12}$.

2. COMPARE on $F_2$ field. Since $H_{11}$ has $F_2 = 0$, this will RESET $P_{1,11}$ leaving only $P_{2,12}$ SET.
3. Write in vertical responders $F_3 = 0$. This will put $F_3$ of $V_2$ (the only vertical responder) ZERO, leaving $F_3$ of $V_1$ equal to ONE so the $F_3$ field of the vertical cells will hold the complement of the $F_2$ field of their $A$ neighbors.
4. Reswap the contents of the $A$ and name fields of all vertical cells. Then SET and compare on the name fields. This will leave $P_{1,1}$ and $P_{2,2}$ SET.
5. COMPARE on $F_3$. This will reset $P_{2,2}$ since $V_2$ has an $F_3 = 0$.
6. Write in horizontal responders (namely $H_1$) $F_1 = 0$. This will leave $F_1$ of $H_1$ equal to ZERO (the same as $H_{11}$'s $F_2$) and $F_1$ of $H_2$ equal to ONE (the same as $H_{12}$'s $F_2$).

A complete simulation of Holland's machine has been done on a machine similar to ORC. Using this type of device, there can be no conflict between pathways and, moreover, transmission of information between non-adjacent neighbors is not dependent upon the "distance" they are apart. In fact, in this machine, there is no distance between cells, except as may be imposed by program.

On the other hand, one cannot fail to notice that the number of intersection points required in ORC will go up as the square of the number of cells.

## ILLIAC IV

No book on computer architecture could be complete without at least a brief discussion of array computers, and no discussion of array computers can exist that does not spend considerable time on Illiac IV.[10]

Illiac IV consists of an $8 \times 8$ arrangement of 64 processing units. Each unit has four neighbors (North, South, East, and West) with which it can communicate. Each processing unit is a full-fledged small digital computer with its own private memory and arithmetic/logic unit but lacking instruction registers. Instructions are broadcast from a central control unit to all processing units, and when central control says "add," all 64 PU's add. Central control is a stand-alone computer in its own right, and it has its own memory for storing its own program and data. One of the things it can do is broadcast instructions or constants to the PU's. Actually, not all PU's must respond to a broadcast instruction. Each PU has a set of flags, and instructions can be sent to be executed contingent on a particular flag's being one or zero. Thus for example, suppose we decide to program heat flow in a slab of metal. Suppose we choose a slab 7 inches on a side and decide that a one-inch spacing of points will give us sufficient accuracy in our simulation. For each interior point we find a new temperature by averaging the old temperature of the four neighbors of the point.

$$T(i, j) = \tfrac{1}{4}(T(i - 1, j) + T(i + 1, j) + T(i, j - 1) + T(i, j + 1))$$

Those processing units that represent the edge points will have their temperatures fixed by the boundary conditions of the problem and hence will not be subject to changes as we make further and further approximations to the interior temperature distribution. To keep these PU's from changing, we will make at least one of their flags be zero, while the corresponding flags of "interior" PU's will be one.

Any problem that can be cast as a two-dimensional array problem with each nodal point influenced by its immediate neighbors can be executed rapidly on Illiac IV. Indeed, those portions of the problem which would have been written as a singly or doubly nested loop to iterate over the points of the array can expect to run 64 times as fast on the 64 unit Illiac IV as they would have run on a comparable conventional machine.

## REFERENCES

1. von Neumann, J. "Theory of Self-Reproducing Automata." Urbana, Univ. of Illinois Press, 1966.
2. Holland, J. "A Universal Computer Capable of Executing an Arbitrary Number of Sub-Programs Simultaneously." *Proc. 1959 Eastern Joint Comp. Conf.,* 108–113.
3. Holland, J. "Iterative Circuit Computers." *Proc. 1960 Western Joint Comp. Conf.,* 259–265.
4. Squire, J. S., and Palais, S. M. "Programming and Design Considerations of a Highly Parallel Computer." *Proc. AFIPS 1963 Spring Joint Comp. Conf.,* 395–400.
5. Foster, C. C. "Parallel Execution of Iterative Algorithms." *Ph.D. Dissertation,* Ann Arbor, Mich., U. of Mich., 1965.
6. Comfort, W. T. "A Modified Holland Machine." *Proc. AFIPS 1963 Fall Joint Comp. Conf.,* 481–488.
7. Fuller, R. H. "Content Addressable Memory Systems." Report No. 63–25, Los Angeles, Calif., Dept. of Eng., U. of Calif., June 1963.
8. Rosin, R. "An Organization of an Associative Cryogenic Computer." *Proc. AFIPS 1962 Spring Joint Comp. Conf.,* 203–212.
9. Lee, C. Y. "Intercommunicating Cells, Basis for a Distributed Logic Computer." *Proc. AFIPS 1962 Fall Joint Comp. Conf.,* 130–136.
10. Barnes, George, H., R. M. Brown, M. Kato, D. J. Kuck, D. L. Slotnik, and R. A, Stokes. "The Illiac IV Computer." *IEEE Trans. on Comp.* C-17, 8, 746–757, (Aug. 1968).

# INDEX